POP CULTURE MANIA

POP CULTURE MANIA

Collecting 20th-Century Americana for Fun and Profit

STEPHEN HUGHES

McGraw-Hill Book Company

New York   St. Louis   San Francisco   Auckland   Bogotá
Guatemala   Hamburg   Johannesburg   Lisbon   London
Madrid   Mexico   Montreal   New Delhi   Panama   Paris
San Juan   São Paulo   Singapore   Sydney   Tokyo   Toronto

1 2 3 4 5 6 7 8 9 0 D O C D O C 8 7 6 5 4

ISBN 0-07-031113-7{PBK.}
ISBN 0-07-031114-5{H.C.}
Library of Congress Cataloging in Publication Data

Hughes, Stephen.
Pop culture mania.
1. Collectibles. 2. Antiques. I. Title.
NK1125.H836 1984   745'.075'0973   83-14941
ISBN 0-07-031114-5
ISBN 0-07-031113-7 (pbk.)

Book design by Roberta Rezk

This book is dedicated to my mother and father, both of whom, in their own ways, shared and encouraged my interest in collectibles.

Contents

Part II.   THE COLLECTIBLES

Foreword

DURING THE LAST 15 YEARS I have been involved as both a collector and a dealer in the incredible phenomenon known today as the collectibles boom. I was there at the start of it all in the late 60's when the word *collectible* was rarely heard, and one had to go searching at flea markets and garage sales if one wanted to collect old comic books, baseball cards, records, or paperbacks. Since that time much has changed, and today these same items, as well as many others, have developed into major hobbies complete with price guides, organized conventions, and professional dealers. The transformation has not been without negative aspects, however, chief among these being an enormous increase in prices. When I began collecting, the price of most collectibles was low, and one could afford to make mistakes, to learn by experimenting in the market. Today, a collector may spend several thousand dollars before he or she is done putting a collection together. It is now imperative for one to learn about the hobby and the market before beginning to buy.

I have tried to write this book with the beginning collector or investor in mind. There are a great number of misconceptions and errors circulating about collectibles generally and specifically. My hope is that this book will dispel many of these notions and that it will serve as a primer providing tyros with a firm foundation on which to begin collecting.

The first quarter of the book is a general introduction that covers all overall details of collecting. One can look there for the who, why, where, when, and, most importantly, the how of collectibles. Following the general introduction are the specific chapters that introduce the reader to 51 different collectible groups.

In each of these I have tried to include enough specific information to get the reader started without becoming too specific and confusing him or her with details readily picked up once one becomes a collector of an item. At the end of each chapter I have included information regarding books, clubs, and publications.

Too many introductory collectibles books have missed the point by concentrating on showing photos of colorful collectibles at the expense of including hard, useful information. I've found that pictures in a general book on collectibles, no matter how well photographed or selected, tend to confuse beginners who often draw the wrong conclusions when viewing a smattering of different objects. I am concerned in this book with presenting principles that pertain to collecting; once a beginner has determined what to collect, specialized books and the marketplace will provide the visual input.

Over the years I have spoken with many people who were fascinated by collectibles and interested in becoming collectors themselves. During these conversations I often wished that there were some way people could instantaneously transfer information to one another. A super machine has yet to be developed, but fortunately we still have books and reading this one will give you access to my accumulated knowledge and experience about collectibles. The transference of information will not be instantaneous, but I do hope it will be profitable and pleasurable.

S.E.H

Acknowledgments

Thanks are owed to the following people:

First, to Ken Stuart, without whose sensibilities, encouragement, and patience the book would not have been written;

to Melanie, for carrying her ill-fitting role of chief conscience so well;

to all the publishers, clubs, and organizations that sent me books, pamphlets, newsletters, and information;

to Jim Johnson, for sharing his collectible resources with me;

to all the dealers who shared their time and expertise with me over the years;

and, lastly, to all the collectors before me whose collective spirit embraced me at an early age.

PART I

An Introduction to
Collecting

CHAPTER 1

Developing
Historical Perspective

BEFORE THE INDUSTRIAL REVOLUTION came to the United States and made possible the mass production of inexpensive objects, Americans had a different feeling about the material things that surrounded them. Something as simple as a handmade child's toy, a piece of furniture, or a farming implement was valuable solely because it served a utilitarian purpose. Life for most of the population prior to 1840 was too rigorous for the frivolity of collecting "things." This was left for the upper class and the wealthy European families who could afford to own ancient coins, rare musical instruments, or 16th and 17th century master paintings.

During the second half of the 19th century the development of machinery that could mass produce goods began to affect the way and quality of life for most of the country. Items that formerly had to be made by hand began to be produced in the tens of thousands and became affordable for all. In all the major cities factories were built, and everywhere people caught in the euphoria of the new way believed that the good life had come. This was the time of the Sears, Roebuck catalog, Horatio Alger's young men, and the traveling salesman.

The Industrial Revolution made it possible for even the indigent to become collectors. Paper goods especially had become very inexpensive to produce, and anyone could afford to collect trade cards, cigarette cards, and other paper advertising items that were given away by businesses as promotions. Thousands of turn-of-the-century scrapbooks have survived, revealing page after page of these souvenirs of long-defunct companies. Among children, marbles, tops, and a variety of other toys were traded, collected, and played with.

Throughout the first half of the 20th century the engines of production continued to improve, producing an ever more sophisticated array of inexpensive objects. Baseball cards, comic books, the Kodak camera, ball-point pens, beer cans, Depression glass, slick magazines, records, radios, and electric trains were all products of the burgeoning movement. As they were produced, many of these items were also collected because they were so inexpensive and available. The production of so many inexpensive goods began to lead to a shift in the mass consciousness of the country. The old way of saving everything, of making use of rather than discarding, began to be replaced by a mentality that said, "Throw away the old and replace it with the new!" With the nation's machines producing to excess, frivolity began to come of age as an option for the masses.

What Is a Collectible?

The word *collectible* has been variously defined during the past ten years. Many of these definitions are incorrect or misleading, and their usage has led to a corruption of the true meaning of what a collectible is. For the sake of clarity, here is a one-sentence definition that is correct. *Collectibles are items originally produced to serve a solely utilitarian purpose that subsequently become, through intense collector interest, objects that transcend their mere utility.* For instance, an automobile is driven and is thus functional in an active way. A figurine is only viewed yet is also functional in a passive way as, perhaps, a decorative element in a home. Neither the automobile nor the figurine is a collectible, however, unless enough individuals decide to regard each one as more than simply a utilitarian object. In this sense, toys and baseball cards, for example, would have remained children's playthings had not enough people begun regarding them differently. Following is a list of the most popular collectibles and collectible categories today:

advertising items	art nouveau items
American Indian pieces	art pottery
animation art	ashtrays

autographs
automotive items
aviation
banks
barbed wire
barbershop collectibles
baseball cards
baskets
Beatles memorabilia
beer and soda cans
bells
bicycles
book plates
books
bottlecaps
bottles
Boy Scout memorabilia
boxes
boxing
buttons
calendars
cameras
canes
carriages
cash registers
ceramics
checks
Christmas
cigarettes
circuses
clocks
clothing
Coca-Cola memorabilia
coin-operated machines
comic books
country store items
crime
cup plates
decals
deco pieces

dinnerware
dolls
electrical collectibles
Elvis Presley
fans
fairs and expositions
family artifacts
figurines
firehouse memorabilia
fishing lures
flags
folk art
fountain pens
furniture
games
gemstones
glassware
golf
greeting cards
guns
hatpins
Hollywood memorabilia
illustrations
insulators
inventions and patents
jackknives
jazz memorabilia
jewelry
jokes and riddles
keys
kitchen implements
knives
labels
locks and keys
light bulbs
magazines
magicana
marbles
matchbooks
Maxfield Parrish

mechanical devices
medals
medical and scientific
menus
military paraphernalia
minerals
movie memorabilia
music boxes
musical instruments
nautical items
needlework and sewing
newspapers
non-sports cards
Norman Rockwell
occult
Olympics
paper money
paperback books
paperweights
patches
pencils
perfume bottles
phonographs
photographic items
pin-ups
pipes
plates
playing cards
police items
political items
postcards
posters
postmarks
premiums
presidents
prints
private mint issues
pulp magazines
quilts

radios
radio shows
railroad memorabilia
recipes
recordings
records
religious items
robots
rocks
rock and roll memorabilia
Royal Doulton
rubber stamps
rubbings
rugs
schoolhouse items
scrapbooks
shaving mugs
sheet music
shells
signs
silver items
space
spoons
sports cards
sports memorabilia
stock certificates
stoneware
straight razors
Teddy bears
telephones
televisions
temperance collectibles
theater material
thimbles
tins
tobacco items
tokens
tools
toothpick holders

toys

trade cards

trademarks

trains

traps

typewriters

Walt Disney

watches

weathervanes

Western Americana items

whirligigs

wine

wood carvings

zodiac items

To become a major collectible then, an item has to somehow cause enough people to begin regarding it differently. But what about objects that were produced for utilitarian purposes but have not generated significant collector interest to become collectibles; where do they stand? The answer is that there is probably some collector somewhere in the world for anything that has ever been produced. I've met a man who collects nothing but prophylactic wrappers; a woman who lives for saving spools of thread; and a young scoundrel who undoubtedly has the largest illegal collection of hubcaps. Should you think these people odd, I've also seen collections of corkscrews, bricks, razor blades, and World War II tanks. If it exists, there is probably a collector somewhere. While mass interest is needed to transform an object from functional to collectible, anyone who desires to can by his very interest in a "thing" elevate it from its mere functional purpose. In fact, some people want to be the first collector of an item. For this reason, a list of some unusual collectibles has been included for those not content to stay with the more established collectible groups.

While anything originally produced for a functional purpose can, through the efforts of even a few people, become a collectible, what qualities make certain objects become major collectibles? An accurate answer to this question could make a person rich. Unfortunately, it is a difficult question because its answer depends on the laws of supply and demand, which are themselves dependent upon man's fickle nature. Why, for instance, do certain pulp magazines from the 20's bring hundreds of dollars while their far rarer counterparts from the turn of the century bring only three dollars? Or why does a Pete Rose rookie baseball card from 1963 sell for more than a scarcer Lou Gehrig card from 1939? To begin to understand what qualities make one object desirable and another not, we must turn to an examination of the causes of the collectibles phenomenon.

The Development of the
Collectibles Phenomenon

As we have already noted, there was a time when people could not think about the objects that surrounded them as anything other than functional. The Industrial Revolution changed this by improving the standard of living and providing the masses with many inexpensive things like trade cards, postcards, and buttons, which a poor man could save in imitation of the wealthy collector. What caused the transformation of such utilitarian objects as baseball cards, comics, and toys into hobbies approaching the same level of mania as such age-old pursuits as rare art, stamp and coin collecting?

One has to go back to the early 60's and the beginning of contemporary inflation. Up until then technology had led Americans to expect to be able to buy better goods each year at lower prices. For this reason the prevailing mentality had become, "Throw away the old model every two years and replace it with the new, better one." This was the American dream; and as long as technology provided new advancements in machinery and production, labor remained inexpensive, and raw materials were readily available, the dream could go on.

During the 60's, however, things began to change. Raw materials began to cost more, labor prices rose, and producers were forced to begin cutting corners by using inferior quality materials and design. People began to see their dollar buying less and the quality of consumer goods declining. As the deficit budgeting of the Vietnam war escalated, causing inflation to spiral even more, there was the beginning of an awareness that the good old days of stable prices and ever-better quality were departing, to be replaced by increasing prices and inferior models. As people became aware of this, some of them went out and began buying whatever old models they could find. Because most of the population still believed that the old was the junk, people who were anticipating what was to come were able to buy "things" for very little. Their motivation was usually the same. They were individuals who recognized the superior design and quality of the older models and felt compelled to save them as emblems of the past.

In saving items, people want things that are symbols of the past, either through their design, quality of workmanship, or composition. Some people want a thing that brings on feelings of nostalgia, transporting them back to childhood, adolescence, or young adulthood.

How Does a "Thing" Become a Collectible?

The comic book is particularly suited as a paradigm of a collectible because it was one of the first common objects to be vested with collectible glamour.

I remember being at one of the first major comic book conventions in 1971. It was held in the Grand Ballroom of the old Commodore Hotel in New York City. My father was with me, and I will never forget his amazement, and mine, at seeing people pay 20 dollars and more for the right to own a single comic. His inability to comprehend these transactions epitomized the mentality of the old school, which had grown up during the Great Depression. For him, comics had been, and were, cheaply made magazines to be read and traded among children. How could people now be willing to pay "big money" to own what he had casually discarded in his youth?

The first comics as we know them today were published beginning in the mid-1930's and had a cover price of 10 cents. *Superman #1* was among the first of the issues coming out in 1939. The medium caught on, and over the next two decades hundreds of different titles were produced under such categories as Walt Disney, superhero, love, crime, war, and horror.

In the early 60's a few comic clubs had formed in New York and San Francisco. The members of these loosely organized groups ranged in age from eight to 80, but all shared a love for comic books. They traded amongst themselves, compiled lists, and shared ideas. At this time one could purchase a first edition of *Superman* for only 20 dollars, and that was considered a lot. There were no comics yet worth more than a few dollars. The going price was based on what this small group of early collectors was willing to pay.

By 1964 the number of clubs had increased, and informal

meetings between clubs were arranged. These affairs were advertised by word of mouth and through newsletters and provided a larger forum for collectors to exchange information. During this period collectors began printing up lists of their duplicates, which they offered for sale to other collectors. Their profits were meager and certainly they were motivated more by the hope of obtaining desired issues in exchange for their duplicates than by an expectation of making money. Their enterprises were part-time, since the demand that would transform the hobby into a big business was yet to come.

Because of inflation, the price of a comic, which had been 10 cents for 25 years, was raised to 12 cents in 1964. The inflation rate continued to increase, and in the next five years the price and quality of comics changed drastically. By 1970 the newsstand price had reached 20 cents, and the comic had fewer pages than when it was only a dime. Six years had seen the doubling in price of an item that had previously been the same price for over 25 years. The implications of inflation in the growth of the collectibles market were enormous. As the country began to see that everything was costing more and not working as well, there was a nostalgia for the old times when things were made better and cost less. Since these old times could not be brought back, at least the goods that had been produced then could be saved. The ownership of collectibles seemed to provide a kind of link to the past, to a time when things were better.

On a monetary level, the early comic collectors began to realize in the late 60's that they could count on seeing a 100 percent appreciation yearly on the comics they were saving. *Superman #1* was now worth over 200 dollars.

Robert Overstreet, a comic collector in his mid-30's, realized at this time that some sort of guide was needed to organize and standardize the hobby. He approached several publishers with the idea but was refused on the grounds that there was not enough interest. Undaunted, he went on to publish the first official publication, the *Comic Book Price Guide*, himself in 1970. It promptly sold out its first printing, and Overstreet went on to revise it and produce a second printing.

The effect of the *Comic Book Price Guide* was to stimulate a wave of buying by collectors, who felt they finally had a tool to aid them in making intelligent purchases. Comics were to become, like stamps and coins before them, accepted as a legitimate hobby complete with price book and professional dealers.

The *Comic Book Price Guide* stimulated demand, and the number of clubs, dealers, and conventions increased geometrically. In Manhattan, where formerly there had been only one convention a year, one could now go to at least one a month. What had been a friendly gathering place for collectors became a competitive marketplace where dealers hawked their books to the throngs of collectors looking for missing issues. In 1971 the second annual *Comic Book Price Guide* was published, and the prices listed had increased so much that collectors were sent into a frenzy. Now the game became trying to locate people who had comics and were not aware of their growing value. It was at this time that the professional comic dealer began to emerge. Typically he was a collector who had recognized the enormous opportunities for profit. The media had not yet made the public aware of the potential value of old comics. It was very easy for a knowledgeable collector or dealer to chalk up large profits, if he could find those who were not aware of what was happening.

Many people were fair and tried to set standard buying prices, but the problem was that the hobby was growing at such an incredible rate that few people knew how to proceed. Amidst the confusion of the early period the two things anyone was sure of was that a formerly valueless item had become a collectible overnight and that there was a lot of money to be made. As a result, many of the collectors who initially began buying and selling as a way to improve their collections eventually abandoned them and concentrated on making comics a second job. This was the ground-floor stage in the business, and everyone was trying to get a little piece of the action.

By 1973 the fourth annual *Comic Book Price Guide* was out and so was the news that comics had value. By this time the media was making regular trips to the larger conventions in Manhattan and reporting on them on network television. At this point comics were still regarded as a fad and the press always focused on the seeming quirkiness of adult interest in comics and the fantastically high prices being paid for certain issues. The media blitz accomplished two things. It brought thousands of collections out of attics and into the marketplace, but more importantly, it made the public aware for the first time that comic books, which were formerly considered junk, were now becoming extremely valuable.

In 1974 the *Comic Book Price Guide* had more than 10,000 copies in print and was picked up for distribution by a major publishing house. Now that it was available in all major bookstores, even laymen could come to some reasonable assessment of the value of old comics. For dealers this meant an end to many of their serendipitous finds. Now they would have to pay reasonable percentages of the retail value in order to maintain their inventories. This forced comic dealers to organize along the same lines as any business. It became crucial to have an accounting system that would determine if the business was profitable. Many of the early dealer/collectors could not make the necessary transition. They had prospered during the initial opportunities but were unable to cope with the new demands. The dealers who remained began developing more sophisticated marketing devices and business procedures for dealing with the growing numbers of comic collectors.

One of the side effects of the overnight appreciation of comic books was the intrusion of the investor. The investors, many of them former collectors, drove up prices through hoarding and speculation. They were drawn to comics and other collectibles as a way of staying ahead of inflation and making a profit. In the early 70's, when passbook interest was only $5^{1}/_{4}$ percent, it made sense to invest in something that was doubling in value each year. In addition, most collectible transactions were in cash, and profits were often not reported as income.

By the late 70's speculative interest from investors and collectors had driven the price of certain comics so high that many collectors became frustrated and began to abandon the hobby. Popularity had been a double-edged sword. As comic collecting gained acceptance as a legitimate hobby, it became so expensive that one had to consider investment potential before buying. The joy of the early pre-profit-motive days was gone, and every collector had to become a wheeler-dealer to effectively build his collection.

In the last few years the comic book market has become even more specialized and subject to the investment cycles normally associated with art and antiques. Particularly in a deflationary economy, collectibles do not do as well as when times are prosperous, and the comic market suffered during the bad economy of 1982.

The Qualities of All Desirable Collectibles

The exaltation of the comic book is typical of the transformation an item undergoes when enough collector interest turns it into a collectible. Understanding this metamorphosis can be helpful to those who are interested in elevating an object to the status of a collectible.

The stages an item goes through in its development from functional object to collectible can be summarized as follows: (1) *Beginning*: The item is valued for its utilitarian worth and, at most, only a small number of people collect it. At this stage it has no collectible value; (2) *Growth of interest*: The item has attracted attention and collectors begin pursuing it, thus creating a supply and demand situation that often drives the price up; (3) *Collectible*: There is a broad base of collector śupport for the item, which is now generally regarded and valued as a collectible.

The speed at which a group of items proceeds through the first two of these stages usually determines how stable the prices for this group will be once it has reaches the third stage and becomes a recognized collectible. History has shown us that when a group does not mature slowly into a collectible, there will be a weak or unsupported market.

This happened with many of the collectibles that became popular overnight once the collectibles boom had begun. For instance, baseball cards had hardly reached stage two when investors rushed into the card market and began speculating. Baseball card prices went way up, but most of these increases were attributable to investor hype not solid collector support. The 1952 Topps Mickey Mantle card, which was worth over $3,000 in 1980, is now worth only $500.

Similar retrenchment occurred in other collectible groups that experienced accelerated growth speeds. The key factor that must be present for a collectible market to be strong is collector-supported demand. Collectors save collectibles because they like them. Inves-

tors only buy with the hope of reselling at a profit. When prices
within a collectible group are supported primarily by investors, a
very dangerous situation exists. Investors usually sell out at the
first signs of a market weakening.

In addition to a gradual maturation through the first two stages,
there are several other qualities that influence the desirability of
a collectible. A look at each of these follows.

Continuity with the present. The more popular collectible groups
usually have present-day counterparts. The link to the present
gives them a vitality lacking in items that are antiquated. Collectors
like to collect things that are still being produced *in some form*.

Attractiveness. Cars are sometimes thought of as sexy. In collectibles, dealers refer to a piece with that special look as having
"sex appeal." The first time I heard this term used it was in reference to a toy, and I thought I was being kidded by the other
dealer. When I thought about it though, I realized that the term
does convey the sensation a collector feels when he encounters an
exciting or unusual piece. These feelings are not unlike the ones
a person experiences near a particularly alluring member of the
opposite sex.

The exact factors that combine to create the overall appeal of
a piece vary according to the criteria of a particular collectible
group. You must become familiar with a group in order to know
when you have encountered "the look." An antique camera that
makes a camera buff swoon might cause a toy collector to yawn.
A feel for "the look" is developed by viewing and handling the
desirable examples within a category. Many collectibles can be
judged using the kind of standards applied to art. For instance,
when looking at a collectible, try to determine if it has an interesting design and you are pleased with its overall visual appeal.
This last consideration is particularly important since it is you who
will have to look at the item if you buy it.

Availability. Some collectibles attain popularity because there
are enough of them around to fuel initial collector interest. Obviously, an object must also have enough merit to draw collectors,
but there are many things that are desirable and yet do not exist
in sufficient quantity to make their collecting feasible by more

than a few individuals. On the other hand, if a particular item were saved by a great many people, it would never become a collectible because it would be so common. For this reason, those who are now saving objects they think will become tomorrow's collectibles are, by their very combined efforts, defeating their purpose. The best scenario for the popularization of an object is for enough of it to exist to stimulate the popular imagination, but not enough to make it common.

Affordability. Most popular culture collectibles fall within the low-value range, which in this book refers to pieces priced between 50 cents and 50 dollars. Of course, within every collectible category there will be those examples that, because of rarity or demand, will sell into the middle- and high-value range. Affordability plays an important role in whether or not an item will take off as a collectible. Most successful collectibles started off rather inexpensively, thus attracting broad collector support. As prices increase beyond the level of the average budget, many collectors depart.

Historical importance. Most collectibles are important historically in that they capture and remind us of how different people's lives were in the past. For instance, radio premiums, which were so popular during the 1940's, remind us that once there were no televisions; straight razors evoke images of a more rugged life before the advent of modern conveniences; Beatles memorabilia brings back memories of what the 60's were like; movie posters from the 20's testify to the silent film; and temperance collectibles make us wonder what Prohibition must have been like. The more a group of items captures the "soul" of a past era or period, the more likely it is that this group will become (if it is not already) a collectible.

The Problems with Instant Collectibles

An "instant collectible" is an object produced specifically to appeal to the general public who has heard of the investment potential of collectibles. Instant collectibles come in many forms and are usually promoted as "limited editions." By 1979 most national publications were carrying several advertisements per issue for instant collectibles like plates, statues, figurines, silver ingots, and medals. The problem with all of these items is that they are not really collectibles. They lack most of the essential qualities discussed earlier that give at item "collectible soul," and, if this is not enough, they bypass the first two critical stages an item must go through to become a collector-supported collectible.

The many instant collectibles produced appeal to the average person who believes he is making an investment in something that is a legitimate collectible. I don't know how many times I have had the unfortunate task of informing people who have bought these items that their prized "limited edition" was not worth even half what they paid for it. The advice I always give is to buy instant collectibles only if you like them as decorative pieces for your home. Purchasing them as investments is unwise, because when it comes time to sell them, there will be no demand.

Philosophy of Collecting

People often complain of being bored, of having nothing to do. This is puzzling, because ennui is self-generated. Those who complain the most of being bored are themselves usually the most boring people. Why are so many people walking around bored these days? The most general answer is because at some point in their lives they have lost their curiosity about the world and have come to depend upon mass-oriented entertainment for their vitality.

For many people, curiosity is stunted in unimaginative school environments, where they begin to dislike learning at an early age. There are also those who have the misfortune of being raised in an atmosphere opposed to intellectual curiosity, where street smarts are often all one needs to move ahead. For others, adult responsibilities such as a career and a family leave little time to pursue outside interests. And then there are those individuals who close off the outside world because of personal tragedy.

Whatever the reason, a person who does not engage in activities that promote personal growth is doomed to live a shallow puppet show of a life. Fortunately, this condition is reversible. It is possible for anyone to rekindle that flame of curiosity that burned within us as children.

The first step is to become willing to disallow some of our acquired assumptions about the world. Most people are very comfortable with putting everything into a category. This enables them to believe that they have mastered that part of the world under their view. How sad that they do not realize that it is their own viewpoint that has become fixed and that the world still remains very much in flux.

The trick is to begin looking at the world with fresh eyes once again, to marvel at the very fact of life and its multitude of fascinating relationships. Seeing the world through fresh eyes is the first step to becoming a more fulfilled and happy person. For some, reaching this point is difficult, often involving battle with an entire lifetime of jadedness. For this reason, one needs to pursue activities that are engaging and rewarding. This is where collecting comes in.

Why Collect?

The purest satisfaction one can derive from collecting comes when, in some way, one's esthetic, spiritual, educational, or cultural impulses are engaged. Because of the virtually unlimited number of ways to collect, there is something for everyone. Examples of some types of collectors are, people who save baseball cards as a way of carrying the joy of childhood fantasies of heroes into the present; the executive who buys antique toys as an anodyne for the pressures of work; the housewife who is interested in learning about the evolution of kitchenware and spends Sundays looking for unusual kitchen implements at flea markets; children who learn that knowledge can be fun and satisfying through their pursuit of comic books, non-sports cards, and dolls; the retired couple who enjoy bottle collecting because it provides them a way to stay active and meet new people; and the scholar who is transported to an exciting fantasy world through the study of philology. These are but a few examples of collector types. Following is a breakdown of some of the benefits that can be derived through collecting.

SEARCHING FOR AN IDENTITY. Just about everyone is doomed to be thought of by those outside their close circle of friends in terms of what they do in life. References such as, "Oh, he's an accountant" or, "She's a secretary" take away from a person's uniqueness. While we can't waste time worrying about how the world will label us, we should all be concerned about our identities. For many, this is a subject unconsciously avoided for fear of discovering insufficiencies or private little horrors, or ignored for lack of introspection. It is a subject that should not be ignored, however, because our identity may be the only real thing we can ever hope to have control of.

Choosing to collect something can be a first step toward enriching the identity we already have from our jobs, relationships, and family backgrounds. It can also be the first step in establishing the identity *we want* for ourselves, as opposed to the one we have merely acquired. Those who take this first step cannot fail, for in their move to action they have already begun to establish their true identity.

BECOMING A PARTICIPANT. The thoughts of an entire generation have been influenced by the mass media. I am constantly amazed at gatherings at the number of people who seem incapable of speaking about anything other than what they've read in the papers, heard on the radio, or seen on television. The implications of Henry Wadsworth Longfellow's statement, "A man is what he thinks about all day" are quite shocking when one considers how much of our daily mental input is from newspapers and television. While a certain amount of this is necessary for us to stay abreast of current events and world happenings, too much of it makes one an observer of life instead of a participant.

Television has become the largest form of mass entertainment. Many people switch on the set as soon as they walk through the door after work and leave it on throughout dinner and the entire evening, never realizing they could be spending their time in a more constructive fashion.

Collectibles can be far more engaging and enjoyable than an evening of television. Moreover, when one is able to pursue an activity in which one is a participant instead of an observer, such things as radio and television lose much of their appeal. In addition, the accompanying shift in orientation regarding leisure time extends into other activities, making one more aware of the quality of time spent. We can become more aware of how we spend our time and try to become doers instead of watchers.

BECOMING GOOD AT SOMETHING. Life is not always fair, and most people must be content to support themselves and their families by working at jobs in which they will never be more than competent. This is, of course, admirable, but many of us want to be great at something, to rise to the top in a particular area. Collectibles offer a unique opportunity for personal excellence, in that one can invent a collectible category, become expert at it, and then begin a club, write newsletters and books, and give talks— in short, become king or queen of that collectible. Recently, there has been a rash of books on such esoteric collectibles as straight razors, milk bottles, radio premiums, and soda cans. Their authors are people who hold regular jobs and shine only in their particular hobby. One does not have to be able to invent a category to become good at. There are many established collectible groups in which one could quickly become very knowledgeable if he or she were willing to put in the necessary effort. Other collectible categories are just waiting for interested parties to discover and master them. There was a time when people chuckled upon hearing that some- one was an expert on say, comic books or baseball cards. Today, however, with record prices being paid, an expert on any collecti- ble is regarded as a useful connection, someone who might one day be able to help determine whether a family heirloom is trash or treasure.

MEETING PEOPLE. A major complaint frequently heard at all levels of society is the difficulty of finding and making friends. After school our lives tend to become more insular as we settle into the routines of family and career. Usually one is not blessed with the kind of job that regularly involves meeting new people. Most of us are stuck with the same co-workers year in and year out. Sometimes, friendships are solidified on the job, but more often they are not since the last person you want to see in the evening or on the weekend is someone connected to your work environment. So where then can one make friends if not on the job, which for most of us takes up better than a third of our lives?

The bar and pub scene is not very practical for anyone who is married or over 30. In addition to which, drinking establishments are notorious for leaving their patrons more desolate by night's end than when they walked in. Single associations are not good, since their focus is on dating and marriage. Organizational activities are slightly better but are often bland or boring. The problem with most of the many forums designed to bring people together is that they attract too large a variety of people. In making friends, the trick is to find an activity you truly enjoy and then to go where others with the same interest congregate.

One of the reasons that "fun runs" and Saturday morning races have become so popular across the country is that they provide an opportunity for runners to get together. After the race, contestants mingle over refreshments, sharing training schedules, diets, and anecdotes. Many friendships begin at these meetings when people decide to try jogging or entering a race together.

We are social animals but need an excuse or initial link to become closer. In the preceding example, running provides this link. Collectibles can also provide it. In fact, nothing is better than a collectible show for bringing together strangers eager to talk about their hobby. At any baseball card, comic book, train, stamp, coin, glass, bottle, gem, art, antique, or jewelry show, one can witness people from all walks of life being brought together by their common interest. Often their involvement will not go beyond the acquaintance level, since, after all, a hobby can only act as an icebreaker, after which personality and desire take over; however, it is astounding how compatible people who collect the same thing are.

It is not surprising that most serious collectors often have as their best friends other collectors. Of course, the truth is that one must also be open to making friends. No forum will help the kind of individual who closes himself off. A collectible show is a perfect place to begin making friends with other collectors, but one must be, at the least, receptive and perhaps even aggressive about talking to those one finds appealing.

For anyone interested in the possibility of finding more than just friends through collecting, I am happy to report that many romances have started through a mutual interest in collectibles. In addition, many marriages have resulted. I know one couple who got married at a World's Fair in celebration of their hobby, Exonumia (the collecting of items from world's fairs and expositions), that brought them together. They even plan to name their children Isabella and Christopher after the historic figures for whom the famous 1893–1894 World's Fair was commemorated.

STRENGTHENING A MARRIAGE. Often, after years of being together, a couple may find that they have drifted apart. The closeness they once had has been supplanted and vitiated by the various demands of their careers, children, and friends. Many people have had the experience of one day waking up to the fact that their spouse has become a stranger. Long before this happens, a couple should reaffirm the friendship that initially drew them together, by participating in activities that encourage their sharing time and exchanging ideas.

Collecting can provide the perfect transport to a stronger marriage. The very nature of a hobby makes it more enjoyable when it can be shared with others; and who could be in a better position to gain from this sharing than a couple trying to strengthen the bond between them? Some of the top collections in the country have been assembled by husband and wife teams. It is not even necessary for both partners to collect the same thing. Each can collect a different item but still spend time together at shows looking for collectibles and sharing enthusiasm for each other's collection. In this way, friendship can be renewed over a mutual pursuit, which can be kept separate from some of the more mundane aspects of marriage.

RELIEVING STRESS. For many people, the stresses of working in the modern age are considerable. The pressure to succeed is on everywhere, and even the strongest individuals are worn down by overwork, anxiety, pollution, poor diets, and many other pressures. One's hobby can be a shady enclave to which one goes for refreshment.

I know one successful businessman who commutes to one of Manhattan's largest brokerage firms. There, he performs admirably, negotiating high-pressure deals involving millions of dollars. To see him in his office dressed the part with his face lined with tension, one could hardly believe that this is the same seemingly carefree man who traipses through toy shows on the weekends looking to add to his collection. His story is far from unique and, anyone, no matter what their job, can alleviate job stress by abandoning their work persona come Friday night and spending part of the weekend in pursuit of a hobby.

MAKING MONEY. While it is not a good idea to enter collecting solely as a way of making money, many collectors have learned that they can significantly augment their collections as well as their incomes by being open to opportunities for using their specialized knowledge. An experienced collector, for instance, can often use his knowledge to pick up bargains from dealers selling out of their field. Many dealers will buy a "lot" of merchandise, paying only for the items they really know about. The other merchandise is "gravy," and often they will not take the time to research it carefully. This lack of effort translates into a bargain for the persistent collector. I know one man who makes a living buying various collectibles around the New York area. One of his tricks, he told me, is to buy paper collectibles from glass dealers, toys from paper dealers, and furniture from glass dealers. He always has the edge in knowledge this way.

To make money, many collectors haunt the various forums that will be discussed in depth further on in this section. Of course, one has to put in the time to learn a field well, before one can expect to pick out that rare piece that has been overlooked by everyone else. A fortunate find is often the result of hard-won knowledge as well as luck. I know of one watch collector who bought what seemed to be a common Waltham pocket watch for 40 dollars at a flea market. The piece lay among many others and had been picked up and examined at least 20 times that day. It turned out to be an extremely rare watch that was made during a brief period when the ownership of the company was changing over. It is worth around $10,000. This man would have walked away from it had he not noticed something unusual in the numbering sequence stamped on the case. For those who have a good eye, learn fast, and do their homework, collectibles offer many opportunities for profit.

Most collectors are content to make a deal here and there as a way of helping finance their hobbies. They often aren't interested in becoming dealers because they fear it would detract from the pure enjoyment of collecting. Some flirt with dealing for years and even try selling from a booth at a show. The nice thing about being a weekend collectible dealer is that the start-up costs are minimal. Anyone can experiment once or twice without risking a major loss. For specific information on how to become a collectible dealer, see pages 72–76.

BUILDING INVESTMENTS. No one should buy a collectible strictly as an investment. The field is too young to have a real track record, and no one can be certain that the country will not wake up one day and decide that paying astronomical prices for items that formerly had only utilitarian value is absurd. The likelihood of this happening is remote, but collectibles are no more reliable than any other investment when it comes to forecasting. A period of severe deflation, economic crisis, or war might quickly change the public's attitude toward buying them. A pure investor should put his money into a sounder medium.

The economic downturn of the early 80's, which resulted from governmental attempts to curb inflation, has brought a modicum of sense to the collectibles market. Prices in many groups have stopped soaring, and on some items there have been corrections downward. There are still many areas where records are being set, but the collectibles setting them are always the rarest and finest examples.

A famous movie producer paid over $60,000 at an auction in 1982 for the balsa wood "Rosebud" sled that was used as a prop in the film *Citizen Kane*. He bought it reportedly because he felt it is an emblem of quality in film making. Emblem or not, if he were to put it back up for sale today, there is no guarantee that it would bring even half as much.

This particular individual is well-heeled enough not to have to worry about such things; however, the average person is not. Most people who begin collecting like to believe that they can get their money back should they need to sell their collection. For those who buy collectibles intelligently, there is a very good chance that this will happen. It is even likely that they will make a profit.

But, there is no certainty, and for this reason I offer this advice: *Buy things you like and will not be unhappy keeping should the market fall apart.* By following this rule you can be assured of never getting hurt in the hobby. It is the people who buy things they do not particularly like, purely as investments, who are stung badly when prices fall and can't even recoup their initial investment.

For those who cannot imagine buying expensive collectibles, I suggest the pursuit of one of the many inexpensive collectible categories. In this way the monetary investment is kept low, and one is freed of having to fret over the future value of items.

For those who, aware of the risks, might still be interested in collecting for investment I offer the following observations.

1. *The collectibles market generally responds favorably to news that the inflation rate is up.* In an inflationary economy people buy "things" at the current price level because they fear that a year later the cost will be much higher. Conversely, during a deflationary period people want to be liquid so that they can take advantage of lower prices. Collectibles and other "things" do not do so well during these times.

2. *In buying collectibles always go for the finest examples in the best possible condition.* As always, the law of supply and demand determines price. The finer pieces are always more in demand and less in supply then their more common counterparts. In addition, the wealthy usually pursue the better pieces, which is an advantage for the seller of quality in a bad economy. When everybody else is tightening their belts, the wealthy can still afford to indulge themselves. For this reason, the holder of top-quality merchandise will still be able to sell when times are rough. This will not be true for those who hold average-quality goods, which, during hard times are very difficult to dispose of at any price.

3. *Always try to buy collectible groups that have continuity with the present.* There is more of a demand for items still produced in some form. Things like comic books, baseball cards, postcards, etc., are alive and have far more supporters than collectibles like straight razors, insulators, and trade cards. An alive collectible can continue bringing new collectors into the fold, which keeps demand up. Dead items attract far less attention.

4. *Stay away from instant collectible offerings*. As discussed earlier, these items are not even true collectibles and have led to the demise of many ill-advised investors.

5. *Lastly, buy with your head and not your heart*. An item that may seem attractive to you might be one of the least desirable types within a group. Always learn as much about the field as possible before buying. Don't rely on smooth-talking dealers for your education. Use all of your senses to acquire the knowledge that will give you power to make the best investments possible.

Before You Begin

Shrewd collecting can be financially profitable in addition to being fun. However, there are some difficulties awaiting those who do not define beforehand what their true motivations for collecting are. We have just discussed some of the benefits one can derive from collecting. Most of them are not mutually exclusive. A person can, for instance, meet people, relieve stress, and become good at something all at the same time. The problems usually start though when one tries to be both a collector and a dealer.

In the purest sense, a collector is someone for whom the ownership of collectibles borders on the religious. A collector worships his collection. A collector will hold, fondle, and stare at his treasures for hours without noticing that time has gone by. A collector's heart races when he is near his beloved possessions. A collector dreams about finding the rarest item in his hobby. A collector would never consider selling his collection unless his family were starving and the rent was due—and then only if he were unable to raise cash in some other manner. Finally, a collector derives a pleasure from his collection that cannot be measured financially.

On the other hand, a true dealer is someone for whom collectibles are *ultimately* merchandise to be bought, sold, and traded. A dealer may become excited about the prospect of obtaining a rare piece. His excitement, though, is more over the thought of dealing the item than of owning it. A good dealer understands that to collect and deal often means working at cross purposes. After all, a collector wants to own the finest pieces—the ones a dealer needs to sell to make his business grow. Therefore one must choose whether to be primarily a collector or a dealer. Not deciding beforehand will deny one the purer pleasures of the former and the profits of the latter.

In today's collectibles market it is very difficult to be a pure collector. Better pieces often cost a great deal, and one needs to wheel and deal as a way of building a collection. My advice is to become a collector, but one who has the best talents of a dealer. That is, someone who utilizes dealers' methods for obtaining collectibles at wholesale but who always keeps the best items for his or her collection, selling only duplicates or what is not wanted. In this way, one can have the best of both worlds.

CHAPTER 2

Collecting

FOR ANYONE CONTEMPLATING COLLECTING, there is a tremendous body of information available about collecting in general. Those who do their homework beforehand will be spared much of the expense of learning through mistakes. The first rule is never to begin buying until you have *handled, read,* and *learned* enough to rely upon yourself. The markets are full of friendly individuals who will gladly take your money for reproductions, forgeries, and damaged items. Buying at one of the collectible forums is not like going into a department store. At the shows, pieces are usually sold "as is," with no return privileges. Remember, *let the buyer beware.*

Things to Know Before You Begin to Buy or Sell

The purpose of reading about and handling as many examples of the collectible one is interested in is to gain a feel for the objects. Having a "feel," as it is called in hobby vernacular, is what makes a collector immediately spot a piece that has been overgraded, tampered with, or is wrong. Obviously, the "feel" is an important skill to pick up, so we will start with grading.

THE CONDITION FACTOR. There is not a single collectible category discussed in this book for which condition is not a major factor in determining desirability and value. Collectors almost always want to obtain the item that is in the best state of preservation. Usually there are fewer pieces extant in the best grade and therefore these command the highest prices. In most fields there are price guides that give condition descriptions for good, fine, and mint. The problem with these guides is that their grading key can never convey the subtle distinctions that make the difference among grades. The price of a very fine condition item may be double that of its very good condition counterpart. Many sellers will wishfully think their wares to a higher grade and price. Grading must be one of the first skills mastered before a collector begins buying.

The way to develop a good grading sense has always been through experience. The dilettante must learn by actually handling enough accurately graded goods. In this case, "handling" means picking up the object, running your fingers over its surfaces to learn the feel of its texture, the quality of its composition. At the same time you should be looking for the fine points of its construction and any distinguishing details it may have. This is the only way. The guide book descriptions of condition are only good for those who supplement them with actual holding, seeing, and feeling collectibles.

For most collectible groups, grading is on a scale from poor to mint condition, with intermediary stages such as good, very good, fine, very fine, and near-mint condition. Never let anyone tell you that grading is on a shifting scale according to age, that the older an object is the less rigorous one has to be in grading it. This is not true. Price guides take into account the relative scarcity of high-grade items by pricing them at several times the amount for similar items in average or low grade. If a seller wants to get the high-condition price, his item must be in that condition and nothing less! With very few exceptions, mint is mint, regardless of age. A piece that is chipped, ripped, marked, repaired, slightly peeling, dried out, or blemished in any other way simply cannot be called perfect. Following is a brief description of the general factors that influence the grading of paper, metal, ceramic, cloth, wood, and plastic collectibles. Any nuances that apply only to a certain collectible will be discussed in the specialized chapters.

Paper: Prior to the industrial advancement that introduced chemicals into the paper-making process, paper could exist for hundreds of years without browning. Today one finds books from the 17th century with snow white pages while pulps from the 1940's have turned totally brittle. One of the most important cri-

teria for assessing paper collectibles is the condition of preservation. A badly browned comic book cannot be handled without
causing flakes of paper to break off. I have seen comics that are
ostensibly perfect, yet when they are opened they reveal heavily
browned pages. Brittleness is to be avoided like the plague. Once
paper has become brittle, there is nothing that can be done to
save it. Eventually it will become dust. This is not true of light
browning however. Paper conservation has become an art, and it
is amazing what the experts can do. Using mixtures like benzene,
they will take a comic book apart and bathe each leaf until the
decomposing chemicals have been neutralized. Stains and Scotch
tape can also be removed through various processes.

Beyond browning, the things to look for that detract from
paper items are rips, tears, creases, stray marks, and soiling. A
perfect paper item will be free of all these. It will be clean and
look the same as it did the day it was produced. If it has one rip,
crease, or penned-in word, it is no longer perfect. There are a
few exceptions to this, and they will be discussed in the relevant
chapters.

When dealing with paper, be aware of the ways in which it can
be repaired, touched up, and made to look perfect. Mold, for
instance, can be eliminated by spraying a light mist of Lysol over
the afflicted areas and then allowing them to dry in a slight breeze.
Worn areas can be recolored using felt-tip pens and watercolors.
Rips can be expertly mended using rice paper (available at art
supply shops) and a thin flour and water paste. Stains can sometimes be removed by soaking the item in warm water, air drying
it, and then flattening it between blotter papers in a book press.
(Improvise if a book press is not available.) Regarding this process,
it is important to test a piece before fully immersing it to make
sure that the inks are fixed and will not run. Most pre-1920 paper
items are safe. To test, hold a corner in the water and check to
see if any dye starts to migrate into the water. If it does, remove
the piece quickly and blot it dry.

Any of the above methods are fine if a collector does not mind
owning a repaired item. In fact, there are even some people who
go out of their way to purchase damaged pieces because they enjoy
doing the work necessary to resurrect them. However, a damaged
or repaired item should be sold as such, and normally a collector

should only have to pay half of what a similar undamaged piece would sell for.

To learn to spot defects and repairs, begin by examining the object inch by inch. By doing this methodically during the early stages of your development as a collector, you will eventually reach the point where close scrutiny will not be necessary and, like other experts, a quick appraisal will tell you what condition an item is in. This ability is part of that quality, discussed earlier, called the "feel."

Metal: Because of their design, major defects are usually pretty obvious on metal objects. It is difficult to disguise a soldered leg or a missing part. But there are a number of small ways in which metal collectibles can be repaired that require specific knowledge and a good eye to detect. For instance, the addition of new parts that closely resemble those that should be there; the repainting of a portion of or even a whole piece; rusted areas that have been scraped and then coated with oil; and heavy polishing, which can make an object appear to be in better shape than it is.

Ceramics: Ceramic objects may be the most difficult collectibles in regard to assessing condition. Particularly in the high-pressure atmosphere of some of the selling forums, it is easy to overlook a hairline crack, a missing piece, or a chip. These are the three most prevalent dangers facing the ceramics collector. The more detailed pieces require especially patient scrutiny in a well-lit area.

Examining carefully means holding a piece in the light and slowly rotating it, making sure to observe everything. Always assume, despite what the seller may say, that there *is* something wrong. In this way you begin playing a game with yourself, the rules of which are that you cannot buy an object until you have proved that it is entirely undamaged. With this attitude you will be more likely to assemble a collection of high-grade pieces.

One repair that beginners often miss is the ground-down lip. The lip of a vase or cup often will be slightly chipped. To remove this imperfection, a craftsman can sand down the entire lip, thus removing the chip and part of the object. Watch for this by always noticing if a piece seems out of proportion.

Regarding cemented sections, on some elaborate pieces locating glued portions is very difficult. Some collectors and dealers carry battery-generated black lights, which when played over an object reveal fissures. This technique may be too much for the beginner but is recommened for those buying expensive items. For the average pieces, the eye is enough.

Glass: Like ceramics, the principal dangers with glass are cracks, chips, and ground-down or glued portions. Glass is easier to examine for fissures because it is generally transparent, and they show up more easily. For the same reason, however, chips are harder to locate. I know one woman who assembled a collection of silver-overlay perfume bottles only to find when she decided to sell them that they all had chips missing in some places. The way to avoid making the kind of mistake she did is to run your fingers over the surfaces of any piece you are considering buying. A chip will feel like a slight indentation. Combine this tactile approach with close eye examination under a bright light, and you will usually find any damage.

Cloth: Amount of wear is usually the key to determining the condition of a garment or other cloth collectible. An item that is still in new condition will appear fresh and supple and have no major mends or stained portions. Some of the most common defects to look for are moth holes or thinning, thread repairs, and brittleness. This last defect applies particularly to animal skins. A pelt that has dried out is practically worthless to anyone. A gentleman once wanted me to buy his raccoon coat; when I examined it, the question of my purchasing it became academic, since the skin side of the fur literally crumpled to the touch.

Wood: Most wooden collectibles were produced by carpenters or cabinetmakers. Their principal output was in the area of furniture. A high-condition piece of furniture is one that is clean and in its original state. This means it has not been refinished, added to, or had major repairs done to it. Much has been written on the art of repairing furniture. There are so many tricks that there is only room here to mention the most common.

Refinishing. A piece that has been refinished can be worth less or more than a similar unrefinished piece. This is based on the factors of rarity, quality of the refinishing, and whether it was in keeping with the style or period of the object.

Marriages. A married piece is one that is not original in the sense that something major has been added to it. An example would be a pedestal table that has had its original top replaced with a different one. As hybrids, most married pieces are undesirable for the real collector.

New fittings. It is very common to find flawed pieces that have been furnished with new fittings. A fitting describes things like hinges, knobs, pulls, etc. New fittings detract from value depending upon how in keeping they are with the integrity of the style or period of the object.

Replaced portions. A replaced portion of wood considerably lowers the overall condition of a piece. Like a marriage, it adulterates the piece in that it can no longer be considered "original." Detecting replaced portions can be very difficult, particularly if the piece has recently been refinished.

In addition to the condition factors just discussed, one should be aware in assessing the condition of any wooden collectibles of stains, chips, deep scratches, warping, and repainting. The presence of any of these factors will lower the overall grade according to severity.

Plastic: Repairs to plastic are usually very easy to detect, and most sellers do not even attempt to work with the material because of the generally low value of plastic collectibles. In examining for repairs, the most common ones to look for are glued sections. In examining for condition, make sure that the plastic is not warped, scratched, or cracked.

A repaired collectible is worth considerably less than its undamaged counterpart; this rule varies, however, depending on the item. A badly cracked glass vase that has been poorly glued together may have only 5 percent of its undamaged value, whereas a camera with a replaced part or a missing handle may be worth only 10 percent less than the full price of a perfect one. Within each chapter, I've indicated how seriously a particular damage reduces value.

REPRODUCTIONS. A reproduction is fine as long as it is properly identified. Once it is offered as the genuine article it is meant to be a copy of, it becomes a fake. Unfortunately, the popularity and value of many collectibles has launched an entire industry of fakes. Comic books, baseball cards, toys, autographs, postcards, furniture, and maps have all been counterfeited. In each chapter I've listed the particular warning signs to look for.

As a general rule, though, the only way to guarantee not getting stuck with a fake is to buy from reputable dealers who are willing to warrant the genuineness of the item they are selling. Make sure that this warranty is written right on the sales receipt. The problem with buying only from reputable dealers is that one will miss out on the possible bargains every collector dreams of. These come from haunting some of the less professional forums for buying and selling collectibles, where deals are done in cash and between strangers, and there is seldom any talk of guarantees or return privileges. My advice is to try and find a balance on the risk/reward scale and always to remember "caveat emptor" before pulling out the wallet. Invariably both beginning collectors and experts will make mistakes. A mistake is an opportunity to learn.

The Best Way to Learn

Employers institute on-the-job training because they know their employees will learn fastest by actually doing their jobs. The best way to learn about the collectibles you are interested in is to read as much as possible about them and go to the collectibles forums. At the forums one has the opportunity to learn firsthand. This experience will enrich and bring life to the things explained in the books. The forums are also places for the beginner to make friends with dealers in order to learn the tricks of the trade. Unlike some skills, which one must pay for to learn, knowledge about collectibles can be had for free if an individual is friendly and inquisitive.

In the next chapter the most popular forums for buying and selling collectibles in this country are examined. Expect that the bigger shows will be better publicized than the smaller regional gatherings, whose promoters often rely more on word of mouth. Invariably, as you enter the collecting ranks, you will make contact with dealers and collectors who will inform you of the dates and locations of shows.

CHAPTER 3

The Collectible Forums

General Antique and Collectible Shows

ESPECIALLY IN THE EAST, antique and collectible shows have proliferated to the point where every community of over 10,000 is sure to have several shows a year. Often they are sponsored by local organizations. These general shows are an excellent place for the beginner to start. At them one has the opportunity to see, feel, and hear about the vast number of things people are collecting today. Often these shows will have a free appraisal booth, an excellent place to observe and learn. To find out where the shows are being held in your area, check both the local papers and one of the national antiques and collectibles periodicals (see list on page 311).

SELLING. Usually, one will do better selling high-quality collectibles to the specialists. This means taking your trains to a train show, your old comics to a comic show, and so on. In this way you will have an opportunity to offer your goods to the highest bidder. At the general shows, specialized items don't bring as much money on the wholesale level. The only items one should bring to them are low-quality collectibles and miscellaneous antiques. Dealers in general antique and collectible merchandise are not as selective because they don't know enough about all the items they sell. Often they will pay more than an item is worth because they think it is better than it is. As you learn more about the group you decide to specialize in, you can take advantage of this fact. Conversely, these dealers often let good material go for much less than it is worth. To take advantage of the possible bargains, always be sure to arrive early on the first day of the show. By noon most of the "sleepers" will be picked over.

35

Garage, House, Rummage, and White Elephant Sales

When sales like these are held in or near the larger cities, they rarely offer fine collectibles at a bargain. The situation was different before the media spread the word that anything collectible has value. What I have found lately is that certain items like comic books, baseball cards, toys, coins, and postcards set off an alarm among pricers when spotted during the preparation for a sale. These items are generally removed until a price can be determined. This determination is usually accomplished by four or five misguided individuals who stand around trading stories about how they have read that this or that particular collectible is very valuable. Ultimately, they offer the items at far more than their actual value. Sellers like this, in trying not to cheat themselves, end up overcharging ignorant buyers.

A typical example is a box of recent baseball cards worth a penny a piece on the collector's market, offered at 25–50 cents each. Even when sellers take the time to buy a price book, they generally make pricing errors due to misjudgment on grading.

My reason for presenting all the bad things that can happen at amateur sales is to protect buyers from themselves. Just as sellers have heard stories of baseball cards worth hundreds of dollars, buyers have heard stories of collections worth thousands being sold for a few dollars. Most of these stories are true, and they still happen but less frequently than before the media blitz. Therefore, if you are a buyer, be wary and cautious and be satisfied if you can buy collectibles you like at reasonable wholesale prices. If you do run into items that have been grossly overpriced, call attention to this fact. Often this kind of situation can provide an opportunity for you to practice the negotiating skills discussed on pages 52–56.

Flea Markets

The grandfather of all modern flea markets is the Marché aux Puces that has been held in Paris since the 1860's. At this market thousands of venders sell everything imaginable, and trash is often stacked next to treasures. Going to one of the larger outdoor flea markets located throughout the United States will amaze even the most unflappable individual. Several hundred dealers congregate at the larger markets, filling an area the size of a dozen football fields. There is always a carnival atmosphere, with barkers demonstrating home improvement products and food vendors selling every ethnic delicacy imaginable. Products new and old are hawked by colorful dealers who are part of a growing number of peripatetic "flea dealers." These dealers sell merchandise that runs the gamut from brand-new watches of questionable background to 500-year-old Persian rugs. An expedition to a market can be anything from a serious search for rare collectibles to a playful jaunt with some friends. Whatever your intentions, when you go you will never leave without buying something.

SELLING. Flea markets are not the place to sell fine-quality antiques and collectibles. Buyers are looking for bargains, and it is hard to get them to pay retail prices for desirable items. For this reason, the best things to sell at a market are inexpensive items that appear to be desirable collectibles. For instance, I know a postcard dealer who separates any stock he buys into two inventories. One inventory consists of quality postcards. These he sells through the mail and at postcard shows. The other inventory consists of poor-conditions and low-quality cards. These he sells at flea markets. So far he has done very well selling these cards to the tyros who show up at the markets. If you would like to try selling at flea markets, see page 72 for advice on starting a collectibles business.

BUYING. Flea market dealers are notorious salespeople and always try to make the buyer think he is getting something for nothing. Such dealers play on the greed of shoppers who have heard stories about thousand-dollar items being bought for a dollar at a flea market. These things do happen but only to collectors who know their fields inside and out, and not with the frequency the public is led to believe. I urge buyers to be cautious at flea markets. As long as one sticks to buying collectibles one is familiar with, there are no problems. If you are a beginner and start to get ideas of the "score" or the "find," watch out, because you are probably getting set for a fall. *Buy only what you know.*

To find the bargains (and possible scores) that appear at every flea market, one must get up very early and be at the site while the dealers are setting up. This usually means arriving by eight A.M.

The *National Flea Market Directory* is a very good source for finding out where and when flea markets are being held around the country. It is published four times a year and is available from Clarks, Rt. 4, Box 151, Milton, FL 32570. (See also *Jersey Devil* on page 314.)

Auctions

Currently, the larger prestigious auction houses in the big cities of the United States will not take consignments in most of the collectible categories we are discussing. The reason they give is that these collectibles do not have the kind of track record wealthy investors want. This statement is belied of course by the fact that these same houses will readily sell movie memorabilia, toy trains, and records. The real answer to why they won't yet carry some collectibles is that they don't understand them and are afraid to venture into uncharted waters where there is the possibility of making errors. Until this situation changes, sellers will have to be content to sell some of their extremely rare or otherwise special collectibles without the tremendous hype a major auction house can generate. Buyers, on the other hand, can benefit from this by attending the many smaller auctions where rare collectibles regularly are sold at wholesale prices.

In the suburbs of the major cities, the outlying areas, and in smaller cities and towns across the United States, small and medium-size auction houses and companies routinely dispose of estates, private collections, and the inventories of bankrupts. For the experienced collectibles buyer, these can be *the* places to pick up tremendous buys. However, they can also be, for the uninitiated, the place for severe disaster. Following is an explanation of some common auction terms and what they mean to both the buyer and seller.

BUYER'S PREMIUM. Some auctions charge the buyer a percentage of the hammer price as a premium. Typically, the percentage has been 10 percent. This policy is frowned upon, particularly by dealers who are often the main constituent at an auction. At the time of this writing, there are several legal suits in New York over the legality of charging both buyer and seller a percentage. The cases revolve around the idea that an auction house that charges both parties is involved in a conflict of interest. At any rate, the smaller auction houses usually do not charge this premium, so that the buyer only has to pay the hammer price plus applicable taxes if he succeeds in winning an item.

SELLER'S CHARGES. Most auction houses charge sellers between 10 and 25 percent of the hammer price for the house's services in conducting the sale. The determination of the exact percentage is usually decided by policy; however, there is always leeway for bargaining, particularly if a seller has a highly desirable collection or single piece. In addition to the percentage of the hammer price, the seller often can expect to pay for things like insurance, photography (if there is a catalog), and so forth. It is a good idea to discuss these matters before signing a consignment agreement. Again, depending on the desirability of your merchandise, certain fees can be waived or reduced. Never assume intransigence on the part of auction representatives. They are out to make money, and if they feel they will lose your material unless they are flexible, they usually will be.

RESERVES. A reserve agreement is the usually confidential agreement between auctioneer and seller that a piece will not be permitted to sell for less than a certain price. If a piece does not sell for a price above the reserve, then it is "bought in" by the desk. Many auctions charge a fee if they buy in a piece. This buy-in charge is another fee that can be waived. The reserve protects the seller from a poorly attended auction. It is recommended whenever a quality item is being sold and is usually set at the wholesale value of a piece. In this way a seller will get at least what he could've gotten wholesale should his item bring only the reserve price.

CATALOG. Many smaller auction houses cannot afford to produce a catalog of the items they will be offering. In lieu of the catalog they will send out brochures and fliers. For the buyer, the lack of a catalog is usually good since since fewer people will actually get to see the goods being offered. For the seller, a catalog improves the chances of netting a high price. One never knows when a collector from across the country will spot an item in a catalog and send in a mail bid or make a phone bid on the day of the auction.

HOW TO BUY AT AUCTION.   The rule at any auction anywhere is to establish beforehand the maximum amount you are willing to spend on a particular lot. This means actually making a list indicating lot numbers and prices, so you will not yield to temptation once the auction begins. Something about the concreteness of having a list has saved many otherwise uncontrolled auction buyers. Auction fever can become a very real addiction. To save yourself the agony of feeling that you have paid much too much, follow the rule about the list and never bid spontaneously.

In addition to the more abstract auction fever, there are several other stumbling blocks for the buyer at auctions. To begin with, while auction prices tend to be wholesale (in that mostly dealers buy at them), this does not mean that certain pieces do not attract undue attention and bring far over their retail value. This is particularly true of collectibles selling at auctions where the buyers are novices in that particular field. I have seen electric trains sell for double and triple their retail prices to naive dealers who thought they were going to score on the seeming ignorance of the rest of the people at an auction.

Typically, this situation occurs when at least two greedy souls spot an item they think is better than it is and bid their heads off trying to get it. To avoid making this mistake, try not to bid on anything you do not know enough about. If you do try to make a buy out of your area of knowledge, never go above that price you've set down as your limit.

Another trick to not getting taken at an auction is to try and forget what most people believe about auctions. They are not forums of pure bargains. Yes, finds are made at them, but more often mistakes are unloaded on unwitting buyers. Usually the temptation is to think that you've spotted that rarity everyone else has missed. This seldom occurs.

SELLING AT AUCTION.   It is probably better to sell your collectibles to a dealer who specializes in them if you are considering an auction as your only other alternative. Unless you own an extremely rare or desirable piece, an auction will bring only the wholesale price for your object. And by the time you factor in the cost of paying the auction house for their various services, the time value of money (most items must be consigned one month before a sale, and settlement checks are not issued until two to four weeks after the sale), and the aggravation of the whole affair, the amount you will receive will be less than what you would have made selling the items immediately to a dealer. Even with finer objects there is no guarantee that a particular auction will be good, and you run the risk (unless you have a reserve) of getting far less than you would had you sold the piece privately.

Collectible Shows

The spectacle of a major collectible show involves hundreds of dealers from all over the country setting up tables covered with toys, comic books, baseball cards, photographica, militaria, or whatever the particular show is featuring. Thousands of collectors come and squeeze their way through narrow aisles, fondling the goods and negotiating deals. The atmosphere is intense and the action is non-stop all day.

The huge collectible shows which feature popular items like books, mechanical devices, bottles, dolls, watches, and clocks, as well as those groups mentioned above, are usually held in major cities across the country. These events are national in the sense that they attract dealers and collectors from all over the country (and world) and are often the highlight of the collecting year for a particular category. Usually they run two to four days and feature special guest speakers, exhibits, seminars, and auctions. For the collector, they provide an extended period of collector reality and an opportunity to buy just about anything within a given field.

The smaller collectible shows account for the major percentage of conventions held during a given year. Usually they last only a day and are primarily forums for buying and selling. There are two types of smaller shows, the ones that feature the more esoteric collectible groups and those that are miniature versions of their larger counterparts. Regardless of the size of the show, there is no better place to see, buy, sell, and trade collectibles. For the beginning collector in any field, the specialized show is a vast reservoir of accumulated knowledge that can be tapped by anyone interested enough to talk to the dealers and collectors in attendance. Along with verbal communication, collectors have an opportunity to learn by examining and comparing items. The collectible show is *the place* to learn about grading and pricing and to pick up savvy about market trends and developments. Nowhere else can one hope to find so many collectors of a particular item in the same room.

STRIKING UP A CONVERSATION. This section is for those shy individuals who are not sure exactly how to start a conversation with another collector or a dealer.

The easiest way is to start with the dealers. As a rule, they love to talk! Since many of them were once collectors themselves (and many still are), the easiest way to get them started is to query them about a particular piece and its provenance. Partly because they hope to sell it to you, but also because talking about it is enjoyable for them, most dealers will ramble on and on when questioned about an item. Don't stop them as you normally might stop a long-winded friend or relative. Some of the most useful information can be gleaned from what might ostensibly seem a boring explanation. Learning about a hobby requires acquiring a foundation, and for most beginners every bit of information can be put to some use. Dealers are particularly eager to talk if a show is slow. Buying them a cup of coffee from the nearest vendor will probably also result in your receiving an additional discount (should you buy anything) and extra words of advice.

The dealers are also very important for another reason. They can be your main source for obtaining items for your collection. If you live in an area where pieces are not easy to obtain, a dealer met at a show can become a mail order source for buying. Many collectors print up "want lists" that also include their addresses and telephone numbers and pass them out at shows. In this way they will be contacted if any of their "wants" are obtained.

SELLING. Selling to dealers at a collectible show can be the most expedient way of disposing of a collection, providing you are satisfied with receiving the wholesale value of your goods. Dealers need inventory, and many count on being able to buy collections that "walk through the door" at shows. The person who wants or needs to sell a collection quickly can take one of two approaches. The first is to price up all the items as a lot and "walk it around" until a deal can be consummated with one of the dealers. This approach is best used when there are only a few good pieces in a collection. It avoids the danger of having the best items "cherry picked" out and being left with the chaff. The second approach, best used when all the items are of the same quality, is to price everything individually and then take it around, allowing the dealers to choose what they want.

TAKING OFFERS. If you are not sure how much you should ask for your items, you can use the "taking offers" approach. This is not favored by many dealers who feel that by making an offer they are cutting off their own noses by giving a seller a base price to work with. There is truth to this feeling. I have watched many people have a dealer carefully go through a collection and come up with a price, only to see these same people bring the collection to a table an aisle away and sell the lot for only ten dollars more. The fairest way for everyone seems to be to bring a lot around with the pre-arranged notion of selling it to the individual who will pay at least 20 percent more than the last highest offer. This technique will quickly identify who the highest payers are. In the area of wholesale prices, you can generally expect to net between 20 percent and 80 percent of the retail value of your items. The actual percentage will depend on things like desirability, inventory turnover time, market conditions, and the mood of the dealers on that particular day.

SELLING TO OTHER COLLECTORS. If there is anything that will get you lynched at a collectible show, it is trying to sell to other collectors if you have not paid for a table to display your goods. Dealers feel very strongly about the fact that they have incurred expenses for transportation, lodging, food, and so on in coming to exhibit at a show and react strongly to non-dealers trying to take away some of their business by selling on the floor. Avoid doing this. If you are interested in the details of becoming a part-time dealer see Chapter 6.

In some cases it is better to sell collectibles at a non-specialized market. This is true when an item, say a comic book, appears to be more valuable than it actually is in its specialized market. In every collectible group there are things that are considered "losers" or white elephants. Trying to sell these items at a specialized show will always result in very poor offers. On the other hand, taking them to a non-specialist, who may think they are more desirable or valuable than they are, could yield a better price. I mention this not to encourage readers to try and rip off dealers, but to make people aware of the fact that within the field of collectibles there are many levels of "being informed." These same dealers who pay too much for collectibles they don't know enough about are also the dealers who pass them on to the next party at even more inflated prices. Therefore, it is very important to try and reach people who are truly knowledgeable about prices and grading before you begin buying.

Consignment Shops

A relatively new phenomenon, the consignment shop is usually a privately owned store where individuals can bring various goods to be sold under the usual terms of two-thirds to the consignor, one-third to the owner of the shop. The quality of the merchandise sold will vary according to the location of the store. Generally, the more affluent the area the better the goods being sold on consignment.

The consignment shop is one of the last places to try to sell quality collectibles. This is because one, the owners of such stores usually don't possess superior knowledge of the collectible markets and as a result are unable to price or represent collectible merchandise properly, and two, "buyers" at consignment shops are usually looking for bargains and will not generally pay the price for quality collectibles. Of course, for this reason they can be used as a place of last resort for disposing of low-grade collectibles. Like their counterparts, general antique and collectible shows, they do generate the "treasure in the trash" hype that has encouraged many buyers to spend more than they should have for valueless items.

If you are persistent, and a bit lucky, regular visits to consignment shops could eventually lead to a serendipitous find.

Estate Sales

An estate sale is not a garage sale, although the latter is sometimes misrepresented as such. Estate sales involve the selling off of a person's or a family's entire lifetime of possessions, minus, of course, items that will be removed for sentimental reasons. Today, estate sales are usually run by individuals or firms that specialize in estate liquidation. For a percentage of the ultimate gross value of the possessions, estate sellers will handle everything from the initial appraisal of the items to the physical selling of them. All advertising costs, labor expenses, and damage responsibility are theirs. The usual commission rate is 25 percent, but on estates over $10,000 in value it decreases. The bigger and better the estate, the more power the contractee has in negotiating. It is always advisable to call in a few of the different agencies in your area and listen to their various pitches.

FOR THE SELLER. Estate sales are fine places for disposing of quality collectibles if the individuals handling the sale know enough about their value and take the trouble to publicize them well enough that collectors become aware of them. I have seen the gamut of price variance at estate sales, from the comic selling at 50 times its real value to the old toy boat selling for $50 instead of $5,000. Assuming that your collectibles are properly researched and advertised, they will do very well at an estate sale, because buyers often get caught up in looking for the exceptional piece that has escaped all but their attention. I have seen quite ordinary pieces bring prices that exceed all rational explanation. With this warning, we will turn to the pros and cons of seeking collectibles at estate sales.

FOR THE BUYER. To avoid wasting time going to sales that do not even have collectibles, check with the firms that run estate sales beforehand. Most include their telephone numbers in their advertisements, and a quick phone conversation can save you a lot of time and aggravation. Be sure to find out exactly what collectibles will be offered and, if possible, how much they will cost. Often the people running these sales are not familiar with selling the newer collectibles, since their primary business is with furniture and furnishings, and they will be vague in their descriptions. Try to force them to be specific. Sometimes, if you sound like you know a whole lot about particular items, you may be invited into the house before the sale to act as a kind of consultant. With this type of arrangement you can usually expect as your fee the right to buy a couple of the best items at whatever price you would like to pay. Clearly, this kind of thing is not legitimate, but it is often done anyway. (The new breed of estate dispersal services is run by private people who are often unprofessional.) Once you have located a promising sale, arrange to get there early, about two hours before the doors open. Most outfits hand out admission numbers one hour before the sale begins. It is not unusual, for really big sales, to find dealers camped out on the lawn of the house a day or two before. If you cannot get to a sale early enough to be one of the first people through the door, you might as well forget being able to buy any bargains. These will have been bought up within the first two hours.

On entering a sale, be ready to move quickly. If, for instance, you see an item that looks as if it might be good, pick it up immediately or in some way stake a claim to it. Those who hesitate at a sale lose their chance. I have seen many lots scooped up right from under someone's nose. To avoid having this happen to you, learn to be fast.

There is a New York dealer who has become infamous at estate sales for his "label system." The clever devil is always one of the first to enter a sale and quickly stakes his claim to the best items by affixing a pressure-sensitive label reading "Sold to Martin Woofstan" (name changed) on them. He will run through a sale, distributing a label wherever he thinks he sees a buy. Later, after he has covered everything, he goes over every piece slowly to determine whether it is really worth purchasing and removes labels from items he doesn't want. I don't condone this rather showy and obnoxious way of staking a claim on items, but I recount it to illustrate the kind of "pressure to purchase quickly" that is on at a sale and also to show that you need not be positive you are going to purchase something when you pick it up.

One last note: The individuals who run estate sales must rely heavily on dealers who return week after week to purchase goods for their inventories. For this reason they are often willing to work with a person who will come back regularly to buy particular items. With this in mind, you may be interested in establishing a buying relationship with one or several of estate sales outfits in your area.

Antique Shops

Antique shops can be excellent sources for obtaining fine-quality collectibles. The prices charged at these shops usually will not be wholesale, but a clever collector can benefit by establishing himself as the person to call when specific items come in. Several years ago antique dealers shied away from collectibles. At that time an item had to be at least 50 years old to be classified as an antique and hence valuable. Today the situation has changed drastically, and most antique-shop owners will actively pursue any collectibles that cross their path.

The best way to establish yourself and your particular interests at antique stores is to hand out a business card listing your name, address, telephone number, and collecting categories. By giving them a card you automatically give yourself more credibility. Most dealers keep a card file divided into item classifications so that when a collection comes in they can easily look up whom to call. They especially like to sell to collectors since dealers will usually only pay them wholesale prices. Follow-up visits are always advisable as a way of reminding shop owners that you are still interested in buying. Often, if you haunt a place enough, you may even become friendly with the dealer, which could lead to your becoming his visiting expert in a particualr area. This is a position you should try to develop since it could lead to your buying some very fine pieces for your collection at reasonable prices. I have always found that, given time, all antique dealers eventually get quality collectibles.

Collectible Stores

There are already stores throughout the country devoted exclusively to the sale of baseball cards, comic books, records, gaming machines, music boxes, toys, postcards, trains, and dolls. In addition, there are hundreds of other stores that specialize in selling a mélange of collectibles. Most of these stores are located in and around major cities and are a dream come true for collectors living close enough to patronize them. The collectible store makes it possible for collectors to walk in and buy desired items without having to wait for a convention or order through the mail. They are also places where collectors can meet and learn.

Collectible stores can be good places to buy if their owners are trying to cultivate a clientele of knowledgeable collectors and not a series of one-time sales to dilettantes. The reason for establishing this difference is that there are stores that take advantage of the public's interest in collectibles by offering items at vastly inflated prices. I have seen comic books, for instance, priced at some stores for up to ten times their true market value. This variance cannot be attributed simply to overhead since there are many respectable comic stores that sell their wares at reasonable prices. Unless you are unlucky enough to stumble into one of the "robber" shops, your experience with buying at collectible stores should be beneficial.

Selling to a collectible store is not as good as selling at a convention. Store owners know that a seller is more or less "theirs" once the seller walks in carrying the items he wishes to sell. This is not to say that one will not receive a fair or even a generous offer from a storekeeper, only that dealers are known to pay more when they have to compete with other dealers waiting to see a collection. There are, however, other ways of utilizing a store to move out part or all of your collection. These ways include consignment, percentage sales, and trading.

Mail Order Dealers

Many collectible dealers have full-time jobs in some other field and devote only weekends and evenings to their collectible business. This usually means that having a store is impractical, and so many use mail order selling as a way to augment their show sales. Buying collectibles through the mail can be an expedient and pleasurable way to buy, especially for collectors who live in regions that do not have many shows or stores.

The most crucial factor in buying through the mail is to ascertain the terms and grading standards of a dealer before placing a major order. This is not always easy. If you've made contact with a dealer at a show, then you may already know the accuracy of his grading and selling terms. However, if you have not, then the thing to do is to try a few inexpensive trial orders. Uusally the results of these will be indicative of a dealer's standards. It is also advisable to try to deal only with those who offer a return privilege.

Some dealers issue catalogs that are valuable as price reference material. Many collectors send away for these specifically as a way of learning about the current market values in their hobby. In this respect these are more reliable for learning prices than the guides. I strongly recommend this approach for beginners.

Museums

Museums can be tiresome. There is always so much to see, and a person is quickly overwhelmed by an overload of sensory input. However, if approached with the correct mental attitude and plan, a trip to a museum can be edifying and enjoyable.

Many collectibles are now part of the permanent collections of major museums. There are also some collectible groups that have generated museums. Among these are comic art, toys, railroad-iana, and marine items. The way to find out which collectibles are housed in the permanent collections of museums near you is to contact the curator or head of a museum. In many instances you may be able to arrange for a private viewing if the items are not on display. For those collecting any kind of printed material that has been copyrighted, and this includes comic books and magazines, the Library of Congress in Washington, D.C., is supposed to have a copy of everything. If you make an appointment and fill out a request form you can see any of the early comic issues from the 40's, the first *Playboy* magazine, and so on. Eventually, some libraries intend to eliminate the physical specimens since they are subject to decay and thievery. Everything they own will be on microfiche; and the collector of the future will not be able to appreciate the true nature of these paper items.

Thrift Shops

Thrift shops are often owned and run by charitable organizations, which rely on the donation of goods from the public to fill their shelves and racks. For this reason one can generally expect to find much in the way of clothing and little in the way of collectibles. What few collectibles do come in are generally of low quality. This, combined with the fact that there are usually insiders who look for potentially valuable donations, makes it unlikely that one will find anything of collectible note at an organization-run thrift shop.

There is, however, another kind of thrift store that is privately operated and where one can sometimes find quality items. These stores buy their merchandise used from private individuals. One famous store, the Ritz Thrift Shop in Manhattan, specializes in high-quality furs, silver, and jewelry. Here, collectors can sometimes buy old toy soldiers, cameras, watches, etc.

Find the better thrift stores in your neighborhood and make yourself known at them by leaving your card (as discussed earlier). If something good comes in, you then have a chance of being called. Sometimes, if it is an item or collection that requires specialized knowledge, you may even find yourself acting as a kind of combination appraiser/consultant.

The general rule regarding thrift stores is that their merchandise usually reflects the economic status of their clientele. A store in a low-income or low-middle-income area will probably not have the rare piece of art glass or Indian jewelry that the store in a high-income area might have.

CHAPTER 4

Buying

SOMETIMES, WHEN I STEP BACK for a moment and cast a mercilessly objective eye on the whole of collecting and collectibles, I am aghast at the utter insanity of people paying sometimes the equivalent of a year's rent to own an old toy or comic book. There is a sense of unreality that presides in most of the collectible markets. People who normally watch their pennies at a supermarket will nonchalantly pay $300 for an old doll that once cost only three dollars. Men who would never play in the stock market will lay out a thousand bucks for a windup tin Buck Rogers ship. One day a particular toy is priced at $50 and nobody is interested. The next day someone important in the antique toy business comes along and says that the item is rare, and a week later it is worth $150. Conversely, the market on Ansel Adams prints may be hot one year and cold the next. The thing every collector must do no matter what he collects is determine the amount of money he can afford to spend on collectibles *because he loves them*. One must forget about things like investment potential when making this judgment. Collectibles should be purchased with the attitude of "I don't care what somebody says it will be worth tomorrow, because it's worth to me what I'm paying for it today." If one adopts this attitude, one will be spared considerable aggravation in the future.

How to Buy

For most collectibles there is some form of published material listing valuations or price records. Generally, the best way to proceed in learning how much to pay is to combine studying price guides, catalogs, and lists with going to the forums to see how the listed prices compare with the marketplace. In every field there are nuances the books don't reveal. A particular baseball card selling at a convention for triple its guide price may not be over-priced at all but rather reflect a market turn or revelation that has yet to be recorded in the book. Or, an item may be selling for more than its book list because the dealer selling it feels it is more rare than the author of the book does. Particularly in collectible fields that are in their incipiency, one will find discrepancies in valuation and in information. Thankfully, the more developed collectible groups can be approached with greater reliance on catalog or guide prices.

Strategy

Following is an example of the kind of situation collectible buyers are often faced with. By examining the responses of two different individuals, we can begin to understand what strategies the wise collector needs to adopt in order to make the best deal.

A garage sale is being held in a residential area, and two people, collector A and collector B, plan on attending in search of baseball cards. A arrives first. He has only recently begun collecting and is unsure of such basics as the pricing structure within the hobby and grading standards. After asking the man running the sale if he has any cards for sale, A is pleasantly surprised to find that the man has three shoeboxes of old cards. A fingers a few cards and then immediately asks what the price is for each. He doesn't try to mask his excitement. The owner, sizing up the situation, believes A to be a knowledgeable baseball card collector who has spotted some good cards. He responds to the question about price by saying, "Just pick out what you want and then we'll discuss it." A complies and goes through the three boxes carefully. He is amazed at how many valuable cards there seems to be. He is sorry he didn't bring his price guide. Without it, he is unsure of how much each card is worth. A selects only those cards he wants very much, because they picture particular players he likes. After he is through A hands the stack he has selected to the man and asks, "How much?" After a cursory examination the man looks up and asks, "Well, what are they worth to you?" This is not what A has been expecting. He is not sure how much he should offer. He is afraid of either paying too much or offering too little and losing the deal entirely. After a few frantic calculations based on the number of cards he has selected, A shrugs and says, "I don't know; I guess I could pay $50?" To this, the owner responds, "I'll tell you what; you had first look and all so I think you should pay $100." After several moments of verbose negotiations a deal is struck, and A exits with the cards, $75 poorer.

On the way out he passes B, who on seeing the cards in A's hand, curses the traffic jam that made him arrive late for this sale. B heads immediately to the man running the sale and inquires if there are any more baseball cards. He is shown the three shoe-boxes and told the cards are priced according to player. As the owner walks away he adds that there probably aren't any good ones left. B says nothing but begins to rapidly thumb through the cards. He cannot believe his eyes but is careful not to let his excitement show. By the time he's finished with the first box, he knows that there are over $1,000 worth of cards. Although he doesn't need all of them, he summons the owner and with a blank face mentions the fact that he might be interested in buying the lot of cards, if they can agree on a price. The owner, more concerned with a young couple who are thinking of buying his old dining room set, quickly appraises the three boxes and asks, "Well, what do you think is a fair price?" B hesitates and looks like he is exasperated and maybe about to walk away. Finally he responds, "Look, they're your cards, you make the price." The owner, thinking that the other collector probably took all the better cards, sighs and with a nervous glance in the direction of the young couple says, "Okay, just give me 50 bucks and you can take them all." B pauses for effect and then smiles saying, "Alright, fair enough." He quickly pays the owner and exits.

Epilogue: On the way home A worries about whether he had paid too much for the cards. As soon as he gets to his house he runs to check his price guide. A is pleased to find that he has made a good deal after all. The cards he paid $75 for are worth around $140. He is sorry he didn't pick out more and begins to consider going back to the sale.

When B arrives home, he, too, goes to the price book but to

get exact figures on a few of the rare cards. He already knows he's made a score. In fact, totaling the value for the three boxes, B finds that he has bought over $1,300 worth of cards. He is ecstatic. Even though he does not collect the particular series he has just bought, he can use the profit he'll make selling them to other collectors to purchase items he does want. The same day he invites two collector friends over for trading.

Back at the garage sale, the man has just finished counting the day's receipts so far and is chagrined to find that he has only taken in $390. The young couple decided not to take the old dining room set.

Without belaboring the obvious, it is clear that A's inexperience as both a collector and negotiator led to his not getting a very good deal on all of the cards. What were some of the mistakes he made? His most egregious error, aside from walking into a sale without having at least brought his reference material, was in assuming the owner knew the value of the cards. Often a seller is in the dark about how to price an item or group and waits for feedback from interested parties. If A had casually waved a hand toward the boxes and asked, "How much?"—indicating them all—the owner would have had an entirely different feeling about his cards. By asking how much each was, A told the owner that at least some of the cards were worth enough to be priced individually. Another major tactical error on A's part was in not forcing the owner to make the first price. A good bargainer always lets the seller make the first price. If it is too high, the buyer can always bargain down. Any seller who won't quote a price is waiting for you to teach him. Don't!

Anyone interested in selling collectibles must be willing to make the same investment of time and money as the next person. If an individual is not willing to, he should not expect to be educated for free by the buyer. In addition, there are many people who are in the business of "picking" at garage sales and other forums and then bringing the goods they have purchased around to dealers and collectors for offers. Only when these individuals are convinced that they finally know the value of their items will they try to sell them, usually at full retail value and not to one of the people whose brain they picked for information. Most people in the trade consider this unacceptable behavior and try to discourage it by refusing to make offers to or answer the questions of those who have a reputation.

In our example, buyer B was the antithesis of buyer A. B was the knowledgeable collector and consummate bargainer. He betrayed no emotion and was careful not to help the seller in any way. By appearing casual, he made the man think the cards were worth very little. While one may question the ethical implications of B's "put on" behavior for the sake of making a good deal, remember that at no point did he lie or give false information. B merely used all the techniques of a good bargainer to get the best deal. It was not his fault that the man decided to sell something without first researching its value.

This example reveals just some of the dos and don'ts in the strategy of buying well. Following is some more information that every collector should know regarding the art of negotiation.

Bargaining

Most antiques and collectibles dealers expect to bargain. Only once have I encountered a person who would not lower his prices. It was at a Manhattan antiques show, and the man had an eclectic group of small antique and collectible items scattered on the tables in his booth. A small candy tin caught my fancy. It was priced at $22, and I held it up to the attention of the man running the stall. When he saw me I asked if he could do any better. I wanted and expected him to say, "Give me twenty," and was therefore taken aback when he shook his head and mumbled something about the prices being as marked. Normally, I would have left the piece on principle, but in this case it seemed silly to cut off my nose, and anyway I was not buying the piece for resale.

A revealing epilogue to this story is that later on the same day I happened to be making a second circuit of the floor, when I heard voices arguing nearby. Looking toward the sound, I discovered that our mumbling friend had succeeded in irritating a woman. Moving closer, I joined the ranks of several other busybodies observing the conflict. Apparently the woman would not accept the fact that he would not lower his prices. She was insisting that he give her a "break" on a ceramic figurine of the Buddha. "This is unheard of," she barked. "I only asked for a 10 percent discount!" Eventually she left, leaving the Buddha. I noticed with some degree of satisfaction that most of the items I had seen on his table that morning were still there. Why was this man unwilling to lower his prices? Had he been smart he would have added 10 percent more to his entire inventory, thus allowing himself a margin to dicker. This is the approach almost all dealers take.

When buying at the shows, always assume you will be able to get at least 10 percent off the marked price. Use this as a minimum discount and then, depending on how much you want the item, try for more. Don't be ashamed to negotiate; and don't be intimidated by people who say, "I don't bargain." Anyone who won't ask a dealer for a better price is either extremely shy or very foolish, because most dealers price their goods with the intent of coming down. I think there are some who would actually have heart failure if a customer just walked up and paid the full asking price on a piece. I know some sellers who actually tack on 25 percent more than they would be happy with. This way they can afford to seem extremely generous and therefore make many new customers.

There is one exception to the rule that you should always bargain. This is when your instincts as a collector tell you that an item is already bargain priced and there are other collectors or dealers nearby. I have seen wonderful opportunities lost by people who try to bargain at the wrong time. If an object is very underpriced, don't try to get it for less. This is offensive to the gods of good fortune, and they will punish you by bringing someone else along, who at just the crucial moment will say, "I'll take it at that price."

One bargaining approach that some buyers have perfected to an art could be called the "denigration act." It involves pointing out real and imagined defects in a piece. The trick is to walk the fine line between pointing out so many flaws that the dealer will say, "Don't take it, then" and making him feel that his item is truly worth a lot less than he is asking. Make sure you know the subject well so that your criticisms sound intelligent. Nothing alerts a dealer more quickly to a phony than a lack of basic knowledge about a subject. The game is to make the seller think you know more than he does. At garage, estate, and church sales this is particularly easy to accomplish. With established antique dealers, it is not so easy.

Trading

Trading can be an effective way of obtaining desirable items at much less than they would cost you if you purchased them. The principle behind maximizing its effectiveness is to find a dealer or collector who has something you particularly value but which means very little to him. An example of this would be finding a general antiques dealer who happens to have acquired a rare autograph you want. Not being a specialist, it is probable that the dealer paid very little for the item and would be happy to trade it to you for some items he is more familiar with. You might happen to have some old postcards or candlesticks you don't want (collectors always have miscellaneous items lying around) that would be perfect for the occasion. Even if all "trade" deals are not as perfect as this example, they all at least provide an opportunity to acquire items without spending money.

Buying Through the Mail

Ordering collectibles through the mail can be risky unless you are dealing with established sellers whose grading and pricing standards you know. A common problem is misgrading. So many people have ordered items cataloged as "fine" only to receive them in poor condition. Most dealers accept returns, but who needs the aggravation of rewrapping a collectible and mailing it back? It is always simpler just to keep it. This is, incidentally, the very strategy behind the major mail order sellers who offer the public a 10-day trial period on things from steak knives that "never wear out" to "miracle" choppers. They know that most people would rather pay the $12.95 than have to wrap up a set of steak knives and take them back to the post office. If you do order through the mail, try a couple of inexpensive test orders to see how reliable a particular dealer is.

Buying at Auction

Buying at auction can sometimes be a good source of obtaining choice items reasonably. Auction prices are generally wholesale, but be wary of the exceptions where certain items are hyped and bring prices far in excess of their market value. Generally, if you are experienced and know your hobby, you will not be burned. Remember, though, auction fever is a very real disease and many otherwise rational people have bid way out of bounds in a compulsion not to be bested. Many auctions also charge buyers a fee of 10 percent of the hammer price. Add this fee to the sales tax, and you end up paying almost 20 percent above the winning bid price. Be careful.

Creating Opportunities to Buy

There are generally two approaches people take in representing their hobby to the public. The first approach is that of the closet collector who relegates his collecting to a secret weekend world of shows where his anonymity is protected. This approach is favored by many professionals who still feel that their reputation could be damaged if word got out that they saved certain collectibles. This attitude has lessened somewhat in the past five years as public knowledge about the high value of some collectibles has spread.

The second approach is that of the collector who integrates his hobby with his everyday life, taking no pains to deny or hide it from his peers. Those who decide to take this approach can benefit from sources they can generate in their daily lives. The various forums are fine for buying, but most don't offer an opportunity for making the really good purchase that most collectors dream about. There is always the element of luck in making a serendipitous find; however, one can make oneself lucky.

The first step is to have a business card printed advertising your specific hobby as well as your name, address, and telephone number. It helps to put something catchy on the card like a design or saying. A business card gives you credibility. People assume when handed one that you are serious about your interest. Hand out cards to anyone who might eventually become a lead or connection to a collection. Never worry about people thinking you strange or odd. This is entirely their problem. Many of the world's leading citizens collect seemingly crazy things.

In addition to developing leads through friends, you should give out your cards to dealers at antique and collectible shows, flea markets, and estate sales. Don't stop there either. Tack up your card on community bulletin boards, on supermarket cork-boards, and anywhere else the public might see it.

Advertising

Despite the fact that public awareness of the value of collectibles is at an all-time high, there are still many individuals who throw out and give away collectibles without ever realizing they may be valuable. In addition to these individuals, there is an even larger group of people who have an idea that the items they own may be special but do not know how to go about selling them. To reach them, the collector has to advertise in the local community paper. Advertisement rates are usually low, and a classified can be run on a contract basis for as little as $10 a month. Below are some examples of good classifieds. Always try to emphasize the idea that your interests are general. Many uninformed people are confused if an advertisement is too specific.

WANTED
Confederate Swords for My Collection. Top Prices Paid! Call 081-079-0344

I Want Antique Wooden and Brass Chairs. I'll pay if you've got them! Call 087-094-0186

Autographs WANTED of Famous People. Lily Frank Box 83 Boston, MA. 02164 or Call 017-077-0392

WANTED
Charlie Chaplin Items Send photo and price to: S. Miller 1500 Broadway, Mineola

DESIRED!
Fine Paintings for Investment. Call Jack at 085-0300

CUP PLATES
Wanted; rare patterns in dark historical blue, spatter and Gaudy Dutch. *Perfect only*. Dan Lovine 076-032-9177

If you live in a major city, I don't recommend the newspaper. In the big city a small personal collectibles advertisement would not be taken seriously. For ambitious city collectors there are the suburban papers. These can be very good for attracting sellers. You may want to indicate that respondees can call collect, since often something as trivial as a toll call will put people off.

In addition to the newspapers, many collectors try advertising in one or more of the antiques and collectibles magazines and newspapers. Through them one reaches people who are already in the business or hobby in some way. A trick to being successful is to try and always advertise in a publication specializing in something outside of your field of interest. For example, if you are interested in buying comic books, don't advertise in the comic newspapers, since you will be competing with dozens of others. Rather, advertise in *Doll News*, in the hope that some doll dealer will have acquired a collection of comics and be anxious to sell them.

The approach to take in designing ads for this forum is different from the one you would take with the city papers. In the specialized publications of the trade, try to get across, in as few words as possible, that you are a serious collector willing to pay well for desirable material. Indicate exactly what that material is. Here you will be reaching people who have a greater understanding of the business.

Dangers

Within all of us there is the dream of one day finding the figurative treasure chest. Especially in the field of collectibles, one finds people who are continually in search of the score, the one deal where they'll make it big, be able to retire, find the bucket of gold at the end of the rainbow. It would be wrong to state flatly that there are no finds in collectibles. Every week I hear new reports of dealers and collectors who have made major discoveries of old and valuable collections. Only recently I spoke with a dealer friend who had just returned from a garage sale with an authentic Indian pawn belt he'd paid only three dollars for. The piece is easily worth a thousand. The truth is, however, that the find is rarer than most people realize, and it is for this reason that I include the following two cautionary stories.

The first happened to a young, inexperienced collector and his wife on their way to a vacation spot in Pennsylvania during the summer of 1980. Their names have been changed to spare them further embarrassment.

Larry and Sandra had left New York around ten o'clock Friday morning and were already three-quarters of the way to the campground where they would be staying for the night. Opting for local flavor, they had decided to leave the highway and were traveling on country roads. Coming through a small town, they noticed several handmade signs giving directions to a flea market. Larry had recently begun collecting autographs and suggested they take an hour out and explore the market.

This particular flea market was a one-day "tailgate" affair and featured over 100 dealers selling everything from new clothes to antiques from their cars. Larry began asking likely vendors if they had any old autographs. None seemed to, and Larry was about to give up when a dealer directed him to a car in front of which a table was set up displaying various paper collectibles. Larry introduced himself and told the man he had heard about a trunkful of old signatures. The dealer was middle aged and looked a bit like a circus barker. He responded by indicating the rear of his station wagon and saying, "Yeah, I have 'em, but I don't think I want to sell 'em yet."

"Can I at least look at them?" Larry asked. The man called for his wife, and the two went to the rear of the wagon and pulled out an old steamer trunk. The woman stayed close by while Larry began to look through its contents. Inside were over a dozen scrapbooks overflowing with pasted-in signatures. He could hardly contain himself when he found a book containing several presidential signatures, including George Washington's. Larry was a beginning collector, but he already knew how valuable a Washington was. In this trunk were the signatures of many people of historical importance, and Larry began to think of strategies for buying the lot. He closed the lid of the trunk and helped the woman put it back in the car.

"Where did you ever get such a collection?" he asked the dealer. The man replied, "I bought 'em yesterday off another dealer at a flea 50 miles from here. He told me that they came from an old man's estate." Larry assessed the information. It seemed right. The collection had obviously been put together in the late 19th century, when signatures were relatively inexpensive. Larry decided that he would have to get this collection before the man found out what they were really worth. He asked the dealer if he would consider selling the collection for a generous offer. The man scratched his head and said, "Look here, I just got these things, and I ain't even sure if they're not worth a lot of money. I don't think we want to sell 'em yet."

Larry frowned and raised his eyebrows. The dealer went to talk to his wife, and Sandra turned to Larry and said, "Do you know what you're doing?" He smiled at her and assured her there was no need to worry. After a moment the dealer returned and said, "Look, we wasn't gonna sell 'em yet, but you go ahead and make an offer and if it rings the bell, you can take 'em." Now it was Larry's turn to consider. He and Sandra walked away from the table and began to talk. "Have you any idea what's there? I saw at least 50 extremely valuable signatures. There's a Washington, an Adams, a Jefferson, and a Lincoln—"

Sandra interrupted him. "But Larry, how do you know they're real? I mean you don't even know the guy or anything. You just started collecting." Larry became exasperated, "Oh, come on, look at that guy. Does he look intelligent enough to fool anybody? Besides, I can tell they're real by the paper—did you see how old and yellowed it was?" Sandra knew Larry well enough to tell he was very excited. She decided against raising any more doubts and instead just asked, "What about the money? If you spend a lot on this collection, how are we going to pay for the vacation?"

Larry smiled and said, "Listen honey, if I get this collection there will be enough money to go to Europe." Sandra looked dubious as they walked back to the dealer's car. Larry explained that he would need to look through the collection once more. He already had an idea what he was going to offer but decided it would look better if he went through the trunk again. After twenty minutes he stood up and said, "All right, I can offer you $850 for the lot." Sandra gasped, as that was almost all they had on them. The dealer looked at his wife who said, "It's up to you, Flint." There was a pause and then Flint said, "Make it a thousand and you've got yourself a deal." Larry was ready for him and rejoined with, "Nine hundred is the best I can do on them." The dealer looked thoughtfully at the collection and finally nodded and said, "Okay, take 'em for nine hundred." Sandra blanched.

All the way back to the city, Larry went on about how much the collection could be worth. "Do you know, Sandy, this collection could be worth three or four thousand dollars." He was ecstatic.

It was eleven o'clock when they finally got home, and the first thing Larry did was call his best friend Mike who had gotten him interested in autograph collecting. Mike arrived half an hour later, and the two spent the next three hours carefully looking over the signatures. Sandra went to bed.

The first inkling of trouble came when Mike noticed something funny about the Washington signature. The more he looked at it, the more he believed it was a forgery. Larry thought this impossible and kept describing the circumstances of his purchase and what little he knew about the provenance of the collection. At one point Mike turned to him and said, "I'm not saying that this guy Flint forged it, it could have been done 120 years ago." Larry froze at this statement. It had not occurred to him that there were autograph forgers even a hundred years ago.

The next morning Mike and Larry took the collection to a noted philographist in the city. Immediately upon seeing the Washington signature he said, "It's not good, and I'm pretty sure it was the handiwork of Robert Spring." As it turned out, not only the Washington but 45 other autographs were forgeries as well. Whoever had assembled the scrapbooks had either been unlucky or else had purposely purchased inexpensive forgeries of the more famous people. According to the expert, it was quite common during the 19th century for forgeries to pass as authentic. The hobby lacked the sophistication it has today. A crushed Larry meekly asked what the collection was worth sans the valuable ones. "About $600, if you can find a collector interested in a lot of characters of minor historical importance," explained the expert.

The hardest part was telling Sandra the bad news. All things considered, she took it rather well, and they restarted their vacation on Sunday morning. This time they took the highway all the way up and once at their destination ignored the many signs they saw advertising a local flea market.

Larry's story is not exceptional. It is, in fact, rather common. Most collectors and dealers have had similar things happen to them. Tragedy always strikes when beginners get too greedy and bite off more than they can chew. The quest for inexpensive treasure has ended rather badly for many people.

Larry's two principal mistakes were (1) buying something that he was too inexperienced to be sure about; and (2) paying too much for it. It is one thing to take a chance on an item you think may be valuable if it costs 10, 20, or even 50 dollars. Nine hundred dollars is another thing. (Of course, the amount you are willing to risk should depend on your income.) Larry assumed that because the dealer seemed honest (and probably was) and the collection appeared old, that it was "right." A beginner should never spend a lot of money on something he cannot be sure is authentic.

Time has shown me that the number of true major finds in the various collectible fields is rather few and getting fewer. For this reason, I seldom get excited anymore when I hear from somebody who claims to have this or that extremely rare item. Invariably, it turns out to be a reproduction, a forgery, or not even the rare thing it was described as. I still dream sometimes of making the discovery of a lifetime, but I have come to be content with the various mini-discoveries I have made. I try to buy only what I know about and let the next person take the chance on the item or collection that *might* be valuable.

The action of story number two takes place at a collectible and antique show being held on the street in Manhattan.

One spring Sunday, John was showing his cousin Vinnie parts of Greenwich Village. As the two made their way, they overheard two people talking about a collectibles show they were going to. John asked them where it was being held and was told that it was only four blocks away. John had been interested in going to a show like this for some time. Many people he knew were collectors, and one friend in particular had a comic collection with issues from the 40's that were worth over 100 dollars. These were his friend's pride and joy and were stored wrapped in special plastic bags. John knew there was money to be made in collectibles and had been thinking of getting into one of the fields.

John and Vinnie reached the show and began looking at the various stalls set up by dealers selling magazines, records, dolls, jewelry, toys, books, furniture, bric-a-brac, old jukeboxes, and things they remembered from when they were boys. As they passed one booth, John noticed an attractive young vendor kneeling beside her table sorting some comics. He nudged his cousin and they approached her. John asked, "Are those for sale?" The young woman looked up and replied, "I guess so." "What do you mean you guess so?" questioned John. "Aren't they yours?" She stood up and said, "Well, actually they're my boyfriend's. He just bought them, and I'm not sure he wants to sell them yet. You can look through them though. He'll be back in a few minutes." John carefully sorted through the comics in the box. They seemed old, and he remembered what his friend had told him about finding the date. He opened one of them and looked at the first page and read, *New Funnies* Vol. 1 #4 1945.

"Gee, these are pretty old," he thought out loud. "How much do you think they'll be?" he asked the young woman. She began to explain that he would have to wait until her boyfriend came back but stopped as the boyfriend walked up to the stall. "He can tell you," she said.

John asked again. The man, who was about John's age, replied, "Which ones are you interested in?" John began to think that the owner of the comics didn't seem to be that sharp; maybe he had no idea how valuable they were. He decided to test him. "Well, I'm not sure exactly. Do you have any others?" The man shook his head. John asked, "Aren't you a comic dealer?" The dealer laughed and said, "Not really, we just do shows once in a while with whatever stuff we happen to pick up at house sales. I just bought this load of comics from an old lady uptown. I haven't even had a chance to go through them."

John tried to look absentminded as he thumbed through the box. He had heard it, the books were just bought—the man hadn't had time to go through them yet. "All right," he said, "how much for all of them?"

The other man's eyes widened a bit, and he didn't speak for a moment. Finally, he said, "There's a lot of money here you know." (John sort of shrugged.) "I mean I'm not even sure what these comics are worth."

There was a long pause during which John tried to emit only feelings of neutrality. He did not want to help the dealer by acting excited. Finally the man said, "Okay, look, give me $150 and you can have the box of them."

Now John smiled; he knew he would get them. Of course he

would pay the $150, he thought. That was nothing. There had to be at least 100 comics in the box, and many of them were from the 40's. "How about a hundred?" John queried. The seller shook his head. John frowned, chuckled, and then said, "Can't you do even a little better?"

The dealer seemed to be getting annoyed and didn't answer immediately. John got nervous and was about to pull out the money when the owner said, "Okay, I won't charge you any tax. But if you don't want them, that's fine with me, too. Once I look up their value the price may go up." John's cousin never saw money change hands so quickly, and before he knew what had happened John and he were walking away from the dealer's stall carrying the box of comics.

On the way back to the car, John, overflowing with confidence and pride, preached to Vinnie about how easy it was to make money if you knew what you were doing. "Yep, Vin, I'd say that this little box here has got, figuring conservatively, at least $1,000 worth of comics in it. Maybe more." "How do you know that?" his cousin asked. "Well, you gotta figure that the average one from the 40's is gonna be worth at least $15. I know they're not all from the 40's, but my friend Bill has got some from the 40's worth over $200. Anyway, I think they'll average out around $10 a piece, and there's at least 100 comics."

The next day after work John's friend Bill came over to look at the comics. He brought with him the *Comic Book Price Guide.* John conducted him to the living room, where the comics were sorted into neat piles. After five minutes' worth of looking, Bill stood up and said, "John, I hope you didn't pay much for these." "What do you mean? Aren't there a lot of good ones there?" Bill shook his head and said, "There isn't a comic here worth more than about three dollars retail. They're all what we call funny animal comics—the kind just about nobody wants."

John was astonished. "But most of them are from the 40's," he said. "They've got to be worth more. Look again." Bill spent the next ten minutes explaining that age was only one criterion for value and that there were plenty of comics from the 40's worth only a dollar or two. "The ones I have that are valuable are *Superman* and *Batman* issues. Everyone wants those," Bill said.

John cursed softly, shook his head, and then was philosophic about the whole thing. "Well it just figures. Here I thought I had skinned this guy, and it turns out that he got me."

For a moment neither of them said anything. Then Bill said, "For $150 it wasn't that bad a deal. If you go by catalog these books are probably worth over $200. Maybe I can trade them off for something I need and give you the money." John shook his head. "No, you're a good friend, but I'd rather keep them to remind me to be more careful next time. I let my greed get to me. I never should have bought them without knowing."

Epilogue: John ended up becoming a comic collector anyway. Two months later he happened to be at a paper collectibles show in the city. As he walked down the aisles he noticed an attractive young woman standing behind a table covered with boxes of comics. It was the same person from the show in the Village. He looked for her boyfriend and, sure enough, he was also there. Moving away from their table, he found one of the friends he had come with and asked him to go over to the table and find out how long the couple had been in the comic business. His friend complied, and it turned out that the two were expert comic dealers and had been selling for three years. "And he told me that he wasn't really a dealer," John sighed.

The incidents in this story are representative of things that can and do happen to beginners in collectibles. I can still remember several times when I was taken in by my own greed, which altered my perceptions and caused me to reason foolishly.

John's mistake was in believing that this dealer, by his own admission a person who occasionally did shows, would sell anything he had not checked out first. True, the dealer lied in saying that he was not really a comic dealer, but sellers in any profession will often bend the truth in order to make a sale. Particularly in the world of antiques and collectibles, one must be very cautious.

The first rule is, Never underestimate the intelligence of dealers when it comes to knowing what they have. No dealer who has been in the business long will sell anything he's unfamiliar with without having it checked out first. This doesn't mean that there aren't any bargains from dealers. Many times a dealer, working out of his field, will receive misinformation about an item. He may then price it too high or too low.

I was able to buy a collection of baseball cards at considerably under their actual retail value because they had been priced by someone using a general antiques guide instead of a baseball card price guide. Especially in the less developed collectible fields, an informed collector will have an advantage over a general antiques dealer. This advantage, however, will be readily dissipated if a collector doesn't approach any potential acquisition with caution and even doubt regarding its potential value. Always go by your own knowledge, and never let a seller's story convince you that a collection or a piece is a great bargain you must have.

CHAPTER 5

Selling

THE BEST WAY TO APPROACH SELLING an item is to follow the same steps of familiarization involved in preparing to buy. In this way one learns at least enough not to "give away" a very valuable piece. The nuances of selling different kinds of collectibles will be covered in the individual chapters. But there are several general ways in which to dispose of items.

To Dealers

The first and simplest way is to sell to reputable dealers who will buy your items at anywhere from a third to two-thirds of their retail value. Most dealers base the percentage they will pay on the estimated turnover time of the item. If a dealer has a ready customer for a high-priced collectible, he may be willing to pay 90 percent of what he will sell it for. On the other hand, if he thinks it will be six months before it sells, he may want to pay only 50 percent of its retail price, or less. Selling to dealers has the advantage of being expedient and easy. Its disadvantage is that you might not net as much money as you might by selling the goods yourself.

To Collectors

If you are ambitious and willing to learn enough to accurately grade and price your collectibles, you can sell them to collectors. The markets vary according to the collectible group (look for specific information regarding publications for selling within the individual chapters), but some of the general ways you can sell are through the mail (by advertising in a collectibles publication), at flea markets, at antique and collectible shows, and through a garage sale. Usually it is not worth the expense of renting a table at one of the shows unless you have enough stock to justify it. In addition to table expenses, there will also be equipment, gas, lunch, supplies, and other costs. The show route for selling can often turn out to be a losing proposition. If there is a poor turnout at a show or the right collectors for your merchandise do not show up, you can actually end up losing money for the day. Whereas a full-time dealer can average out the bad shows, an individual attempting to do just one show can be devasted financially.

A much better way to sell to collectors, therefore, is through the mail. You have the option of advertising in the classified section of one of the specialized or general publications for collectibles. If you have an item that is especially rare or desirable, you can try offering it up for sale to the highest bidder within a set time schedule. Mail auctions often prove very successful for those wishing to sell. There are two things to remember if you choose to sell through the mail. One, don't send out any merchandise until the buyer's check has cleared at the bank; and, two, always wrap a package carefully and send it registered or insured mail.

At Auction

It is advisable to sell at auction only when you are disposing of a particularly valuable piece that would benefit from the exposure and competition an auction can generate. Most of the larger houses (Sotheby Parke Bernet and Christie's for instance) now have a minimum commission rate of $50 or 15 percent, whichever is higher, on lots under $1,000. In addition, the consignor is charged for such things as storage, insurance, photography, and, if an item does not sell, the buy-in fee. Aside from all the fees, the consignor must be willing and able to wait for months to receive his settlement check. Add to all these pitfalls the fact that except on better lots auction prices are wholesale, and you can understand why

auction selling is not recommended. Should you decide to inves-
tigate this method of selling, it is helpful to remember that auction
houses, despite their sometimes pretentious facades, are there to
serve you and will often be willing to adjust some of their fee
schedules and rules to accommodate you. On most lots, they will
be willing, for instance, to waive the buy-in charge if you allow
them to set a reasonable reserve on your lots.

CHAPTER 6

Starting a Collectibles Business

At least once, any collector of long standing has probably considered becoming a dealer. From the collector's standpoint, dealers seem to have all the fun. They can buy collectibles at half price or less, choose to keep the best material and sell off the junk, travel all over the country on the business expense account and get other tax write-offs, do appraisals, and make new friends.

While most of these things are true, what many collectors do not realize is that the shift from collector to dealer often results in losing one's ability to savor the joys of pure collecting. A business is a business, and collectibles are no exception. Being a successful dealer, even at the part-time level, requires a significant amount of effort in many areas. Following is a look at what it takes to become a part-time show dealer.

The typical show dealer has a full-time job not related to collectibles and spends only evenings and weekends being a collectibles dealer. Assuming you wanted to become such a dealer, you would have to be informed about the following things:

1. Acquiring inventory: Depending on the collectible group you intended to sell, you would need anywhere from $1,000 to $10,000 worth of inventory just to begin. Many collectors use their own collections as their beginning inventory. This spares them the initial acquiring costs; however, they still need to develop sources for buying once their starting inventory is depleted. The typical dealer complaint is that it is easy to sell and difficult to

72

buy. Any starting dealer will quickly find that the trick to staying in business is in being able to locate inventory at the right price. Unfortunately, collectibles can't just be ordered from a jobber. They must be sought out at shows, auctions, estate sales, and any other place that seems promising. In acquiring inventory, be careful not to tie up all of your capital in low-profit items. I have known dealers who have not had the money to make advantageous deals because they had put it all into collectibles on which they were making only a small percentage. A smart dealer sets up his cash flow in such a way that he always has money should the "score" come along.

2. *Renting a table or booth:* In selecting a show or market to exhibit at, you have to consider three points: one, the theme of the show; two, the amount of competition you will have; and three, the past success or failure record of the show itself. To find out which shows would best suit your particular merchandise, talk to experienced dealers. Most of them will be very quick to voice their opinions about show promoters and their shows.

If you have no dealers to consult, follow these guidelines: Do indoor shows over outdoor ones because of the rain factor; pick a show being held on a weekend when there are no other shows being held; and always try to go with promoters who have good track records.

Booth rental fees vary according to the quality of the show and can range from $30 a day at some flea markets to over $1,000 at some of the prestigious antique shows in the big cities. The fee sometimes includes the rental of a display table. Make sure to find out what is being provided by the promoter. Arrangements for things like showcases, electrical hookups, and so on usually must be made several weeks in advance.

3. *The tax number:* Most show sponsors now require that you indicate your dealer resale number. Mere mention of the tax man usually scares everyone, but in this case it is not so bad. Essentially, the resale number is a certificate that empowers you to collect tax and exempts you from paying tax on goods you are buying for ultimate resale. The former is a pain, the latter the benefit everyone loves and unfortunately abuses. To obtain a resale number you need only contact your state bureau of taxation.

They will send you the necessary forms regarding tax collection and remittance. An option for those who only want to get their feet wet is the temporary tax number. This is available from the state and enables the seller to function for 90 days before the number must either be renewed or changed over to a permanent certificate. Some show promoters provide the application for a resale number as a way of encouraging first-time sellers.

4. *Tax Collection:* As mentioned earlier, taxes are generally considered a great annoyance for those in the business. No dealer likes to charge them because they complicate selling. The fact is that at most of the collectible forums throughout the United States, the state tax departments have been unable to effectively control and enforce tax collection. The situation that exists presently includes dealers who collect no tax and have no resale number; dealers who have a number but only collect tax on some items (and then do not necessarily file them); dealers who falsify a list of sales that totals far below what was actually sold; and dealers who record all sales, and pay tax on them.

Generally, dealers who are new to the business pay less attention to the rules. Many of the collectible forums are also less well regulated then their antique counterparts, and there is a greater incidence of tax abuse at them. To combat violations, the state tax departments send out undercover teams (it's true) to the larger, well-publicized shows. These teams, often spotted the moment they arrive, move through the shows posing as collectors. They try to catch dealers selling pieces without charging tax. Usually, the dealers who are caught get off easily and simply have to begin collecting tax at that particular show. However, some states have threatened to get tough with violators who, the states claim, are siphoning off millions of taxable dollars from the government.

5. *Preparation for the show:* Major preparations, such as pricing inventory, making up signs, etc., should be done weeks before a show. It is usually the minor details that one leaves to the last moment. If you want your show day to go smoothly, take care of the little things. Items like coins for change, bags, tape, markers, labels, business cards, food, washcloths, paper, drinking water, checkbook, plastic tarpaulins, etc., always get left behind. To avoid having this happen, start making up a checklist a week

before the show. Add to it every day, and then the night before you set out, pack everything into the car, checking off each item as you go. By being loaded and ready the night before, you can at least get a good night's sleep before the onslaught.

6. *Pricing inventory:* Pricing is always tricky for the beginner. There are generally two kinds of dealers: those who tend to price very high intentionally, leaving a large margin for bargainers; and those who price near the fair retail and are willing to discount a little. I favor the second approach because it tends to scare fewer people away—even though it may result in more arguments with people who want to know why you are not willing to be more flexible. Always leave some margin for discount. Buyers of collectibles derive psychological comfort from knowing they did not pay the full price. If you attempt to deprive them of this comfort, you will do less business.

7. *Hidden costs and how much to pay for inventory:* For those seriously considering beginning a part-time collectibles business, it is important to know that there are going to be hidden expenses that often surface just in time to undermine what might have seemed to be a profitable enterprise. To begin with, in addition to booth rental fees, you must figure on expenses for transportation, food, accessories, and time. Some dealers have figured out that after all expenses, they end up with less than the minimum hourly wage. For this reason, you must figure your own time as an expense in order to see if the business is profitable.

Most show dealers find that the expenses of the business require that they buy inventory they will be able to mark up 100 percent. If they think they can sell an item for $5, it has to cost them only $2.50. Most sellers have trouble understanding why a dealer has to make this high a markup. These individuals don't realize that by the time an item is sold (usually at less than the full price), many expenses have been incurred in carrying it. Because of the attitude of some sellers, many dealers find it difficult to purchase merchandise at the appropriate price level for making a profit. Many dealers resort to paying more for inventory. This is a mistake! It is much better to hold your capital until the right deal comes along than to tie it up on items that are not profitable enough. Eventually, many of the sellers who initially feel they ought to get more for their items come around to selling them to dealers.

8. The show itself: Nothing can replace the feeling of actually standing behind the table as a dealer. When the morning of the big day arrives, many people become nervous. Up until then they have always been the buyer or the onlooker. Now they are actually going to be the dealer. By noon on their first day, most are already casually standing around like the veteran dealers, waiting to help customers. The trick to being successful at shows lies in the personality you cultivate. If you are friendly, helpful, and happen to have desirable merchandise, you will do well. Table display is important. Your collectibles should be arranged in an orderly and attractive fashion. Always price each item. It helps to lay a colored tablecloth or a piece of felt under the items.

The dealers who do not do well are often the ones who have unpleasant personalities. As a frequent buyer at shows, I appreciate a friendly, helpful dealer, the way I appreciate a good waiter or waitress. When spending money, people like to be treated well. Dealers who act aloof, disinterested, or superior turn customers off. I often wonder why some dealers who act as if they hate what they are doing even bother to show up. As a dealer, one needs to learn how to handle the variety of buyer personalities one will encounter. Patience is usually the hallmark of successful sellers. Some customers will make you want to strangle them with their wheedling buy ploys and aggressive questions. Stay calm, centered, and stick to your policies. Aggressive people will often back off if they see you are sure of yourself. There are some buyers who like to waste a dealer's time by bargaining over an item they don't intend to buy anyway. Learn to spot this kind of behavior and avoid it. The interesting thing about being a seller, even if you only do it once, is that you can learn a lot about human nature and yourself. I guarantee you that after one experience as a seller, you will feel differently the next time you are in the position of buyer.

CHAPTER 7

Starting a Club

MANY COLLECTORS find it difficult to learn about items that are still in their infancy as collectibles. Beyond instinctively knowing what to charge, dealers are often ignorant about such items, and other collectors are sometimes difficult to find. Clubs often are the result of one collector reaching out to contact other people interested in the same thing. They can be the perfect forum for sharing information, trading items, and developing friendships based on a common interest.

The first step in starting a club is to decide whether there is a need. If you collect comic books, there is probably already a club in your area. If you collect golf balls, there probably is not. Assuming there is a need, begin by choosing a name or title, making sure to incorporate the particular collectible's name into your heading. Next, advertise in the classified ad columns of one or more of the leading national publications for collectibles. Below are a few fictitious examples of what you could write:

1. Razor Collectors Unite! For information on joining a sharp new club, write Jack Panch at 381 R.D. New Hampshire. Please include a SASE.

2. Soapstone Fanciers of America is forming—send for membership info to Box 39, Farmington, NY.

3. The United Federation of Beer Can Lovers Wants You! Write to Ethel Kelley at 38 Curvy Lane, Sullivan, NM.

As in example number one, it is a good idea to ask people to include a self-addressed, stamped envelope with their response. The initial package you can have ready to send to respondees could be simply a photocopied letter describing yourself and your aspirations for the club. With any luck, you will hook up with people who have been thinking of starting a club also, and they will help to structure the organization.

Many clubs decide to print up a newsletter at certain times during the year. A good newsletter includes information about club members, the latest discoveries within a collectible group, and a market report. Some clubs allow members to submit classified ads listing particular interests for trading, buying, and selling.

CHAPTER 8

Displaying, Storing, and Insuring a Collection

SOME COLLECTORS go to great lengths in displaying their collections. They build special cabinets, install unusual lighting systems, and even designate entire rooms solely for exhibition. If your hobby is an important part of your everyday life, it should be seen and not relegated to a closet or attic. To display your collection safely follow these simple rules:

1. Keep collectibles away from direct sunlight, which can fade or discolor just about anything.

2. Avoid storage areas near radiators, heaters, or fireplaces.

3. Take care not to display items near where moisture or excessive dampness could damage them.

4. Make sure to prevent layers of dust from accumulating.

All of these rules may seem obvious, but it is surprising how many fine pieces are ruined by people who are not careful.

REGARDING PAPER COLLECTIBLES. There are many products on the market that are manufactured specifically for safely exhibiting comic books, baseball cards, magazines, broadsides, playbills, etc. Most of these products are plastic derivatives and offer inexpensive protection from moisture, dust, and handling. Advertisements for them can be found in any of the major antiques and collectibles publications. In addition, archival-quality conservation materials can often be obtained from art supply stores.

STORING A COLLECTION. Collectors sometimes find it expedient or necessary to store some or all of their collections. General rules regarding home storage are:

1. Try to avoid basements unless they are secure from flooding (use of a dehumidifier is a good idea).

2. Always store items off the floor.

3. Avoid attics that become extremely hot in the summer.

4. Store items where there is no chance of rodents getting at them.

5. Pack all collectibles in secure boxes, wrapping ones made of glass or other fragile materials in paper or strips of cloth.

6. Avoid any environments that tend to get damp. Moisture can cause rust, mold, mildew, and warping. Paper collectibles should never be put in cardboard boxes unless they are individually wrapped in acid-free plastic wrapping. The problem with boxes is that they are made with unstable paper, which, as it breaks down, releases acidifiers that can migrate to paper items with which they come into contact, causing these items to turn brown and eventually decay. Acid-free boxes are available from some of the companies that sell conservation supplies.

SAFE-DEPOSIT BOXES. Most banks have a safe-deposit box room where various size boxes can be rented. These are ideal for the long-term storage of smaller more valuable collectibles. The boxes are made of metal, and the temperature and humidity in the vault are constant. Vault boxes can be a good alternative to insurance. Only rarely does one hear of a safe-deposit room being ransacked, and then the thieves are after cash and jewels, not collectibles.

SPACE IN WAREHOUSES. For those who find their collectibles becoming too large to manage or who are forced under a spouses's ultimatum to remove their collections from the premises, there is the cooperative warehouse. Co-op warehouses offer the rental of individual stalls at yearly rates. They are secure and most will provide insurance at an additional charge.

INSURANCE. Whether your collection consists of baseball cards or old American quilts, it usually can be insured under a *fine arts floater*. This floater might be available as an endorsement on your present policy. If it is not, you must be willing to do the necessary work to find a company that will insure your goods. Collectibles are not the favorite insurable items of many companies, and you may have to expend a good deal of effort. Following is important information for insurance seekers.

To insure your collectibles under a fine arts floater you must have them appraised beforehand. This is because a fine arts floater is a "valued policy," which means it sets the amount you will be paid in the event of a loss. Should your property be stolen or destroyed, you would be reimbursed for the "set," or formally agreed upon, value. This differs from the haggling one hears about in regard to *personal property coverage*, where a value range is established.

One of the problems you may encounter is in finding a qualified individual to appraise your collectibles. There are two appraisers organizations that have members throughout the United States: the Appraisers Association of America, 60 East 42nd St., New York, N.Y. 10165, and the American Society of Appraisers, which has its main office in Washington and can be reached by writing Box 17265, Washington, D.C. 20041. Contacting one of them would be a good way to begin locating someone with expertise in the area you need. It is very important to find the right person. A problem frequently encountered by those desiring to have collectibles appraised is dealing with an appraiser who pretends to know about collectibles but is really only winging it. Insurance companies usually will accept the appraisal only of someone who is a member of one of the larger organizations or who is generally regarded to be an expert in a field (evidenced perhaps by authorship or a degree). Appraisal fees are either *flat rate* or percentage. Currently, most people favor flat rate because it does not encourage "padding" the appraisal.

Once you have had your collection appraised, you can bring

it, along with a photographic inventory, to the insurance agent. Here, it is important to make sure you deal with someone who is respectful of your needs and does not act as if he were doing you a favor to insure your collectibles. Remember, the agent or representative you deal with in the beginning will usually be the one helping (or not helping) you in the event of loss. Measure your agent by how attentive he is in going over the items in your collection. Stay away from the ones who look at you disbelievingly when you show them a picture of a comic or other collectible worth $500.

Rates vary greatly, depending on the experience of a particular insurance company. Shop around. Some collectors have paid exorbitant rates because they accepted the first quotation. The range you can expect for coverage of fine art is between $30 and $80 for every $15,000 of coverage. These rates will vary for each collectible, however. A paper item is more vulnerable than a bronze one, and so forth. Fine arts floaters usually cover your property only at a set location, say your home. If you intend to exhibit your collection or travel with it, make sure to buy the endorsement that covers this activity.

PART II

The Collectibles

Introduction
to the Collectibles

A LOOK AT OVER 50 of the most interesting and popular collectibles being saved today follows. The general format for each item is: a quick-reference box showing the value range, the most popular items, and good sources for the collectible; an introduction to the item, its history, and how it is collected; and, finally, a list of the books, clubs, and periodicals that relate to the collectible.

In compiling these lists I tried to include as many relevant names, addresses, and sources for further information as possible. To accomplish this I sent out several hundred letters requesting information. What I found, unfortunately, was that many of the clubs, societies, and organizations had disbanded, changed their locations (with no forwarding address), or refused to answer. Quite possibly some of the ones I have listed also will have ceased functioning by the time this book is published. Regrettably, there is nothing I can do about this. On the more positive side, however, many new clubs will have formed, and a collector can find out about these by subscribing to the collectibles publications.

Value-Range Key	
Low	= $.50–$50
Medium	= $51–$250
High	= $251–$999
Very High	= $1,000 and over

ADVERTISING ITEMS

Value range: low—very high. Pre-1900 high-quality tin, glass, and paper advertising are expensive and generally cost over $250. Items produced between 1901 and 1946 can be obtained for less, depending on size, composition, and attractiveness. There are many collectible pieces available for under $50, and there are a vast number of items currently being made that can be obtained for nothing.

Most popular items: pieces that have the "look" or "feel" of their era, are colorful, and display popular motifs, such as children at play, beautiful women, automobiles, aircraft, animals, factories, and products such as Coca-Cola, Hires, Dr. Pepper, Schlitz, etc.

Good sources: antique advertising shows, general antique and collectible shows, and private connections.

ADVERTISING DESCRIBES AN extremely broad range of items produced or ordered by American companies since the mid-1800's to promote their products. Advertising items have been made of paper, wood, tin, porcelain, glass, and celluloid and have taken the form of signs, calendars, mirrors, trays, ashtrays, plates, containers, lamps, clocks, scales, mugs, and dozens of other everyday objects.

HISTORY. As the Industrial Revolution swept across America, creating companies that produced products they believed to be special and different from other similar products, competition developed. The earliest forms of advertising were paper signs promoting a particular brand of beer, tobacco, whiskey, or soda. These were posted in general stores as early as the 1840's. As the century progressed and more and more products were created, new forms of advertising were developed. One of these early forms was reverse painting on glass, which was done by skilled

artists who were able to produce exceptionally beautiful advertisements. By the 1880's color lithographic techniques had been
developed to transfer brilliant color images onto paper and tin.
Large, colorful signs began to adorn storefronts, railway stations,
and hotels. Smaller signs, calendars, handbills, trays, and a number of other items were produced to be used promotionally wherever people congregated.

During this time porcelain signs with glazed lettering began
arriving from Europe. Plates and china soon followed. Some companies even contracted to have extremely costly leaded stained
glass signs made. From the late 19th century through the Second
World War, countless attractive advertising items were produced.
Beginning in the 1940's, however, the quality and appeal of many
of these items began to change as plastics and less expensive lithographic techniques were utilized. The colors became less brilliant
and tin trays began to be replaced by plastic ones. Today, most
collectors feel that the heyday of advertising was before the Second
World War.

COLLECTING. While some post-1946 advertising items are
collected, and in some cases are very attractive, most collectors
save only those items produced before the end of World War II.
The most popular types of advertising are tin and paper signs,
calendars, trays, and pieces made between 1875 and 1925, which
display the brilliance of early color lithography. The great majority
of these pieces were produced or ordered by beer, tobacco, whiskey, and soft drink companies, as they had the largest advertising
budgets. Candy, milk, meat, medicine, gum, insurance, automobile, and hardware companies also turned out advertising items.

The subjects collectors most want to see illustrated are beautiful
women, children, animals, trains, factory buildings, and automobiles. Value varies according to composition, size, and the appeal of the advertisement. Examples of very good pieces would
be large (over 1' x 1') tin signs featuring a pretty girl holding a
glass of beer with the beer company's logo or catch phrase printed
as part of the design; a colorful illustration of a cherubic child at
a soda fountain reaching for a glass of some popular brand of
pop; a picture of a hunting party relaxing at a lodge drinking
whiskey with a particular brand promoted along the border of

the sign. Collectors judge advertising pieces by how tastefully the product is promoted. An ideal piece has balanced graphics, colors, and wording.

The best place to purchase antique advertising items is at a general antique or collectible show. Frequently, the dealers there will not have developed a sense of what is good in advertising, and a collector with an eye can pick up bargains. Desirable large tin pieces from the period between 1875 and 1925 can bring up to several hundred dollars. Paper signs are generally less costly, but an especially attractive one advertising a recognizable product like Coca-Cola or Hershey's chocolate can bring $500. Collectors on a budget may therefore want to stick with calendars or smaller signs that can be purchased for under $100.

Another alternative is to collect modern advertising items. Some collectors feel that the plastic whiskey and beer promotions that presently line the shelves of bars and taverns are going to be very valuable one day. In many cases they can be obtained for free if one makes friends with the owner or barkeep.

Another area of advertising that has not yet become hot is neon signs. During the last 20 years their use has declined because many store owners find them awkward and difficult to repair. There are thousands of slightly damaged neon signs gathering dust in the storerooms of businesses throughout the country. Aggressive collectors locate and purchase them for a song, have them repaired by a company specializing in neon (there is usually one in every city), and end up with rare and beautiful examples of an advertising medium that may be extinct in another 20 years.

There are an infinite number of items currently being produced that qualify as advertising and may one day be worth money. For the young collector who can't afford expensive pieces, items like tumblers, plates, trays, playing cards, game cards, games, totes, medals, toys, matchbooks, key chains, and signs can be picked up for free at fast food restaurants, gas stations, supermarkets and hardware, department, electronics, and sporting goods stores across the nation. I know of one boy who had been collecting McDonald's advertising promotions for over five years when he was approached by a scholar who was doing a dissertation on the artifacts of popular culture and wanted to research how McDonald's had changed the nature of its promotions to suit the times.

BOOKS

Cope, Jim, *Old Advertising*, 1980.
  Available from: The Great American Publishing Co., 5513 Highway 290 West, Austin, TX 78735.

Petretti and Munsey, *Official Coca-Cola Collectibles Price Guide*.
  Available from: The Nostalgia Publishing Co., 21 South Lake Drive, Hackensack, NJ 07601.

CLUBS

Coca-Cola c/o Jean Gibbs
3306 Yellowstone Drive, Lawrence, KS 66044.

  1 yr./$15, includes 6 newsletters, free want ads and classifieds, etc. This is an international organization of people dedicated to the study of the history and collecting of Coca-Cola memorabilia.

National Association of Breweriana Advertising
2343 Met-to-Wee Lane, Wauwatosa, WI 53226.

  1 yr./$20, includes quarterly newsletter and other mailings. The club is for collectors of all items of breweriana, but the emphasis is on advertising pieces.

The National Association of Paper and Advertising Collectibles
Box 471, Columbia, PA 17512.

  1 yr./$10, includes monthly copy of *P.A.C.*, a newspaper with buy/ sell ads.; a certificate; and a membership card.

MAIL AUCTIONS

The Nostalgia Company's Coca-Cola Auction.
21 South Lake Drive, Hackensack, NJ 07601.

  $3 will bring you 3 profusely illustrated auction booklets featuring all kinds of Coca-Cola and other soft drink advertising collectibles.

ART POTTERY

Value range: low–very high. The majority of pieces found at
general shows sell in the low–medium range. Higher-priced
examples are usually sold at auctions and from antique stores.

Most popular items: vases and bowls designed and produced by
one of the companies listed below.

Good sources: general antique and collectible shows, dealers
who specialize in art pottery, and at auction.

HISTORY. Art pottery production began in the 1870's. Before
that pottery (which can be any kind of ceramic, including stoneware and porcelain) was produced either by studio potters, who
created pieces for their own enjoyment and use, or by enterprises,
which mass produced standardized crocks, vases, pitchers, etc.,
for utilitarian purposes. While the quality of the items in this latter
group was good, the pieces lacked originality. They were all the
same and lacked artistic expression.

The production of art pottery began in the 1870's as an off-
shoot of the Arts and Crafts movement, which was a reaction to
the ascension of the insipid industrial product. The people behind
the art pottery movement wanted to produce items by hand that
would reflect individuality. They realized, however, that they would
have to work within the framework of a commercial enterprise if
they were to become economically viable.

Paul Evans, in his *Art Pottery of the United States*, defines art
pottery as those pieces that were produced as a result of the unique
tension created by commercially supported individuality. The
companies and individuals listed below, which began to produce
art pottery in the 1870's, created bookends, bowls, jars, pitchers,
planters, plates, platters, teapots, tiles, and vases that were functional as well as artistic.

LIST OF ART POTTERY COMPANIES

Arc-en-ceil   Avon
Arequipa   Avon Works

Bennett
Biloxi
Brouwer
Brush Guild
Buffalo
Cambridge
Chelsea
Cincinnati
Clewell
Clifton
Cowan
Craven
Dallas
Dedham
Deldare Ware
Frackelton
Fulper
Grueby
Hampshire
Haviland
Hull
Jervis
Kenton Hills
Lonhuda
Low

Marblehead
McCoy
Merrimac
Middle Lane
Newcomb
Niloak
Ohr
Overbeck
Owens
Pauline
Pewabic
Radford
Robineau
Roblin
Rookwood
Roseville
Shawsheen
Stockton
Teco
Tiffany
Van Briggle
Volkmar
Weller
Wheatley
Zanesville

The wares produced by these companies were often conceived, thrown, and decorated by the same person, who then signed his name or initials under the company name (some companies worked in assembly-line fashion but still emphasized the artistic uniqueness of the product). Once the objects were ready for sale, the normal methods of commerce were utilized.

The exigencies of enterprise unfortunately led to the softening of the ideals of the Arts and Crafts movement. By 1910 many of the companies were forced to begin standardizing their product by casting and uniformly decorating it. By 1925 most of the true art pottery producers had either switched over to what Evans calls "industrial artware" or had gone out of business. Few companies producing art pottery survived into the 30's.

COLLECTING. Ironically, the collecting world has broadened the strict definition of art pottery to include any pottery made by one of the aforementioned companies as well as the pottery produced by firms that only made industrial artware. At shows, most of what is offered for sale as art pottery is really, in the strict sense, industrial artware. While art pottery purists may be upset by this, the average collector entering the hobby today is either not aware of the distinction between art pottery and industrial artware or is unable to afford the former and so is content to collect the latter.

My feeling is that collectors should collect what they like and that many of the industrial artware pieces are bargains in comparison to the price tags on desirable art pottery.

The qualities to look for, whether you are buying an expensive Weller vase or a $20 Roseville planter, are attractiveness of form and decoration and excellent condition of preservation. The most popular kinds of decorations include the metallic look produced by high-gloss glazes; the irridescent appearance also produced by mixtures of glaze; and the painted decoration in the form of a scene, figure, or motif painted under the glaze. The richness of color achieved by the artists and potters is often astounding. In terms of condition, collectors are advised to buy only undamaged pieces. A bowl or a vase that has even a chip missing is considered undesirable. Look over pieces carefully, since many sellers try to hide defects with amateurish repairs. Hairline cracks must also be watched for. These, which appear as thread-thin lines up and down or from side to side on a piece, indicate cracks in the glaze and, unless they were purposefully caused as part of the pattern, usually reduce value.

BOOKS

Denker, Ellen and Bert. *Warner Collectors Guide to North American Pottery and Porcelain*. New York: Warner Books, 1982.

Evans, Paul. *Art Pottery of the U.S.* Hanover, PA: Everybody's Press, 1974.

Grayson, Joan. *The Repair and Restoration of Pottery and Porcelain*. New York: Sterling, 1982.

Kovel, Ralph and Terry. *The Kovels' Collectors Guide to American Art Pottery*. New York: Crown, 1974.

PERIODICAL

The Glaze
Box 4929, G.S.
Springfield, MO 65808

1 yr./11 issues/$12. For collectors of all kinds of earthenware.

RELATED COLLECTIBLE—STONEWARE. Unlike art pottery, which was a much later functional art form, stoneware accompanied the colonists to the New World. Stoneware differs from other ceramics in that it can be made only from clay that can hold its form under the intense heat necessary to vitrify it. Unlike earthenware (a classification describing clays fired at lower temperatures), which needs a glaze to make it non-permeable to liquids, properly made stoneware is dense and impermeable. The potters among the colonists almost immediately began making utilitarian stoneware crocks, jugs, jars, pitchers, churns, and mugs. These pieces were made simply and decorated in a primitive fashion.

Collectors can find various examples of stoneware at general antique shows. Except for the exceptional early pieces, most examples can be obtained in the low to medium value range. When buying, look for the piece that was hand formed (or thrown) and primitively decorated. Be careful of factory-produced 19th and early 20th century examples, which are frequently offered as early pieces.

BOOK

Greer, Georgeanna H. *American Stonewares: The Art and Craft of Utilitarian Potters*. Exton, PA: Schiffer Press, 1981.

AUTOGRAPHS

Value range: low–very high. Desirable autographs usually fall in the medium–high range. Autographs of people who will one day be famous can often be obtained for free. Important historical items penned by the great international figures of the past and present often bring tens of thousands of dollars.

Most popular items: autographs of presidents, movie stars, and Nazi leaders.

Good sources: from reputable autograph dealers.

DESPITE THE POPULAR NOTION that an autograph is merely a signature, the fact is that *autograph* refers to anything written by the hand of a person. For this reason, autographs are often collected because of a kind of link they provide between collector and subject. Philography is the hobby of collecting letters and documents of historical and cultural importance, and it differs from mere signature seeking. A philographer is someone who feels brought into contact with the individual whose documents he is collecting. The hobby has been traced back to the Roman Empire.

COLLECTING.   The simplest way to begin collecting is by writing to celebrities to request an autograph. Celebrities' addresses can often be obtained by looking through *Who's Who* in the library. Lists of addresses can also be purchased from other collectors and dealers. When you have decided whose autograph you are going to request, you must remember to include a self-addressed, stamped envelope, an index card, and a letter explaining why you are writing. Most celebrities will send back their signatures. To get something more, you have to think of interesting and relevant things to say that might prod them into responding with a short note, or more.

One good technique is to ask them their opinion about something. People, no matter how famous, are usually flattered by fan curiosity and adulation. Always represent yourself as an adoring fan or a respectful supporter. Celebrities don't like to sign autographs for or write to people they feel are simply interested in acquiring a valuable signature. Be as solicitous as possible without being unctious.

Some questions that have worked before are: Who was your favorite movie star when you were a child? Who is your favorite writer, actor, performer, etc.? Who do you think was the best president of the United States? The kinds of responses collectors have received using these questions range from one-word answers to three-page letters. You can never be sure how to approach a celebrity. There are some who simply will not sign.

Before buying autographs you must become familiar with price levels, categories, and terminology. The best sense of the market can be achieved by carefully looking over the retail prices for items listed in the catalogs of autograph dealers. There are several categories into which autographs fall. These are *signature, document signed, letter signed, autograph letter signed, autograph quotation signed,* and *signed photograph.* The most expensive autographs are the ALS's because they are done entirely in the hand of the individual. A DS or an LS is a piece that has been done by the hand of a secretary or has been typed, which in either case takes away from the value.

The most important factor influencing the value of an autograph is demand. A person could be or have been extremely important in his field, but if collectors aren't interested in him, his signature will be worth only a few dollars at best. The second most important factor is supply. Certain celebrities are known to have signed so much that their signatures and short notes are far less valuable than those of someone equally famous but not known to have been a "signer." Of course, there are some known signers, like Albert Einstein, who are so popular that their autographs still command steep prices and are in constant demand.

Collectors pursue the following categories: athletes, authors, artists, black leaders, composers, Colonial and Revolutionary leaders, criminals, entertainment personalities, explorers, financiers, inventors, Jewish leaders, jurists, lawyers, military men, Nazis, photographers, politicians, presidents, religious leaders, royalty, scientists, signers of the Declaration of Independence, women leaders, and world statesmen.

Value is not determined by age. A friend of mine once made the mistake of buying a legal brief (of a case involving a counterfeiter in New York) dating back to 1773 because he thought its age would certainly make it valuable. He paid $100 for it. He ended up giving it away when he learned it was valueless. No one considered important today had signed it.

The greatest dangers for beginning collectors are the autopen and the secretarial signature. Many busy celebrities, particularly politicians, make use of a mechanical device to duplicate signatures. The user signs his name once and the autopen robot can then duplicate it as many times as is needed. The resultant signatures cannot be distinguished from the original. Unlike a photomechanical reproduction, the autopen actually signs each letter or document fed into it. Autopen signatures are worth practically nothing to collectors. Secretarial signatures, because they, too, lack the special quality of the personal signature, are another bane of collectors. Distinguishing a secretarial or autopen signature takes experience. The secretarial signature is usually easy to distinguish because most secretaries don't make a conscious effort to forge their employer's signature. One merely has to compare a legitimate signature or a facsimile to the one in question to be able to tell. The autopen is trickier, however, because some celebrities are known to vary the signature they program into the robot. As a result, several variant autopen signatures may exist for the same person. The only way one can be sure that a signature in question is genuine is to compare it to copies of known autopen signatures. The best way for the beginner to avoid being burned is to buy only from reputable dealers or from sources where there can be no doubt as to an item's authenticity. It is the job of dealers to know whether a signature is "right" or not.

Presidential autographs have always been popular. A good letter by John F. Kennedy would sell in the high value range. A Nixon signature now brings around $50. Collectors also actively pursue autographs of notorious characters, such as presidential assassins and Charles Manson. Nazi autographs and documents are also very much in demand. The most popular categories are Hollywood stars, scientists, literary figures, and world leaders.

While prices for the most desirable items may be high, the average collector can obtain many nice autographs for prices within the low value range.

BOOKS

Hamilton, Charles. *The Book of Autographs*. New York: Simon & Schuster, 1978.

————. *The Signature of America*. New York: Harper & Row, 1979.

CLUB

Universal Autograph Collectors Club
Box 467
Rockville Centre, NY 11571

   1 yr./$12, includes a year's subscription to the bimonthly newsletter *The Pen and Quill*, as well as other mailings.

AUTOMOTIVE COLLECTIBLES

Value range: low–medium.

Most popular items: antique car advertising, license plates, and promotions.

Good sources: garage, tag, and estate sales and from dealers at "automobilia" shows.

THE AUTO WAS RESPONSIBLE for a change in the way Americans thought of distance between cities, towns, and states. Within 25 years most of the country had gone from horses to cars. Cars symbolize the restlessness that marked the early 20th century. They enabled us to become a nation of people in motion, constantly prowling, searching. Today, few people in the United States remember what it was like without cars, and few are immune to the auto's allure. For teenagers, the first use or ownership of a car still represents adulthood. Becoming a driver is an American rite of passage. The popularity of the automobile in conjunction with the collectibles boom led to the development of automobilia. Following is a list of items and categories collectors of automobilia pursue.

Advertising	Hubcaps
Books	License plates
Car models	Owner's manuals
Car parts	Promotions
Hood ornaments	Spark plugs

Collectors save items by period, type, make of car, and country of origin. Period refers to the years in which a particular make of car was produced. No period is really more popular than another. However, collectors usually favor the cars and related items they remember from their youth. Collectors usually specialize by collecting a type of item, like advertising or hood ornaments.

There have been dozens of different makes of cars since 1900. Following is a list of some of them:

Buick	Nash
Cadillac	Oakland
Checker	Oldsmobile
Chevrolet	Overland
Chrysler	Packard
DeSoto	Plymouth
Dodge	Pontiac
Dusenberg	Rambler
Ford	Stearns
Hudson	Studebaker
International Harvester	Stutz
La Salle	White
Lincoln	Winton

Through the years, many of the companies that produced these makes went out of business or merged with General Motors, Ford, or American Motors. After the United States, England and Italy are the countries most favored by automobilia collectors.

ADVERTISING AND PROMOTIONS. Auto advertising describes anything printed in a magazine or newspaper or distributed at the dealership for the sake of promoting an auto. Saving old car advertisements from magazines is very popular because it is inexpensive, interesting, and easy. Most collectors begin by choosing a particular make or "look" to pursue. To determine the look you like, go to the library and look through books that contain photos and information on cars.

Some collectors favor the open touring car, others like the airflow look, and still others fancy the closed sedan. Once you know the look or make you want to collect, you can begin going to shows and sales and searching for old magazines and newspapers carrying car advertisements. Magazines usually provide better-quality ads. Magazines like *Fortune*, *Life*, the *New Yorker*, and *Time* are especially good and should cost, at most, only a few dollars an issue. There are virtually dozens of other magazines that contain desirable car advertisements. When looking through issues at a show or sale, always go for the ones that contain full-page ads and ones in color.

Once you have acquired some magazines, you can begin assembling your collection. Most collectors remove the advertisement from the magazine and place it in a polyethylene bag backed by a piece of cardboard. ("Polybags" of different sizes are available from mail order dealers who advertise in the collectibles publications.) Mounted ads are then organized according to look, make, period, etc., and stored in cartons. Some collectors like to track down corresponding historical information, such as how much the car cost new, how many were sold, how long the company was in business, and then type it up and place it inside the polybag on the back of the cardboard.

Other forms of auto advertising like posters and bar displays are not that common because the auto industry found out years ago that their advertising funds were best spent reaching the public through publications and radio and, later on, television.

Promotions are any items given away by the auto companies to serve as advertising for their cars. Promotions include postcards, pens and pencils, ashtrays, ink blotters, key chains, leatherette car garbage bags, stickers, nodders, and more. Because promotions are not nearly as common as car ads, promotion collectors usually don't specialize. Pieces marked with the car company logo are especially desirable.

HUBCAPS. Hubcaps are very popular and are usually collected by design, size, or make. I once found and brought home a Mercedes Benz hubcap. For years it sat in my garage. One day an automobilia collector happened to see it and told me it was worth $40 because it came from a popular sports model Mercedes. Most hubcaps cost between $5 and $25 and are often sold at automobilia shows. Some collectors go to gas stations and junk yards looking for bargains.

LICENSE PLATES. Many states require that license plates be turned in once they are no longer registered to a particular vehicle. Over the years, however, plates from all over the United States have made their way to the automobilia market. The most desirable ones date from before 1940 and are from states that had relatively few licensed vehicles at the time. Midwestern states are generally good. New York and California plates are common. Most of the older plates are easy to date because the year is embossed and painted right on them. License plates from pre-statehood Alaska are especially desirable and can bring over $100. Most other plates sell for between $5 and $35, depending on condition and scarcity.

CLUBS

Auto License Plate Collectors Club
Box 712
Weston, WV 26452

1 yr./$14, includes 6 issues of their newsletter, which contains info, photos, and articles on plates and related subjects.

Sparkplug Collectors of America
Box 2229
Ann Arbor, MI 48106

1 yr./$6, includes two issues of *The Ignitor*, which offers a wealth of info on antique sparkplugs and related items, as well as ads.

BASEBALL CARDS

> Value range: low–high. Most collectible cards are in the low value range with exceptional or rare pieces bringing into the high and very high range.
>
> Most popular items: rookie cards of today's popular players. Cards of any Hall of Fame player.
>
> Good sources: new cards wholesale through the mail; old cards from friends and their families.

BASEBALL CARDS HAVE been produced in some form for over 100 years. They are one of the quintessential collectibles because their vitality derives from an entirely American phenomenon. Baseball was created and developed in the United States. It is on everyone's list of top American pastimes. Children collect the cards produced each year because they are affordable and provide a psychic link to the players. Many adults collect the older cards for reasons of nostalgia. Others collect cards because of their graphic appeal or their investment potential.

HISTORY. Baseball cards today are generally thought of as the modern full-color variety, with a photo of the player and his statistics back to back on $2^{1}/_{2}''$ x $3^{1}/_{2}''$ pieces of cardboard that are packaged with chewing gum in a waxy colored wrapper. Cards did not always come like this, however.

The first baseball cards were issued around 1886 by Goodwin

and Company of New York, a manufacturer of Gypsy Queen, Old Judge, and other cigarette brands. These issues were about a third the size of today's cards and featured a black and white photo of a ballplayer on one side and a list of the cards available on the other. They were included as a promotion in the small, slide-opening cigarette boxes.

Other cigarette companies saw that the cards helped sell cigarettes, and from 1890 to 1895 many varieties of cards were produced. Most were of the small size, but some companies offered large cards known as "cabinets." By 1895 the American Tobacco Company had claimed such a large share of the market that it decided to discontinue the inclusion of baseball cards as a promotion.

For the next 15 years, only a smattering of cards was produced. It was not until 1909 that any major series were begun again. This began the era of what are known in the hobby as the "T" and "E" card series (T standing for tobacco, E for candy).

During the period from 1909 to the late 1920's, every conceivable shape and design of card was made. There were cards that came folded over and when opened amputated the legs of the top player and revealed a different player standing on his friend's legs (these are known today as "double folders"). There were cards called "triple folders" that were miniature baseball triptychs showing an action scene flanked by illustrations of heads of two players. An improved version of the cabinet card was issued, and was so strikingly colorful (chromo-lithography at its best), that today's collectors consider them the most beautiful cards ever produced. In 1915 the tobacco companies stopped including cards because they felt the cards were not serving as an inducement to buyers. The candymakers, however, continued giving away cards through the teens and 20's, and thus an unbroken chain of card production was insured.

The early 1930's saw the introduction of cards most like the ones we know today. The Goudey Big League Gum Series was a major set issued in 1933. It consisted of 240 players, 40 of which are now in the Hall of Fame. Other gum companies joined Goudey during the 30's, and many beautiful color sets were issued. From 1942 to 1947 almost no cards were printed because of the war and paper shortages. It was not until 1948, when the Bowman Gum Company produced a 48-card set, that baseball cards began to make a resurgence that has lasted until today. Bowman dropped out in 1955, but by then the Topps Company, which had begun producing cards in 1951, was already on its way to becoming the world's largest manufacturer of cards. Today they dominate the market, producing over 300 million cards a year.

COLLECTING. By the mid-1970's, baseball cards had become extremely popular. In 1979 the first identification and price guide was issued, and it served to codify values and organize the hobby. Today, the most popular ways to collect baseball cards are by year set, player, team, and Hall of Fame standing. To collect by year set means to try and complete the whole issue of a particular card company for one year. In 1976, for instance, Topps Gum Cards issued a 660-card series, which consisted of American and National League players. Some collectors try to assemble this set by purchasing cards by the pack. Other collectors simply buy the set already made up from one of the wholesale mail order dealers who specialize in cards.

Collecting by player or players means that you try to obtain every card ever made of a certain player. Many younger collectors select a player who has only recently entered the major leagues. This makes obtaining all the examples of his card much simpler and cheaper.

Saving cards by team involves obtaining all the players of a particular team. Many collectors favor this approach and choose their own city's team. This, incidentally, is what accounts for the fact that Yankee cards always sell for more in New York, Dodger cards for more in Los Angeles, and so on.

Collecting by Hall of Fame standing means saving only the cards of players who have been elected to the Hall of Fame in Cooperstown, New York. This type of collecting is favored by investors who figure that cards of the superstar players will appreciate faster than those of the average player. The last seven years has proven them correct. As a result, many collectors try to figure out ahead of time which of the players currently playing will eventually make it to the Hall of Fame. The cards of these possibles are then hoarded in anticipation of appreciation.

The condition factor is extremely important with baseball cards. A high-grade card commands several times the price of its low-grade counterpart. To be considered ex-mint (the designation for high grade), a card must be clean, have retained its original gloss, have four sharp (as opposed to rounded from wear) corners, and have no tears, creases, or foreign substances attached. One must be wary of cards that have been cut down on a paper cutter to improve their condition. A cut-down card is considered damaged and should never be sold for the ex-mint price. The easiest way to spot a card that has been tampered with is to carry test cards, which can be laid under the one you are considering buying. If the test card is larger than the one being tested, you know to stay away. The condition factor is most important for investors and collectors who are only satisfied with perfect cards. The less demanding collector can benefit, therefore, in being able to purchase lower-grade cards for much less.

To date, there have been several instances of more expensive baseball cards being faked. The Pete Rose rookie card, for instance, was counterfeited once its price rose over $75. To make sure you don't get caught with an ersatz card, read the current literature in the baseball card publications and consult with dealers (they are up on the subject since their livelihood depends upon it).

The best forum for buying cards is the convention. The hobby is very popular throughout the U.S., and on any given weekend there are 10 shows across the country (check the publications for dates and locations). Other good ways to buy include through the mail and from friends and relatives.

BOOKS

Beckett, James, and Dennis Eckes. *The Sport Americana Baseball Card Price Guide*. Published in 1982 by Den's Collectors Den, Box 606, Laurel, MD 20810

Erbe, Ron. *The American Premium Guide to Baseball Cards*. Florence, AL: Books Americana, 1982.

PERIODICALS

Baseball Cards Magazine
Krause Publications
700 E. State Street
Iola, WI 54990
    1 yr./6 issues/$12; sample, $2. Articles and ads.

Baseball Hobby News
Box 128
Glen Cove, NY 11542

   1 yr./12 issues/$17. Packed with buy/sell ads.

Card Prices Update
Box 500
Seldon, NY 11784

   1 yr./12 issues/$6. Issues a monthly list of price fluctuations on Topps
   and Bowman baseball cards.

Sports Collectors Digest
Krause Publications
700 E. State Street
Iola, WI 54990

   1 yr./26 issues/$13.50. Ads and articles for baseball cards and other
   sports memorabilia.

The Trader Speaks
3 Pleasant Drive
Lake Ronkonkoma, NY 11779

   1 yr./12 issues/$16. Ads for buy/sell.

BEER CANS
AND BREWERIANA

Value range: low–medium.

Most popular items: early examples (pre-1950) of "cone top" and
   "flat top" cans.

Good sources: for free at abandoned dump sites; for trade at
   recycling stations; for sale at beer can conventions.

IT SHOULD COME as no surprise to anyone that Americans should want to collect beer cans and items that relate to brewing and selling beer. From practically the moment the first colonists landed in the New World, malt liquors have been consumed with gusto. Small wonder then that the cans that have encased the foamy beverage since 1935 are becoming very popular.

HISTORY. The American Can Company invested in many years of research and development before a can could be produced that would not impart a metallic taste to the beer. In 1935 a specially coated can was developed that did not alter the taste of beer. The Krueger Brewing Company of Newark, New Jersey, began buying cans in which to package their beer. That same year they were joined by several other brewers, among which was the Schlitz Company, which put its beer into what collectors call a "cone top" can (it resembles the can brake fluid comes in today). Over the next 45 years the design of the beer can underwent several changes as new alloys and opening methods were invented. Today, there are no more cone tops, and beer drinkers all quaff from similar "flat top" varieties.

COLLECTING. Beer can and breweriana collecting is fun and easy to get into. Most collectors start by buying up as many local varieties of canned beer as they can. Your local supermarket or package store is as good a place as any to begin. These cans serve as the start of a collection that can grow anytime you are able to locate a new variety. Drinking the beer is permissible, but *make sure to open each can from the bottom* so that the "flip tab" or "push-in" is kept intact. Beer can collectors very much value the pristine facade when displaying their collections.

After you have acquired as many current cans as you care (or are able) to, the time comes to start searching for old and exotic varieties. One of the best places to look is the abandoned village, city, or town dump. Some of the best beer can collections in the country have been taken from the bowels of dumps. If you go this route bring gloves, a shovel, and plastic garbage bags. If the idea turns you off, you can try looking at the nearest recycling station. Often old or strange beer cans turn up there and can be obtained by trading two for one with the station employees. I know one collector who spent his entire vacation going around to recycling centers in his state. He ended up with a good collection of cans.

A way of obtaining some of the very rare varieties of cans is by attending one of the many "canventions" held across the country by beer can clubs. A canvention is an unusual visual experience, with collectors stacking hundreds of cans for sale and trade on tables. Some especially rare pieces bring over $200. To bring top dollar, cans usually have to be *clean*, *dent free*, and have *no major scratches or rust*. Rust is the bane of collectors and seriously detracts from the value of all but the rarest of cans. A trick collectors use to prevent the spread of small rust spots is to rub a little general purpose oil into the afflicted areas.

The most popular categories of beer can collecting are *size*, *brand name, era, region,* and *design*. Some people collect only cone tops (expensive), others only collect Schlitz or Miller, and some collect only southern or northern beer. If you travel a lot, you can easily pick up examples of cans sold in different states. One executive who travels all over the world never comes home without a few new additions to his collection of worldwide beer cans.

Anything in anyway connected to malt liquor production is considered breweriana. Items in this category consist of such things as advertising signs, trays, calendars, mugs, coasters, napkins, and brewery hardware like meters, regulators, and plaques. I once received a call from an elderly gentleman who claimed to have been the brewmaster at Pabst and wanted to sell one of the original barrel plugs the company used. One of the most important criteria for assessing the desirability of breweriana is its appeal. An original barrel plug, however rare, is not nearly as appealing as a large, colorful advertising placard for a particular brand. The barrel plug, therefore, will not command as high a price in the marketplace.

CLUBS

Beer Can Collectors of America
Box 9104
St. Louis, MO 63117 and 747 Merus Court
Fenton, MO 63026

Eastern Coast Breweriana Association
961 Clintonville Road
Wallingford, CT 06492

National Association of Breweriana
Willson Memorial Drive
Chassell, MI 49916

National Association of Breweriana Advertising
Robert E. Jaeger
2343 Met-to-Wee Lane
Wauwatosa, WI 53226

> 1 yr/$20, includes current directory of members, dealers, breweries, etc.; certificate; and subscription to their quarterly newsletter. The club is for people who collect any item of breweriana.

World Wide Beer Can Collectors
Box 1852
Independence, MO 64055

PERIODICALS

The Beer Can Advisor
Box 146
South Beloit, IL 61080

Universal Beer Can Collectors Guide
Capt. Jack, Inc.
1360 7th Avenue
Marion, IA 52302

BOOKS

Toepfer, Thomas. *American Beer Can Encyclopedia.*
   Paducah, KY: Collector Books, 1976.

The Beer Can. Published by the Beer Can Collectors of
   America, 747 Mesus Court, Fenton, MO 63026. They also sell a guide
   to U.S. beer cans.

The Register of United States Breweries 1876–1976
   Order from: Donald Bull, 21 Frelma Drive, Trumbull, CT 06611.

BOARD GAMES

Value range: low—medium. Except for some very rare mid—19th century games, which sell for $100—$300, most collectible games can be bought for $5—$30.

Most popular items: games made by McLoughlin Brothers of New York City between 1850 and 1915. These are popular for their beautiful color lithographed boxes. Also, games that depict early aviation, baseball, and railroading.

Good sources: general antique and collectible shows.

NOW IS THE TIME to begin collecting antique and modern board games. They are attractive and reflect the era during which they were made. The best thing, though, is that most can still be purchased for a pittance and are sure to appreciate considerably once more people become aware of what bargains they are.

HISTORY. The W. & S. B. Ives Company of Salem, Massachusetts, was one of the first to begin producing board games. In 1843, when they brought out The Mansion of Happiness, many people felt board games were frivolous. Ministers often spoke out against board games, referring to them as "devil games." It was for this reason that many early board games included a small dradle-like device painted with numbers (called a teetotum) instead of dice, which were associated with Satan, to advance players on the board.

During the 1850's the McLoughlin Brothers of New York entered the game business. Their games became popular quickly because of the attractiveness of their color lithographed boxes. After the Civil War several other companies began producing board games. Among these companies the most famous today are Milton Bradley, Selchow and Righter, and Parker Brothers, All three achieved success through the vision and drive of their founding owners. George Parker, for instance, began as a clerk but was able to make his way because of his fertile mind which was forever thinking up new games. The burgeoning industrial movement provided a reservoir of models and ideas for the game companies. As the automobile and aviation industries developed, games began featuring cars and biplanes as markers and playing pieces.

COLLECTING. Games are generally collected for the attractiveness of their boxes. For this reason the most popular examples are ones that have stunning color lithography picturing people, animals, steam engines, sports, paddle boats, airplanes, automobiles, and science fiction or fantasy illustrations. Of all the early companies, the McLoughlin Brothers consistently make the most beautiful games. (The company merged with Milton Bradley in 1920.) For collectors, McLoughlin games typify what is desirable.

In addition to collecting for beauty alone, other popular collecting categories are by *theme, company, genre,* and *period.*

Saving by theme describes the collection built around a particular motif such as trains or airplanes. A collector of either would only buy board games that pictured or involved railroad or aviation scenes.

Collecting by genre means saving games that are played in a similar fashion; for instance, games that use only dice or teetotums or cards to advance play. I know one man who had been saving genre games for years and had become an expert on the ways games can be played. His expertise payed off when he was selected over 50 other applicants for a position with Milton Bradley's research and development department.

The periods of game collecting coincide for the most part with eras of industrial and scientific advancement. For example, some people only collect games produced prior to the automobile or during the period of early aviation or the invention of radio. Some collectors save games from the 50's and 60's that depict rocketships launched to outer space and the moon. Other collectors go after games that involve television. For the most part, however, the popular periods of game collecting are before the 1950's.

Considering the relative scarcity of games made prior to the

1940's, their general availability in the $5–$30 range at antique and collectible shows is amazing. I attribute their present bargain status to three factors: one, that a definitive price guide has yet to be published for board games; two, that many collectors want objects that are more durable and easier to display; and, three, that the public is not yet aware of how few of these games have survived. Games made by the Bliss, Singer, Sowden, or Crandall companies are especially rare and should be quickly purchased.

When buying any board game, always look for top condition in the box. The most common damage one finds is separation at the joints and edges. To repair these, use acid-free restoration tape (available at art supply stores and through the mail—see index) and work from the hidden side. Nothing hurts a collector more than seeing the original appearance of a game marred by tape. The inner pieces like the markers, cards, and spinners are also important. Always make sure that there are no pieces missing. Missing pieces lower the value of a game.

BOOKS

Value range: low–very high. Many collectible books are available in the low value range.

Most popular items: first editions of adult fiction (in dust jacket) by popular authors; well-illustrated children's books; and non-fiction books on hunting, fishing, the military, sports, and other subjects (see end of section for list).

Good sources: garage, estate, and library sales. Secondhand bookstores and mail order dealers.

ONE OF THE MOST WIDELY collected categories of books today is modern first editions. This category is divided into three eras: *1900 to World War I, between the wars,* and *post–World War II.*

Most of the books one encounters date from one of these eras. Pre–20th century books can be collected but will not be covered here.

COLLECTING. The path to becoming competent at book collecting is fraught with pitfalls and frustrations. I remember the time I bought 100 books from the early 1800's at a garage sale. Thinking that they were extremely valuable, I called a book dealer in New York, compiled a detailed list of what I had, and began making plans for an early retirement. As it turned out, the books were practically worthless, and after being turned down by everyone, I ended up donating them to a library sale. This experience taught me that age alone seldom gives a book value. With the exception of incunabula (books printed before 1501), a book must have much more than age going for it to be valuable.

Another mistake I made was in buying a beautiful early 19th century leather bound Bible. I nearly broke my back carrying it home and was crestfallen when I learned that, except for several extremely rare Bibles (like the Gutenberg), religious books are generally undesirable and sell for only a few dollars (which, however, does not stop them from being collected).

I was at a bookstore a few days after I had been told that a first edition of Joseph Heller's *Catch-22* was worth over $200, when I spotted the very same book on a shelf. Quickly examining it, I determined (with the little experience I had) that it was a first edition. The price was only $15. Feeling like a criminal, I walked over to the cash register, trying to look casual. The clerk smiled at me and said, "Good book," as she slipped it into a bag. I thought to myself, You wouldn't be saying that if you knew the mistake you were making.

When I got home I made an appointment with a local book dealer for that afternoon and began to decide how much I would try to get for the book. Three hours later I walked up to the man who specialized in 20th century first editions and proudly drew my find from the bag. "Where's the dust jacket?" he asked immediately. I looked at him and there was a long pause. Finally, he opened the book to the title page and then handed the copy back to me. "It's a first all right," he said, "but without the dust jacket it's worth about ten bucks."

How could a piece of paper make that much of a difference? After checking with several other dealers, I learned that without the jacket (or dust cover or dust wrapper), a 20th century first edition is worth only a fraction of its dust-jacketed value.

The major factors in determining whether a book is valuable are (1) Is it a first edition?; (2) Is it authored or illustrated by a desirable person?; (3) Is it in collectible condition (including the dust jacket)?; and (4) Are there any other features that make it especially desirable, i.e., was it inscribed by the author or is it a limited edition?

A collector must become proficient at ascertaining the first three factors. To illustrate the way to go about determining a book's value, let's take the hypothetical situation of being at a garage sale where an entire wall of books is being offered for sale. How would a collector go about determining which, if any, of the books were collectible?

The first step is to scan the spines of the books, looking for known authors or illustrators. "Known authors" refers not only to the names one thinks of, like Hemingway, Fitzgerald, Faulkner, Miller, Cheever, Updike, Bellow, or Styron, but to any 20th century authors, famous or not, who wrote a work of fiction. Learning names requires time in studying dealers' catalogs and looking through thousands of books.

Popular illustrators include Maxfield Parrish, Arthur Rackham, Howard Pyle, N.C. Wyeth, Edmund Dulac, Kate Greenaway, and others. (A list of the most collected illustrators is included at the end of this section.)

Once a name has been spotted, you should check to see if it is a first edition. Determining whether a book is a first or not is important. A second edition of a famous work of fiction, even with a dust cover, is worth only a fraction of the first-edition price. This is not as true about illustrated books. A second edition of a beautifully done children's book will be less valuable than a first edition, but the difference will not be as substantial as in the case of a work of fiction.

First editions are not always easy to distinguish. Book dealers and collectors refer to the characteristics that identify a first edition as "points." Some books are very easy to check for edition. All you have to do is to see if there is a date on the title page and whether it matches the copyright on the reverse side of the title page. If it does, the book is almost surely a first. In other books the copyright page will specify "First edition" or "First printing." (An edition of a book may include many printings; if it has only one, the first printing is the first edition.)

On some books, however, one must look for the points. A point can be as minor a detail as a misspelled word on page 92 that was not corrected until the second printing. A point could also be a detail concerning color of the binding. There are bibliographies that list these points. For first editions, *American First Editions* by Merle Johnson is widely used. Unfortunately, it is only good for books published before 1941. However, there are bibliographies for specific authors that also list points, and collectors can always call or write to a specialist in first editions for information. Once a collector has been at it for some time, determining the edition becomes second nature.

One more point, be wary of book club editions. These may seem to be first editions but are not. If you spot the logo of a book club, such as Book-of-the-Month Club or the Literary Guild, on the top of the inside front flap, you know you have a book that is not collectible. If there is no dust cover, a club edition can be identified by looking for a small circular indentation in the bottom right-hand region of the back cover of the book.

Back to our garage sale. If a book has passed the first two steps, meaning that it has been authored or illustrated by a name and is a first edition, the next step is to check its overall condition. Any marks, rips, scuffs, stains, or damage to either the dust cover or the book itself will detract from the value. Check the hinges of the book and its spine. Is there separation or heavy wear? Are the pages of the book heavily worn or yellowed? Is there writing anywhere in the book? Collectors of modern first editions are very picky and in most cases will only buy a book that is in fine or better condition. Condition is especially important for books published since 1950. They are expected to be in better shape because they are not that old or hard to find.

Two other desirable features are an inscription or signature by the author and limited editions. An inscribed or signed first or subsequent edition will be worth more than an unsigned copy. If an author was known not to give autographs (J. D. Salinger and Vladimir Nabokov are two examples), a signed copy of one of his books becomes valuable, even if it is not a first edition. Limited-edition books are also desirable. Many times a book is published in only a limited number. Often these copies are signed by the author. Some collectors save only "limiteds." The limitation is indicated by a statement printed on either one of the first or last pages of the book, reading, "The edition of this book is limited to 500 copies, of which this is number ———."

While these factors influence the value and collectibility of 20th century books, one need not collect only books that are valuable. Many collectors choose to save later editions or first editions without dust covers because these books can be purchased for so much less money and are in no way less suitable for reading or owning. Some collectors, however, steadfastly refuse to buy anything that is not a first edition in mint condition with a dust jacket. Book dealers encourage this type of collecting by competing with each other to offer books in the most pristine condition.

Books are generally collected by *genre, author, illustrator,* or *period.* Since popular authors and illustrators have already been discussed, and the three periods have already been mentioned, the only category left is genre. The most popular genres are *fiction, history, biography, science fiction, fantasy, horror, crime, suspense,* and *erotic.* A list of popular categories is included at the end of the chapter.

The best places to buy books are at garage, estate, and library sales. You may have to go through a lot of chaff to come up with desirable editions, but the price is right since books at these three forums seldom sell for more than between 25¢ and $1. Many valuable first editions have been found by "pickers" who spend weekends going to sales. Library sales are a particularly good source. Be careful, however, not to buy ex-library books as these, even if they are first editions, are undesirable since they usually have library stamps and other condition problems.

A more expensive alternative for buying books is to deal with a mail order dealer or a secondhand bookstore. From them one can obtain almost anything. Prices can be steep, though, and few first editions of popular authors sell for under $25. Most first-edition dealers feel that if they cannot charge at least $25 for a book, it is not worth listing in their catalog. The secondhand bookstore can be a good source if one is interested in second or subsequent editions or books without dust jackets. Many booksellers have bins and shelves loaded with such books, which collectors can pick from at a dollar or two an edition.

POPULAR ILLUSTRATORS

Abbey, Edwin
Benton, Thomas Hart
Bonnard, Pierre
Brundage, Frances
Chagall, Marc
Chappell, Warren
Christy, Howard Chandler
Crane, Walter
Dali, Salvador
Deakin, Edwin
Denslow, W.W.
Dixon, Maynard
Dulac, Edmund
Fisher, Harrison
Fogarty, Thomas
Frost, A.B.
Gorey, Edward
Greenaway, Kate
Hanforth, Thomas
Humphrey, Maude
Hurd, Peter
Kent, Rockwell
Lawson, Robert

Matisse, Henri
Miller, Alfred
Nailor, Gerald
Parrish, Maxfield
Paxson, Edgar Samuel
Picasso, Pablo
Potter, Beatrice
Pyle, Howard
Rackham, Arthur
Remington, Frederic
Rockwell, Norman
Russell, Charles M.
Schoonover, Frank
Sendak, Maurice
Seredy, Kate
Sewell, Anna
Shepard, Ernest
Smith, Jessie Wilcox
Stahl, Ben
Szyk, Arthur
Williams, Garth
Wyeth, Andrew
Wyeth, N.C.

POPULAR NON-FICTION CATEGORIES

American art
antiques
automobiles
aviation
black history
cartoons

cats
chess
cinema
Civil War
cooking
crafts

dogs
feminism
fishing
guns
history
horses
humor
hunting
Indians
magic
military

music
occult
opera
photography
printing
railroads
ships and sea
slavery
sports
Wild West
yachting

PRICING GUIDES

American Book Prices Current, 115 Central Park West, New York, NY 10023
   This is an expensive set, and a collector may find that it is preferable
   to use it at the library.

The Book Collector's Handbook of Values by Van Allen Bradley.
   Published by G. P. Putnam's Sons, New York. An indispensable value
   guide to the majority of collectible books.

Bookman's Price Index: A Guide to the Value of Rare and Out of Print Books. Available from: Gale Research Company, Book Tower, Detroit, MI 48226

Dealers' catalogs: Send for the catalogs of dealers who specialize in modern
   first editions. These are the best reference for current market prices.

The Used Book Price Guide by Mildred S. Mandeville.
   Order from: Price Guide Publishers, 525 Kenmore Station, Kenmore,
   WA 98028

PERIODICALS

A B Bookman's Weekly
Box AB
Clifton, NJ 07015

The American Book Collector
The Moretus Press, Inc.
274 Madison Avenue
New York, NY 10016

> 1 yr./six issues/$18.50.
> Sample, $3.75 plus postage.

> Includes articles on authors, publishers, illustrators, etc., as well as advertisements. They also publish the *Directory of Specialized American Bookdealers*.

The Book Mart
Box 481
Pinellas Park, FL 33565

Bookseller
412 North Palm Street
Turlock, CA 95380

The Book Sheet
Box 1461
Lawton, OK 73502

Sent free on request.

In addition to these periodicals, look in the classifieds of the general antiques and collectibles publications (see page 311) for the solicitations and buy/sell ads of collectors and dealers.

CLUBS

International Society of Bible Collectors
Box 2485
El Cajon, CA 92021

> 1 yr./$5, includes 4 copies of the quarterly, *The Bible Collector*.

> A club for those interested in collecting translations and versions of the Bible.

International Wizard of Oz Club
Fred M. Meter
220 North 11th Street
Excanaba, MI 49829

> 1 yr./$10, includes subscription to *The Baum Bugle*, a magazine featuring scholarly articles on all aspects of Baum's creation.

NEWSLETTERS

Yellowback Library
2019 S.E. 8th Street
Des Moines, IA 52401

Published six times a year, it covers all aspects of children's series book collecting.

The Mystery and Adventure Series Review
Fred Woodworth
Box 3488
Tuscan, AZ 85722

Published quarterly, it features articles and ads on the many children's books issued in series from the late 19th century on, e.g., *Tom Swift, The Hardy Boys.*

BOOKPLATES

Value range: Low–very high. Most bookplates were made through photo-mechanical processes and sell for between 50¢ and $5, depending on age, condition, and visual appeal. The plates that bring substantial prices are those drawn by 16th century artists (like Albrecht Dürer) and those once owned by famous personages, e.g., George Washington, Paul Revere, John F. Kennedy.

Most popular items: photo-mechanically produced bookplates drawn by popular late 19th and 20th century artists like, Maxfield Parrish, Rockwell Kent, Arthur Rackham; plates once owned by persons of note; and any visually appealing pieces.

Good sources: ephemera dealers, book dealers, classified sell ads in the general antiques and collectibles publications.

A BOOKPLATE IS THAT relatively small (2"–4" x 3"–5") printed or engraved rectangle of paper that is pasted on the end-paper or the first page of books to signify ownership. The golden age of bookplates began in Europe in the 1600's, when the ownership of books was largely restricted (because of scarcity, value, and limited literacy) to nobility, and custom required people to use bookplates. These early plates were much more than identification tags. They afforded those of wealth an opportunity to express themselves and what they stood for. Owners worked closely with the engraver who would execute a design and a motto on a copper, silver, or wood plate. If the design was satisfactory, engravings were made. Some even had their bookplates hand drawn. Examples of such plates done by Albrecht Dürer or other major artists can be worth thousands of dollars today.

The first bookplates in America came with their Dutch and British owners across the Atlantic. English craftsmen were the masters of the bookplate throughout the early colonial period. The earliest American bookplate engraver was Nathaniel Hurd, who worked in the Boston area. Examples of his work have been found dating back to 1748. Other engravers, including Paul Revere, produced bookplates to meet the demand of America's fledgling aristocracy. Many of the pre-Revolutionary pieces from the New England area reflect the patriotism of the time with mottos like, "Never Despair," "I rise after defeat," and "Liberty or Death."

With the development of photo-mechanical means of reproducing images in the late 19th century, the bookplate entered into general usage. Books were no longer the exclusive property of the wealthy, and many middle-class book owners began buying plates. During this period many children's book illustrators began designing and drawing bookplates that were then reproduced in the tens of thousands and sold to the general public at bookstores. These new plates differed from their predecessors in that they were made with the public's taste in mind. On these mass-produced bookplates, the space where the owner's name was usually engraved (in the case of a commissioned plate) was left blank to be filled in by the eventual owner. The popularity of the photo-mechanical bookplate has not stopped the wealthy, individualistic, or nouveau riche from commissioning bookplates.

CLUB

American Society of Bookplate Collectors and Designers
605 N. Stoneman Avenue #F
Alhambra, CA 91801

1 yr. $35, includes a copy of their yearbook and a subscription to the quarterly *Bookplates in the News*.

BOTTLES

Value range: low–medium. Exceptionally rare or important bottles can bring into the high value range and more.

Most popular items: bottles that have paper labels featuring interesting products; bottles of unusual shape or color; and very early 19th century bottles.

Good sources: dealers and antique bottle shows for rarer and more expensive pieces; flea markets and general antiques shows for common examples; for free at dumpsites.

THERE ARE OVER 20 categories of bottle collecting, and each one has its own books, clubs, and nomenclature. The most popular categories are *Avon, Barber, Beam, Beer, Bitters, Cologne, Figural, Flasks, Food, Fruit, Infant Feeders, Ink, Medicine, Milk, Mineral Water, Miniature Liquor, Modern, Poison, Sarsaparilla, Scent, Soda,* and *Whiskey* bottles. Bottles are collected because they have aesthetic appeal, tie in with the history of the contents they once held, and are historical examples of the technology of the glassware industry for a given period.

The best way to determine which bottle category interests you is to go to a general antiques show or bottle convention. Once there, examine some of the bottles being offered. Ask questions. Don't leave without having gained a sense of what is available. Combine this with a trip to the library and a look at the books on glass and bottle manufacture. Once you have narrowed down the categories you are interested in, you can begin to collect.

One way of obtaining old bottles is to dig for them at abandoned village, town, or city dumps. The location of such places can usually be tracked down by talking to old-timers and checking old survey maps in the library. Nineteenth-century dumpsites are particularly good because they offer the chance of finding some rare bottles. It is wise to get local permission before you start digging. Always bring a shovel, spade, garbage bags, newspaper, *and* gloves. Searching through decades of old refuse is not easy work, but important bottle collections have been built in this way. In addition to old dumpsites, you can try researching the locations of old mountain hunting lodges and hotels. Many of these were built to accommodate tourist traffic in the late 1800's and then torn down after 20 years.

Another way of obtaining old bottles is to dive for them. If you live near water, you more than likely are near some place either on the shore or out on the water that once disposed of its refuse by dumping it into the drink. I met one bottle collector who had found a location in the Long Island Sound off City Island over which an entertainment barge had been moored during Prohibition. Diving with a companion, he had brought up over 500 unbroken whiskey bottles, some of which were fairly valuable. If you are water oriented and would like to try this approach, you can find out about likely locations by talking to local skin divers (who are usually familiar with where certain objects can be found underwater) and consulting old newspapers for the locations of seaside restaurants and entertainment barges. If you decide not (or are unable) to take the unconventional approach to obtaining bottles, the best place to buy them is at antique bottle shows and flea markets. Always buy examples that are in the best possible condition, and look carefully for chips along the lip and bottom of the bottle.

CLEANING. If you acquire a collection or a few pieces that are caked and filled with filth and slime, the best way to clean them is to start by letting them soak overnight in a pail. (Never soak a bottle that still has its label, though.) Once this is done, use a long test-tube brush (available from a hospital or laboratory supplier), a mild liquid soap, and tepid water to clean out the bottles. Dry them carefully and then lay them on their sides on a towel. It usually takes a day or two for all interior moisture to evaporate. For bottles that have their original labels intact, use a funnel to fill them full of warm, soapy water. After they have soaked overnight, empty half of the water and then gently shake the bottle, taking care not to splatter the label. Spill out the dirty water and then rinse the bottle out using the funnel once more. For the outside of the labeled bottle, use a damp cloth and carefully wipe away any dirt, avoiding the label itself if it is very fragile. If it is not, you can carefully dab at it with the cloth to clean it up.

Following is a look at the histories and nuances of collecting Avon, Beam, bitters, ink, medicine, soda, and whiskey bottles.

Avon Bottles

HISTORY. The company we know today as Avon was founded in 1886 by a 28-year-old entrepreneur named David McConnell and his wife. Operating from their Manhattan apartment, they named themselves the California Perfume Company and immediately began their famous tradition of having saleswomen sell door to door. By 1928 their business had grown tremendously, and they introduced a new line of products they called "Avon."

COLLECTING. Avon collectors save anything that was produced by the California Perfume Company or Avon. The most popularly collected items are novelty perfume and cologne bottles in the shape of vehicles and animals, old jars and bottles bearing an Avon of California Perfume label, and literature distributed by the company to advertise its products. Buying and selling Avon collectibles is mostly done through the mail, and there are two clubs with members across the country.

Jim Beam Bottles (modern variety; for old, see *whiskey bottles*)

Colonel James Beam came to work for the Jacob Beam Whiskey Company in 1880. The company later adopted his name and is still known by it today. Since 1955 the company has been producing a series of Beam novelty bottles made of glass, china, porcelain, and plastic. These have become very popular among collectors. The Executive royal porcelain decanter was the first novelty bottle the Beam Company produced. They brought it out during the Christmas season of 1955, and it was a resounding success. The next year they followed it with another and then another, until the popularity of the bottles made them marketable all year round. Soon Beam was joined by Ezra Brooks, Kahlua, Grenadier, Wild Turkey, Lionstone, and other companies that wanted to capitalize on this interesting way of selling liquor.

The best way to begin collecting is to walk into your local liquor store and see what is currently available. Don't be surprised if they have only a small selection, since many of the bottles are special-order items. Ask the store owner to show you a catalog. The most popular novelty bottles are ones in the shape of antique cars, but there are a vast number of varieties to choose from. In recent years some of the companies have shown their slightly eccentric sides in producing bottles in the shape of car batteries.

Older bottles can be purchased at flea markets and through the mail from dealers who specialize in them. To bring top dollar, a bottle should not be chipped or heavily worn. Whether it still retains its original contents affects the value only slightly.

Bitters Bottles

Bitters may evoke thoughts of Angostura for some people, but for bottle collectors, it refers to the great number of patent medicines that were produced and sold before the "pure food" regulations came into effect in 1907. Bitters were quack remedies that were often claimed to cure anything. Companies and individuals made them from herbs added to a potent alcohol base. They were sold in brightly decorated and unusually shaped bottles. Hundreds of different brands are known today. All were sold by general stores and traveling salesmen. Their heydey was between 1875 and 1905.

Bitters bottle collectors save only those bottles that have the word *bitters* embossed on the glass or featured on a label that is still attached to the bottle. Examples of some of the names bitters were

called are, Kaufmann's Celebrated Anti-Cholera Bitters, Fowler's
Stomach Bitters, Clark's Compound Mandrake Bitters, Dr. Blake's
Aromatic Bitters, and Lash's Kidney and Liver Bitters.

A collection of bitters bottles is very pretty and historically
intriguing when one considers that our ancestors relied heavily
on the alleged curative powers of these potions. The best place
to buy them is at a general bottle show. There are especially rare
ones that have brought over three figures, but most can be bought
for between $8 and $20. Always try to buy the ones that look the
most interesting and have their original labels.

Medicine Bottles

The most popular medicine bottles are ones that were manufactured between 1845 and 1907. Collectors pursue these for the
curious ailments they promised to cure, their historical importance
as examples of early glass manufacture, and the aesthetic appeal
of their design and color. Examples of the kinds of unusually
labeled bottles that are available are, Barker's Poison Panacea,
Heine's Golden Specific, Allen's Lung Balsam, Baker's Vegetable
Blood and Liver Cure, Bonsail's Worm Syrup, and Chaul-Moo-
Gra, The East India Cure. Bottles with unusual labels like these
are sought after.

Collectors also go after medicine bottles that are unusually
shaped or colored. A hexagonally shaped bottle is preferable to
any ordinary flask design. A light red bottle is better than a clear
one. When examining old bottles, buy the ones that appeal to your
taste. Most common "medicines" can be bought for prices at the
low end of the low-value range.

Although not as popular as their ancestors, "medicines" sold
between 1908 and 1935 are also collected. The most popular are
ones that contained medicines still in use today. These provide
an interesting link with the past.

Ink Bottles (Inkwells)

The first inkwells were made of ceramic and imported to the
United States around 1810. Eventually American glassmakers be-

gan producing them. The maker always had in mind the idea of producing something that was both functional and attractive. Early ink bottles came in a vast variety of sizes, shapes, and colors. All were designed not to topple easily. Most manufacturers were proud of their product and incorporated their name and location into the mold.

There are essentially two kinds of collectors of old inkwells: those who buy the inexpensive ones and those who buy the expensive ones. To be a member of the former group, all you need to do is go to the next local flea market or general antiques show and look around for attractive wells that strike your fancy as well as your pocketbook. Many interesting and attractive 19th and early 20th century inkwells can be purchased for under $20.

If you decide, however, that you would like to buy the quality inkwells that often fetch hundreds of dollars, the first place you have to go is the library to read as much as you can find on the process and nature of early American glass manufacture. The world of high-priced inkwells is sophisticated and tricky. Before you buy even one expensive well, make sure you have attended auctions, antique bottle shows, and looked at the stock of many dealers in addition to reading. When you do buy, do so from a reputable dealer who will warrant the piece he is selling you. There are many reproductions of rare inkwells in the hands of collectors who believe they own authentic pieces.

Soda Bottles

Soda refers to the various carbonated drinks that were the precursors of today's popular soft drinks. For bottle collectors, it also refers to any of a number of other carbonated beverages, including club soda, that were consumed from as early as 1840. Because many city water systems were contaminated or filthy, the affluent drank bottled soda water. From 1840 to 1850 the bottles were made of stoneware; from 1851 on they were made of glass. Hundreds of varieties of these bottles exist, and none are very expensive. A soda bottle collector can obtain many unusually shaped and colored bottles for around $3 to $8 from dealers. They can also be found at old land and water dumpsites.

Whiskey Bottles

The most desirable whiskey bottles date from between 1800 and 1900. Some are valuable, and the beginning collector must learn to assess age by reading up on early glass manufacture and attending shows at which old bottles are sold. Before 1860 the shape of whiskey bottles varied dramatically from very small bottles to jeroboams. After 1860, however, the industry began to sell whiskey in the familiar "fifth" size. The standard colors became amethyst, clear, amber, green, and cobalt blue. Most surviving specimens have lost their original labels. Common examples can be purchased for $20. For rarer pieces, deal with an established seller until you become competent at age appraisal and fake detection.

BOOKS—GENERAL

Kovel, Ralph and Terry. *The Kovels' Bottle Price List.*
New York: Crown, 1982.

Montague, H.F. *Modern Bottle Identification and Price Guide.*
Available from: H.F. Montague Enterprises, Box 4059-7919, Grant, Overland Park, KS 66204.

BOOKS—SPECIALIZED

Avon: *Avon Bottle Encyclopedia* by Bud Hastin, 1980.
Available from: Bud Hastin, Box 8400, Ft. Lauderdale, FL 33310.

Fruit Jars: *The Collector's Guide to Old Fruit Jars*
by Alice Creswick. Available from the author at: 0-8525 Kenowa S.W., Grand Rapids, MI 49504.

Milk Bottles: *Glass Milk Bottles: Their Makers and Marks*
by Jeffrey L. Giarde. Available from: Time Travelers Press, Box 366, Bryn Mawr, CA 92318.

Miniature Bottles: *Miniature Beer Bottles and Go-Withs*
by Robert E. Kay. Available from: K & K Pubs., 216 N. Batavia Ave, Batavia IL 60510.

James A. Triffon. *The Whiskey Miniature Bottle Collection*
Available from: Brisco Publishers, Box 2161, Palos Verdes Peninsula,
CA 90274.

PERIODICALS—GENERAL

Antique Bottle World
5003 West Berwyn
Chicago, IL 60630

1 yr./12 issues/$11.50. Articles, ads, and information on bottle
collecting.

Old Bottle Magazine
Box 243
Bend, OR 97701

1 yr./12 issues/$7.50. Articles, ads, and information on bottle col-
lecting.

PUBLICATIONS—SPECIALIZED

Beam Bottles: *Pictorial Bottle Review*
Box 2161
Palos Verdes Peninsula, CA 90274

1 yr./6 issues/$10; sample, $2. Articles and ads on fancy liquor de-
canters and novelty bottles.

Miniature Bottles: *The Miniature Bottle Collector*
Same address as above.

1 yr./6 issues/$10; sample, $2. Ads and articles relating to miniature
liquor and beer bottle collecting.

NEWSLETTERS

Fruit Jars: *The Fruit Jar Newsletter*
Dick Roller
607 Driskell
Paris, IL 61944

1 yr./12 issues/$14. Features articles and information on fruit jars
and their collecting. Also buy/sell/trade columns.

Milk Bottles: *The Milk House Moosletter*
Box 366
Bryn Mawr, CA 92318

 1 yr./10 issues/$10; sample, $1. Includes articles and information of
 interest to milk bottle and dairy memorabilia collectors.

The Milk Route
4 Oxbow Road
Westport, CT 06880

 1 yr./12 issues/$10; sample, $1. Newsletter on milk bottle collecting.
 Has buy/sell/trade ads.

Miniature Bottles: *The Miniature Bottle Mart*
24 Gertrude Lane
West Haven, CT 06516

 1 yr./10 issues/$10. Newsletter features articles and buy/sell ads for
 miniature whiskey bottle collectors.

CLUBS

Avon: Western World Avon Collectors Club
Box 27587
San Francisco, CA 94127

 1 yr./$11.50, includes 6 issues of their newsletter. They also publish
 books on the hobby of Avon collecting.

Beam Bottles: International Association of Jim Beam Bottle and Specialties
 Clubs
5120 Belmont Road, Suite D
Downers Grove, IL 60515

 Write for information. They also publish a guide to Jim Beam bottles.

Infant Feeder Bottles: The American Collectors of Infant Feeders
Rosalind Berman
540 Croyden Road
Cheltenham, PA 19012

 1 yr./$20, which entitles members to Keeping Abreast, a quarterly
 newsletter featuring articles and information on feeder bottles.

Miniature Bottles: The Lilliputian Bottle Club
Harry Ford
5114 Maytime Lane
Culver City, CA 90230

   1 yr./$7.50, includes subscription to the bimonthly newsletter *Gulliver's Gazette*, which contains classifieds, club news, etc.

BOY- AND GIRL-SCOUT COLLECTIBLES

Value range: low. With the exception of early handbooks and Jamboree badges, most items can still be purchased for under $20.

Most popular items: The Boy Scouts of America was founded in 1910, the Girl Scouts in 1912, and the most desirable collectibles of each are items that date from the first 20 years of each organization.

Good sources: collectible shows and mail order dealers.

   HISTORY.   The first scouting organization was started in 1907 by an Englishman named Robert Baden-Powell. In 1910 it crossed the Atlantic with an American, William D. Boyce, who expended a considerable amount of energy introducing and popularizing the organization as the Boy Scouts of America. In 1911 Baden-Powell came to New York to speak at the first annual meeting of the American contingent of Scouts. The following year the Girl Scouts of America was founded by Juliette Gordon Low. By 1916 the clubs had grown so large that Congress granted each a charter. In 1920 the Boy Scouts held their first Jamboree, or international meeting, in England. Since then, one has been held every four years (except during World War II). Today, both the Boy Scouts and the Girl Scouts have become worldwide organizations with members in almost every developed country.

COLLECTING. Scouting memorabilia was overlooked until recently. Today, anything associated with scouting is collectible. Among the more popular items are badges, buttons, books, coins, medals, mugs, stamps, supplies, and uniforms. Presently, most of these items can be obtained for under $20. The exceptions are leather copies of the first handbook, which, because of extreme rarity, can bring thousands of dollars, and early Jamboree badges, for which some collectors will pay up to $400. Beginning collectors are advised to go after any of the early (pre-1930) items. As more people enter the hobby, memorabilia from the early days of scouting is expected to go up in value. Items that display the Boy Scout and Girl Scout logos are especially desirable, as are any pieces that were rendered by popular artists (like Norman Rockwell) or designers.

PUBLICATION

Scout Memorabilia
Harry Thorsen
7305 Bounty Drive
Sarasota, FL 33581

> Sample available for free by sending a SASE. Devoted to examining the history of the scouting movement and providing collectors with a forum to buy/sell/trade scouting items.

CLUBS

The Scouts on Stamps Society
Carl R. Hallmann
253 Sheldon Avenue
Downers Grove, IL 60515

> 1 yr./$5, includes a subscription to the monthly *SOSSI* journal. The society is for anyone interested in scouting from the philatelic standpoint.

DEALERS

The Stevensons
90 W. Thacker
Hoffman Estates, IL 60194

Dealers in Boy- and Girl-Scout collectibles, books, and related memorabilia. Ten issues of their catalog costs $5 and includes announcements for swap meets and conventions.

CANDY CONTAINERS

Value range: low–high. Desirable containers made between 1905 and 1935 can sell for as much as $1,000, if they are in original mint condition. Many pieces from the same period, however, are worth as little as $5. Most average pieces fall in the $20–$75 range.

Most popular items: containers made prior to 1935 by one of the companies listed at the end of the chapter.

Good sources: from dealers and collectors who advertise in the general antiques and collectibles publications and at toy shows and auctions.

HISTORY. In 1875 the first glass candy containers were produced in the shape of Philadelphia's Liberty Bell and Independence Hall. These were filled with candy and sold at the Centennial Exposition of 1876 in Philadelphia. By 1920 novelty glass candy containers had become popular sellers at candy shops, soda fountains, and five and dimes; and several glass companies were involved in producing an ever-growing number of containers in the shape of animals, airplanes, automobiles, banks, clocks, comic strip characters, figures, lamps, lanterns, musical instruments, ships, telephones, and dozens of other things. The glass companies made their basic forms with glass, but most incorporated other materials like paint, tin, and celluloid to add to the attractiveness of their containers. While the heyday of the glass container was between 1905 and 1935, some companies continued to produce containers after this time, incorporating plastics into their ornamentation.

Collecting candy containers is especially difficult because (1) better examples easily bring hundreds of dollars; (2) reproductions have been made that are quite good; (3) identification as to age and company is difficult; and (4) there is not a ready supply of examples "in the field" for collectors to examine and learn from.

I recommend, even more strongly than usual, that collectors learn as much as possible before beginning to buy. This can be accomplished by attending toy auctions and shows where glass candy containers are being sold and by contacting collectors who advertise in the various antiques and collectibles publications. Following is a list of the most popular glass candy container manufacturers. Unless otherwise indicated, most of the companies marked their containers either on the closure (cap or lid) or in the glass.

Cambridge Glass Company (did not usually mark their containers)

Jeanette Glass Company

L.E. Smith Company (some of their containers were marked)

J.H. Millstein

T.H. Stough Company

Victory Glass Company

West Brothers

Westmoreland Glass Company

BOOK

Long, Jennie D. *An Album of Candy Containers.*
  Order from author at: Box 552, Kingsbury, CA 93631.

CHRISTMAS COLLECTIBLES

Value range: low—medium.

Most popular items: early German hand-blown baubles, hand-made wax angels, any composition Santa Claus figurines, and early Christmas seals and postcards.

Good sources: No shows yet. Best bet is to go to flea markets, general antique shows and shops, and advertised house sales and auctions.

CERTAINLY NO OTHER collectible group has more nostalgic appeal than beautiful glass Christmas ornaments and Santa Claus figurines.

HISTORY. The first glass ornaments were produced in Germany in the 1800's. These were made by a large cottage industry usually consisting of entire families. The system operated with a middleman who would take orders for particular ornaments and then farm the work out to the families. These families would then hand produce the goods. The majority of them made the ornaments in the following manner: The glass blower began by taking a bit of glass and heating it until it became a molten glob. This was then placed at the bottom of a plaster of paris mold (the mold being in the shape of the ornament) and blown into the mold until it was spread evenly. What emerged after cooling was a transparent glass article in the shape of a figure, globe, or object.

The next step was handled by another member of the family whose job it was to fill the glass shape with a silver nitrate solution that would coat the inside. Once done, the outer surfaces would be dipped into a dye bath for coloration, and then the ornament would be hung to dry. The final stages involved the application of a lacquer coat (through more dipping) and then finally the addition of a painted design, glitter beads, or other material.

A lot of effort went into the production of even a single ornament, and it is a testament to inexpensive labor that these decorations were eventually sold for only a nickel or a dime. The processes described above were used to make ornaments until the late 1930's. The German ornament industry was the major producer of Christmas baubles from 1870 to 1939. Millions were produced primarily for the U.S. market. In addition to Germany, Austria, Czechoslovakia, Poland, and Japan produced ornaments prior to World War II. Each country's product can be identified by a characteristic quality. Japanese ornaments, for instance, were inexpensive but poorly made, while Austrian ornaments are known for their exquisite craftsmanship.

Right after the war, companies in the United States and Japan dominated the Christmas market. The German ornament-producing region had been decimated during the war and was further affected by the division of the country in 1949. It took several years for the West German ornament producers to start up. Today, they are once again a major supplier along with the United States, Japan, and Italy. Mexico and Hong Kong also produce Christmas lines, but they are generally of inferior quality and therefore unpopular with collectors and connoisseurs.

COLLECTING. Christmas collectibles have only recently become popular. The hobby is still young, and there is much misinformation regarding what is good, pricing structure, and place of origin. Generally, collectors go after three categories: (1) *old glass ornaments*; (2) any *figures related to Christmas*, such as Santa, reindeer, elves, angels, made of wax, cloth, paper, bisque, or china; and (3) related paper items, such as Christmas seals, postcards, advertising items, and so on.

The most popular ways of collecting ornaments are by *era*, *motif*, and *country of manufacture*.

The motif category breaks down into numerous designs. There are animals, autos, bells, birds, cones, churches, crosses, elves, flowers, fruit, hearts, houses, icicles, musical instruments, Santa Clauses, snowmen, stars, toys, and trees. The most popular and desirable baubles are the ones made in Germany before World War I. These are not always easy to distinguish from similar ones made 50 years later in Austria.

Learning to distinguish ornaments takes time and a lot of questioning of knowledgeable dealers. When buying old ornaments, always try to obtain ones in very fine condition but be willing to overlook a hairline crack, flecks of missing paint, or a chipped end if the price is reasonable. Ornaments can also be repaired at home by using a bit of ingenuity and creativity. A small puncture in the glass, for instance, can be repaired by gluing a thin cotton patch over the aperture and then painting it to match.

In the second category of Christmas items, collectors most highly prize figures of St. Nicholas. Thousands of varieties were produced, made from every conceivable composition. Many were designed as candy containers and come apart at the head or stomach.

Size and superior workmanship are the major criteria in determining desirability. Larger Santas (bigger than 10 inches) have brought prices in the medium to high value range at auction. Size and quality are also a factor in assessing the value of other figures such as angels, elves, and reindeer. There are some Victorian wax angels that with their finely formed bodies and expressive hand-painted faces are works of art. In comparing what is available, a collector will quickly learn the difference between the poor, average, and first-rate piece.

Paper Christmas items are usually collected as tie-ins with an ornament or figure collection. The most popular paper items are postcards, Christmas seals, and hanging ornaments. The best are the late 19th century and early 20th century pieces that display lithographed colors of a brilliance and quality never duplicated since.

In the early 70's several companies began producing collector series ornaments. These have been marketed with the same strategy as have other instant collectibles. If you like them, fine. Otherwise, it is unwise to buy them as investments since they are not rare, not in demand by collectors, and are not nearly as well made or beautiful as original hand-blown ornaments, which can be bought for less.

BOOK

Rogers, Maggie. *The Glass Christmas Ornament, Old and New.* 1977. Order from: Timber Press, Box 92, Forest Grove, OR 97116.

CLOTHING

Value range: low—medium.

Most popular items: clothes that epitomize their era, e.g., cloche hats and piano shawls for the 20's, zoot suits for the 40's, etc.

Good sources: goodwill, thrift, and Salvation Army stores, as well as estate, church, and tag sales. Vintage clothing dealers are more expensive than these secondhand forums.

THE CHARACTERS NATHAN and Sophie in William Styron's novel *Sophie's Choice* loved to dress up in old clothing and parade through the streets. It was a way they could call attention to themselves in a glorious and grand manner. Today, more and more Americans are doing the same thing after first searching for and then assembling outfits of vintage clothing. Clothes collecting has been gaining in popularity for several years. Managers of thrift and goodwill shops in and around major cities like New York and Los Angeles are used to seeing wealthier types looking for vintage chic from the 1920's on.

Collectors usually come in two varieties: those who collect period clothes (from as far back as the 1700's) and those who collect 1920's to 1950's clothing to wear on special occasions and just for the fun of it. Clothes from the 20's to the 50's are most popular with collectors because they are generally inexpensive and easy to find. The best place to look for them is at goodwill, thrift, and Salvation Army stores. Old clothes are donated regularly to these stores, and a diligent collector can eventually find anything. Church, tag, and estate sales can also be good sources for vintage clothes. Following is a look at some of the general characteristics of clothing from the four most collectible decades.

1920'S

Women: The Roaring Twenties were so named because they marked the beginning of a new moral consciousness for the country. Recently emancipated, many young women wanted to prove that they could do just what the men could. This proving took the form of drinking, smoking, swearing, and wearing fashions that broke with previous ideas of femininity. The 20's fashions included short skirts, short hair worn under cloche hats, tube dresses that de-emphasized a woman's curves, small handbags with geometric designs, ostrich-feather fans, shawls, bugle beads, fringes, and glitter. Flappers typified the look of a stylish 20's woman.

Men: For everyday wear, the smart man of the 20's wore trousers that tapered from the waist to the ankle, sweaters with argyle patterns, caps, and knickers. For formal occasions of the kind described in Fitzgerald's *The Great Gatsby*, tuxedos were de rigueur.

1930'S

Women: The daytime look of the 30's was more conservative, and the well-dressed woman wore clothes that complemented her femininity. Skirts dropped to mid-calf, and dresses, belts, and waistlines came back. Evening clothes were quite stylish with floor-length, shoulder-revealing gowns of satin and velvet, worn with mink, ermine, and silver fox wraps.

Men: For the men who still had money left after paying for the furs, three-piece suits in pinstripes, caps, derby hats, overcoats, and ballooned riding pants were in vogue. For evening, the tuxedo was still in, but lapels were much narrower than in the 20's.

1940'S

Women: The war placed fabrics at a premium and halted the flow of Parisian inspiration. For daywear, women wore two-piece suits (knee-length was back), simple leather pumps, and a hat. For the beach or play, halter tops with matching shorts became popular.

Men: Men's clothing was conservative throughout most of the 40's. The zoot suit, which appeared shortly after the war, was an exception with its bizarre combination of long coat and very baggy trousers. Mostly, men wore sports coats and matching pants and three-piece suits of tweed, wool, and linen.

1950'S

Women: The range of styles was broad, with full skirts and clingy blouses equally popular. Ballerina-type slippers were in and so were fairly high-heeled pumps. Costume jewelry became the rage. Hems were generally down, but for play, women wore short shorts and tight-fitting slacks.

Men: The fashions also ranged widely. "Pegged" and "rogue" pants were hot and so were Bermuda shorts. Men in business continued wearing the styles of the 40's.

After this sketchy summary of some of the looks that flourished during the four most popular decades for collectors, the best way to learn about what was being worn is to look through period magazines. Issues are generally available for a few dollars at flea markets and secondhand magazine outlets and can provide, beyond just a visual catalog of period clothing, ideas for putting together outfits. There are no set costumes. Once you have learned the general guidelines for an era, you can experiment. Part of the fun of this hobby is creating your own special look.

The prices for vintage clothing from the 20's on varies according to the condition and quality of the item. For women's clothing, the ranges are as follows: dresses $5–$100; blouses $4–$35; fur wraps $25–$200; hats $5–$30; shoes (when available) $4–$20; and miscellaneous articles from $2–$30. For men, the biggest bargains are the suits, which usually run between $25–$100. (I know one middle-aged writer who has never bought a new suit in his adult life. He wears only the very best of vintage suits. His secret, he once told me, is in showing up the day the stores hang new stock.) Men's shirts usually run $3–$15, ties $2–$4, and pants $8–$20.

Collectors who have tailoring abilities are very fortunate because one cannot ordinarily expect to wear a used article off the rack. Beginners should note that professional alterations can be expensive, and their cost should be considered when deciding whether or not an item is a good bargain.

COIN-OPERATED MACHINES

Value range: low–very high. See chapter for pricing ranges according to category of machine.

Most popular items: machines that have physical beauty and interesting mechanisms.

Good sources: from dealers who specialize in coin-operated machines, auctions, collectible shows.

ALL OF US USE coin-operated machines daily, but most of us never think about the origin or evolution of such machines. Enter the coin-operated-machine collector. In the last 10 years, the ranks of collectors of slot machines, trade stimulators, and amusement and vending machines have been steadily growing.

Following is a look at the hobby that prompts otherwise sane men and women to spend sometimes thousands of dollars on the purchase and restoration of old coin-operated machines.

HISTORY—VENDING MACHINES AND TRADE STIMULATORS.

The earliest coin-operated machines were produced in the 1860's by merchants who attached coin mechanisms to automatic musical instruments like the disc music box, calliope, and orchestrion. For a penny, a patron could activate one of these machines, and they would play for a designated period of time. During this period other coin-operated machines included automatons in glass-walled boxed stands, which would perform an action(s) (sometimes with accompanying music) when a coin was fed through the slot.

By the late 1880's developments in industrial technique began to suggest using machines to dispense products. During this time the first primitive vending machines were built. They were designed to vend gum in the form of sticks, balls, and nuggets to customers at bars, stores, and train stations. As they grew in popularity and proved viable, new machines were designed for selling cigars, collar buttons, and matches.

During the 1890's trade stimulators also began to appear in public places. These were mechanical games, activated by a coin, that offered a customer the chance to win more than his money's worth in product. For example, a person could put a nickel in The Fairest Wheel, which was a countertop wheel-of-fortune-type device marked all around with the numeral one, and four of the numeral two. The insertion of a nickel would set the wheel spinning, and if it stopped on a two the customer would receive two five-cent cigars instead of one. There were no zeros on the wheel, and a customer could not lose. Merchants liked these devices because they provided an enjoyable motivation for customers to part with the spare change they might otherwise have kept.

As the number and popularity of vending machines and trade stimulators increased, their makers, in order to compete for counterspace, began to make them more attractive and interesting. This was accomplished through the use of colorful paints, cast-iron decorating, and clever mechanisms the customer could watch. By 1910 there were thousands of machines on countertops in bars, tobacco shops, poolrooms, and hardware stores.

The popularity of the vending machine has continued to increase throughout the 20th century. Today, we buy every conceivable item from so-called automated servants. No one who has ever been at a rest stop on one of the nation's highways will forget seeing a bank of machines dispensing everything from hot sandwiches to rain hats. Some companies have recently begun producing machines that speak to the patron, wishing him a good day and asking what he would like. The vending machine seems certain to be around in the 21st century. The trade stimulator, on the other hand, was on the way out by the late 30's, doomed by the illegal use gamblers made of it. By 1952 it was virtually extinct.

HISTORY—SLOT MACHINES. The first slot machines began appearing in the 1890's. Unlike trade stimulators, which required the active participation of the shop owner, "slots" paid the winner off automatically in coin. The first slot machines differed from the standard three-reel machines seen today.

Most of the earliest machines were large (standing $4\frac{1}{2}'-5\frac{1}{2}'$) upright devices consisting of a wheel, different-colored coin slots, and a payoff chute. A gambler would insert his wager into one or more of the colored slots and then move a handle that set the wheel of fortune spinning. If it stopped on his color, he would be compensated in proportion to the amount of his wager.

It was not until 1905 that the first three-reel machine with the familiar side lever was created—by a California inventor named Charles Fey. His slot could sit on a countertop and was an immediate hit because it was exciting to play and offered many more winning combinations than the earlier machines.

Fey's machine revolutionized the way men gambled their change. By the 20's all manufacturers were designing and building machines based on the three-reel slot. To compete for store space, they made their machines works of art, combining rich woods, painted cast iron, bronze, and shiny aluminum. Many of the machines were also designed to provide a non-gambling service in order to circumvent state laws. This was often accomplished by having the machine dispense a product or play a song (music-box mechanism). The ingenious kinds of machines devised to defeat the changing laws were a testament to the popularity of the slots.

By the mid-50's, however, slot machine makers ran out of

alternatives. All states, except Nevada, banned their use and made it a serious offense to own a machine. Transporting slots across state lines became a federal crime. For the next 25 years those who collected slot machines had to take great pains not to let anyone, other than trusted friends, know about their collection. It was not until 1976, after years of lobbying, that a law was finally enacted providing that collectors could own pre-1941 machines.

HISTORY—AMUSEMENT MACHINES. The space-age sounds, fluorescent-colored plastics lit by brilliant lights, and the amazing variety of games at a modern amusement arcade all have antecedents in the penny arcades of the early 20th century.

The penny arcade came about in the 1890's and was so named because patrons could amuse themselves with a multitude of devices that cost only a penny to operate. The sounds then were not the electronic ones heard today but rather the boisterous carnival music produced by the suction-powered orchestrions and steam-generated calliopes. For a penny you could also listen to one of Edison's first phonographs.

In the beginning, the penny arcade was an exotic place where families could go to play with the latest technical wonders. Patrons could look into the mutoscopes and see moving-action scenes of faraway places or naughty French frolics. For more active individuals, there were machines that challenged one's strength of arm, grip, and endurance. Among the most popular of these was a colorful iron torso of Uncle Sam offering his hand for a shake. For a penny you could clasp Sam's hand as fiercely as possible and then check a meter to see your score.

Another popular machine, in a world where electricity was just reaching the masses, was the electrometer, which promised to cure rheumatism and other illnesses by providing a jolt of electricity. The bravest man was the one who could hold the steel contacts longest. For those who wanted the excitement of winning a prize, there were the electric scoop machines, where one would try to maneuver a derrick with a claw hand to pick up a prize and transport it to the reward slide.

During the early part of the 20th century, the complexion of the arcade began to change. Increasingly, it became the hangout for seedy types. When pinball entered the scene in the early 30's and became a game the "characters" liked to gamble on, the arcade's reputation further declined. Between 1940 and 1970 the number of arcades steadily dwindled. It has only been in the last five years that the amusement arcade has begun to make a comeback, aided in large measure by video games and high-tech pinball.

COLLECTING. Slot machines are generally the most expensive of the coin-operated machines. Some very rare and desirable slots like the Caille Big Six Lone Star Wheel (1904) and the Charles Fey Liberty Bell (1905) have sold for over $25,000 in top condition. Many other early machines bring as much as $5,000–$10,000 in restored condition. The average collector, therefore, will probably want to stick with the later machines (1920–1941), of which there are many that can be purchased for around $1,000.

Collecting slots is not like saving postage stamps, and many collections consist of only two or three pieces effectively showcased in a living room or den. This is also true of trade stimulators and amusement machines. Although they are generally much less expensive than slots (nice examples of each can be obtained for under $500), most collectors choose to acquire only a few representative examples, sometimes trading these off for others after a few years. Vending machines are the least expensive of the "coin-ops," and few cost more than $300.

WHAT TO LOOK FOR. The most desirable coin-ops combine an interesting mechanism with structural and surface beauty. Remember, after the early stages in the development of the coin-operated machine, makers competed with one another by designing better and better looking machines. The cream is usually the machine that boasts the most interesting and attractive look.

CONDITION. *Do not* buy any machine that is broken or otherwise suffering from damage or serious cosmetic flaws unless you are (1) mechanically inclined, with some knowledge of restoring metal; (2) the relative of someone who is; or (3) getting the machine at a bargain price and have someone lined up who is capable of restoring it. Coin-ops are wonderful to play with and look at when they are operating and clean. A broken machine, however, can quickly lead to a triple migraine when you start to find out how difficult and expensive it can be to get someone to repair or restore it. Machines are heavy and awkward. Most restorers require that you deliver—no fun, believe me. And when you find out how much it costs to fix certain problems, having the machine restored may lose its appeal. Therefore, unless you fall into one of the three categories mentioned above, always go for the machine that has already been restored or is in working order when it is time to buy.

HOW TO COLLECT. I recommend that interested collectors begin by seeing what is available at coin-op conventions, collectible shows, and auctions. Beginners often make the mistake of falling in love with the first machines they see, not realizing that they may feel differently once their appreciation has matured. Making a mistake about a 200-pound machine is much worse than buying the wrong comic book, baseball card, or record. In addition to in-person viewing, look at the books and publications that feature pictures and articles on different kinds of coin-ops. Read them. Only after you have spent some time becoming familiar with the hobby should you consider purchasing a machine.

BOOKS

Ayliffe, Jerry. *American Premium Guide to Coin Operated Machines.*
    Florence, AL: Books Americana, 1981.

Bueschel, Richard M. *An Illustrated Price Guide to the 100*
    Most Collectible Slot Machines. Order from: Coin Slot Books, Box 612,
    Wheatridge, CO 80033.

——— *An Illustrated Price Guide to the 100*
    Most Collectible Trade Stimulators. Order from: Coin Slot Books, Box
    612, Wheatridge, CO 80033.

Christensen, David G. *Slot Machines, A Pictoral View.*
    Vestal, New York: Vestal Press, 1976.

PERIODICALS

Coin Machine Trader
Box 602
Huron, SD 57350

    1 yr./12 issues/$18. More of a newsletter, this publication features articles, information, and ads for all coin-ops.

The Coin Slot
Box 612-C
Wheatridge, CO 80034

 1 yr./12 issues/$25; sample, $3. The magazine for collectors of antique coin-operated machines.

Loose Change
Mead Publishing Company
21176 S. Alameda Street
Long Beach, CA 90810

 1yr./12 issues/$40; sample, $3.50. Magazine with articles, ads, and beautiful photos of slot machines and other gaming machines.

COMIC BOOKS

Value range: low–very high. The majority of comics being sold fall into the low-medium value range. Certain #1 issues from the late 30's and early 40's have brought several thousand dollars.

Most popular items: old and current Marvel and D.C. comics, any comics with exceptional quality artwork and/or story lines.

Good sources: new comics through the mail from dealers who sell wholesale; older comics at comic conventions and through private connections.

COMIC BOOKS WERE one of the first modern collectibles to develop into a major hobby. Today there are over 100,000 fans nationwide who buy, sell, and trade old comics. Hundreds of comic stores have opened in and around larger cities. The popularity of comic characters has led to the making of motion pictures (*Superman, Wonder Woman*) and dozens of television cartoons.

HISTORY. The story of the comic book as we know it today begins in May 1934 with the publication of *Famous Funnies #1* by the Eastern Color Printing Company. This was the first comic magazine to be offered on the newsstands, and it sold very well. During the next few years other companies joined in producing comics, which were for the most part reprints (in comic book form) of the popular newspaper strip cartoons of the time. In June 1938 *Action Comics #1* was published by National Periodical Publications. This comic, featuring the debut of *Superman*, began what is referred to as the Golden Age of comics. The immediate and tremendous success of the *Superman* character led to the creation of *Batman, The Flash, Hawkman, Sheena, Captain Marvel, The Submariner, The Human Torch*, and dozens of other heroes. Comics featuring these wondrous beings captivated the popular imagination and were a cheerful anodyne to the uncertainty and tension of the early war years. Though D.C. National had the two most popular characters on the market (*Superman* and *Batman*), other publishers did quite well with their ideas, and the 40's saw the debut of such famous comics as *Archie, Walt Disney's Comics & Stories, Wonder Woman, Captain America, Daredevil, Classic Comics,* and many others.

By the early 50's many of the comic characters that had sold so well during the 40's were gone. Certain of the more popular titles were still being published, but sales were not as strong as they had been. At this time the Educational Comics Company began publishing a line of books that was to become famous for its magnificently drawn and written stories. Their most popular books featured imaginative science fiction, fantasy, and horror tales. Much of E.C.'s popularity derived from their horrific titles like *The Haunt of Fear, The Vault of Horror,* and *Crime Suspense Stories,* which featured grisly scenes of carnage and death. For five years E.C. set the standards for the industry and had many imitators. Unfortunately, E.C.'s lifespan was shortened when in 1954 a book, *Seduction of the Innocent,* was published that was a severe indictment of the comic book industry. Its author, Frederic Wertham, maintained that certain of the more gruesome and sexually suggestive comics were corrupting the youth of the country and helping to spawn juvenile delinquency. In order to protect themselves, the comic companies joined together and created the Comic Code of Authority, whose job it became to review and censor all material being produced before approving it. The old line of E.C. titles was too violent to be approved, and the company was unsuccessful in an attempt to publish toned-down comics. (Their popular *Mad* comics, however, switched to a magazine format in order to escape censorship.)

In 1956 D.C. National sought to rejuvenate the failing comic business by reviving several popular 40's characters. This revival continued with marginal results through the late 50's. The next milestone in the evolution of the modern comic book did not come until 1962, when Marvel Comics came out with the first issue of *The Fantastic Four*. This comic featured humans who were suddenly given super powers and had to learn how to deal with them in a modern age fraught with neuroticism and emotional tension. Marvel came out a year later with comics featuring the Amazing Spiderman, the Incredible Hulk, and the Mighty Thor, all of whom were plagued with some kind of emotional/psychological concern relating to the period. Marvel comics became extremely popular because they dealt with relevant issues instead of staying with the hackneyed plots that had helped to ruin some of the other companies.

In the last 10 years Marvel and D.C. comics have dominated the market. The 70's have seen many comic characters develop into extremely valuable commercial properties.

COLLECTING. The best way to begin collecting comics is to go to your local stationery, candy, or drugstore and examine the current product. The two biggest companies are Marvel and D.C., and each produces around a dozen different titles. Some of the D.C. comics being done today are continuations of titles begun over 30 years ago. *Superman* and *Action*, for instance, have been printed continuously since the late 30's. By seeing what is being printed today, you can get an idea of what you would like to collect.

The most popular ways of collecting are by *character*, *title*, *company*, and *first appearance*.

Collecting by character means saving the various comic issues that include your particular superhero. Spiderman, for instance, appears in his own comic as well as in several other issues where he teams up with other characters. If you collected just by title, you could choose to save only *Spiderman Comics* or *The Incredible Hulk*. Collecting by company is seldom done because comics have become so expensive. During the early to mid-60's, when comic books were only a dime and then 12¢, it was possible to buy all the series of a particular company. Today the average price for a comic is 75¢, and most collectors have to be selective.

For investors, collecting by first appearance or first issue is very popular. If a series succeeds, the first issue usually becomes the most valuable. For this reason many collectors and investors hoard multiple copies of first editions. I know one young man who parlayed an initial investment of $100 into $10,000 by buying only first editions. It took him only three years, and he did it while he was still in high school.

At some point you may want to purchase the back issues of your favorite titles. The comic convention is the best place to obtain them. At one of the larger shows a collector can buy just about any comic ever produced. Prices at the shows are generally fair and reflect the true market value of comic books.

In this hobby there are three different sets of values. There are the values listed in the *Comic Book Price Guide*, the ones set by convention dealers, and the ones set by mail order dealers. Of the three, the convention values are the most accurate because they are based on what the market will bear at a given moment. The *Comic Book Price Guide* is very good, however, for getting an idea of which books are valuable and which are not.

The values the beginner must be wary of are the ones set by mail order dealers who make a living by selling issues through the mail at up to 10 times the amount charged by a convention dealer. Many of these overcharging mail dealers advertise in the classified sections of current comic books. They victimize collectors who have just become interested in acquiring back issues. To protect yourself, buy through the mail only when you have become familiar with the back issue market. It is also better to have already dealt with the dealer in person before you place a mail order.

Comic collectors who save for investment are extremely fussy about condition. Their books must be almost perfect. The collector who is more interested in reading his copies can benefit from the vast spread in price between the low-grade condition and the mint. A mint copy usually sells for four times as much as a low-grade one. The near fanaticism of some collectors to acquire the perfect copy does not make sense to the collectors who feel the hobby is about reading and enjoying issues.

Within the hobby there are specific genres that are more popular than others. Generally, the most popular comics are ones that feature *superheroes, science fiction, horror, fantasy tales,* and *good girl art.*

The least popular comics among collectors are ones featuring romance, Westerns, war, funny animals, and teenage humor stories.

BOOKS

Kennedy, Jay. *The Official Underground and Newave Comix*
  Price Guide. Order from: Boatner Norton Press, 99 Mt. Auburn Street,
  Cambridge, MA 02138.

Overstreet, Robert M. *The Comic Book Price Guide.*
  Order from author: Overstreet Publications, 780 Hunt Cliff Drive
  N.W., Cleveland, TN 37311.

PERIODICALS

Amazing Heroes
Redbeard, Inc.
196 West Haviland Lane
Stamford, CT 06903.

  1 yr./12 issues/$24; sample, $2.50. Features coming attractions on new comics, articles, dealer ads, and buy/sell classifieds.

The Comics Buyer's Guide
700 E. State Street
Iola, WI 54990.

  52 issues $19; sample, $1. This is *the* tabloid for comic collectors. Delivered weekly, it is full of buy/sell ads for comics and related collectibles, information about fan organizations, and editorial material.

The Comics Journal
Fantagraphics, Inc.
196 West Haviland Lane
Stamford, CT 06903.

1yr./9 issues/$16. A magazine of news and criticism of comics, it features articles and interviews about comics as well as ads for wholesale comic dealers and supply sellers.

The Comic Times
250 Mercer Square
Suite 1003B
New York, NY 10012.

1yr./12 issues/$20. Articles on comic books, their writers, artists, and editors, as well as information on science fiction and horror films; dealer ads.

CRACKER JACK TOY SURPRISES

Value range: low–high. The average novelties sell for only $5–$20. It is the extremely rare early examples in paper, cast iron, wood, tin, and lead that can bring hundreds of dollars.

Most popular items: pre-1948 novelties that have the Cracker Jack name or logo printed on them.

Good sources: from dealers who run mail order auctions of radio premiums and related collectibles and through private connections.

THERE ARE FEW PEOPLE who can't recall having had the pleasure of opening and searching through a box of Cracker Jack for the little toy surprise. The prize inside has become an American institution, and today many people collect examples of prizes from the company's 70 plus years of production. A collection of colorful little Cracker Jack trinkets and toys has a tremendous amount of nostalgic appeal.

HISTORY. Cracker Jack was invented (but not named) sometime around 1871 by F.W. Rueckheim, a German immigrant who made his start in Chicago by selling his mixture of popcorn, peanuts, and molasses from a streetcorner vending cart. The confection sold well for him, and by 1893 he had done well enough to introduce his product (still unnamed) at the Columbian Exposition. The name Cracker Jack came three years later when a salesman tasting a recently improved batch of the product exclaimed, "Boy, that's cracker jack!" Rueckheim had the name registered as a trademark that year and also had the expression, "The more you eat, the more you want" copyrighted.

Once the confection was named and packaged, it began to sell well. It was particularly popular at ball games, and in 1908 the national hit, "Take me out to the ball game," with the line, "Buy me some peanuts and Cracker Jack . . ." brought the company success outside of Chicago. Rueckheim was a shrewd businessman and was always looking for new ways to promote his creation. He experimented with giving away coupons that could be redeemed for prizes. These worked well, and in 1912 he thought up the idea of putting a surprise right in the box. The rest is history. Once children began to spread the news that every box of Cracker Jack held a toy surprise, stores could not keep the product in stock.

The early novelties were made of wood, tin, cast iron, lead, ceramic, and paper. They included things like tops, cars, figurines, yo-yos, baseball cards, puzzles, coloring books, buttons, and charms. Until 1933 they were packed loose with the product, and children had the thrill of suddenly discovering their surprise amidst a handful of candy. After that, however, they were wrapped in paper to prevent accidental consumption. The company tried to always have several hundred different prizes in circulation. This was to ensure that a child always got a different toy. In 1948 plastic novelties began to make an appearance. It was becoming too expensive to include surprises made of wood, tin, cast iron, and lead. The product had sold for only 5¢ from the very beginning, and the company had to cut corners somewhere. In 1956 they finally raised the price to 10¢, where it remained until the inflation of the 60's. The company was acquired by the Borden Company in 1963.

It has been estimated that in the last 70 years Cracker Jack has bought and distributed over 15 billion novelties. During the same period there have been over 10,000 different toy items. The company has a collection of most of the novelties they have used, but each year new ones are found that are not in the collection.

COLLECTING. Because of their small size, fragile composition, and the fact that most novelties were played with for a short time and then discarded, a relatively small number of the billions of trinkets put in Cracker Jack have survived until today. Some are so rare in fact that there are only one or two known examples of them. Therefore, the beginning collector should start by being willing to buy anything that was once in a Cracker Jack box. The most desirable toys are ones that were made before 1948 and are marked with either the name or trademark of the company. Novelties that are unmarked are difficult to distinguish from some of the trinkets dispensed by gumball machines. The collector will learn dating and identification by becoming familiar with the kind of toys Cracker Jack liked to include.

A tip about dating: The company always tried to buy items that reflected the times. Therefore, a flip-book with a silent film star would be a 20's vintage item; a set of comic strip character tin standups a 30's item, and soldiers, insignia, artillery pieces, and other war toys are 40's and 50's vintage items. Novelties from the 60's and 70's are more readily identifiable, as they are made of either paper or plastic and include pinball games, paper cut-outs, paper jokebooks, tattoos, and stickers. Plastic always means post-1948, since the company did not start buying plastic novelties until that time.

The best place to buy Cracker Jack prizes is from one of the mail order auction dealers who specialize in radio premiums and other small giveaway items (two are listed at the end of this section). You should also see if your friends have any old undisturbed toy boxes as often a few dusty trinkets can be found at the bottom of the box. Dealers at general collectible shows sometimes turn up a few pieces when they buy an estate or collection.

Prices range from a few dollars for common examples to several hundred for unique or extremely rare pieces. Generally, the most difficult toys to find are the early paper items. Being the most fragile, very few of those made before 1945 have survived.

In addition to collecting the novelties, there are many collectors for the old advertising signs featuring the familiar sailor boy with his dog Bingo. These signs can be quite expensive ($300–$700) if they are pre-1940 and very colorful. Some people also try to collect early examples of Cracker Jack boxes. Very few have survived, however, and pursuing this avenue of collecting will soon become frustrating.

MAIL AUCTION DEALERS

Hake's Americana and Collectibles
Box 1444
York, PA 17405

Four well-illustrated catalogs that feature Cracker Jack premiums in addition to many other collectibles/$8.

Historicana
1632 Robert Road
Lancaster, PA 17601

Small company that issues a mail order auction catalog thrice yearly and sends it free to interested parties. Some Cracker Jack items are listed.

MAJOR COLLECTOR

Wes Johnson
1725 Dixie Highway
Louisville, KY 40210

Wes Johnson owns the second largest collection of Cracker Jack items in the world and will be glad to assist beginners.

DOLLS

Value range: low–very high. Quality bisque dolls made between 1840 and 1940 generally sell for $500 and up in high
grade. Dolls made of other materials, like wood, cloth, and
wax often sell for much less depending on their condition
and quality.

Most popular items: French bisque dolls with paperweight eyes
are generally thought to be the most beautiful ever made and
are actively sought by dealers and collectors.

Good sources: For quality dolls the best sources are reliable doll
dealers who will guarantee their merchandise. Some collectors have been fortunate to find bargains at flea markets and
garage sales, but the beginner should be wary at these
forums.

HISTORY. There are examples of ancient art depicting doll-
like toys in the hands of children. It has been surmised therefore that some form of doll has existed since earliest times. Before
1840, however, there were few manufactured dolls. Prior to this
time dolls were either made by hand by craftsmen for the children of royalty, or by skillful parents who carved them out of
wood or fashioned them from scraps of cloth. After 1840 more
and more "production" dolls began appearing in France, Germany, and the United States. Production dolls and doll parts were
partially made by machines. Usually their facial features were
painted by hand.

By the late 19th century dolls had become the rage among the
rich in Europe and America, and parents spent inordinate amounts
of money buying dolls and doll clothes for their children. Usually
the dolls were bought unclothed and then outfitted with handmade accoutrements that minutely replicated the latest Parisian
fashions. Often dolls' clothing cost as much as their owners'. By
1900 dolls were being made of many different materials including
wood, cloth, metal, wax, bisque, composition, rubber, gutta-percha, celluloid, and porcelain.

COLLECTING. The majority of the dolls collected today were made between 1840 and 1939. Dolls made after the war are considered modern and, with few exceptions, are not as desirable. Dolls are generally collected by *material, maker,* and *type.* A doll is usually made of several different materials. For this reason the material of which the doll's head is made is used to classify the doll. For instance, a composition head on a cloth body would put the doll into the composition category, and a china head on a composition body would place the doll into the china category. Of the various material classifications, bisque dolls are the most popular and the most valuable. The beauty of many of the German and French bisque dolls with paperweight eyes is extraordinary, and recently some very fine examples have been fetching prices in the thousands.

There have been many different makers of dolls. The most famous are Jumeau, Kestner, Simon and Halbig, Schoenhut, Fulper, EFFanBEE, Madame Alexander, Kammer and Reinhardt, Armand Marseilles, Bru, and Heubach. Not every doll made by one of these companies is a treasure, as often the company would sell several lines of dolls, each varying in quality and price.

There are two ways of determining the maker and age of a doll. The first is "marks." Marks describes a letter or numerical identification code the manufacturer stamped, incised, embossed, or wrote somewhere on the doll (usually the head or shoulder). Marks are an important key to identifying dolls but, unfortunately are not always present.

A collector must learn enough about a particular manufacturer to be able to use secondary characteristics to identify the maker and age. Secondary characteristics include style, materials, overall look, and feel. Every maker has certain qualities for which it is known. Once collectors begin seeing and handling dolls, they become able to recognize these qualities.

There are dozens of different types of dolls. Following is a list and description of 16 of the most popular.

Bald head. A doll with a smooth, hairless head that is fully molded.

Ball-jointed. Describes a doll that is fully "articulated." This means that it has joints at the shoulders, elbows, hips, knees, and wrists.

Boudoir dolls. Fashionably dressed lady dolls that became popular with women during World War I. They were usually kept on the night table in the bedroom, hence the name.

Character dolls. Bisque-headed dolls made beginning around 1900 to look exactly like a human being.

China head. A doll with a glazed porcelain head.

Closed-mouth. A doll that has a closed mouth. Fewer closed-mouth dolls were made and are usually more desirable than open-mouthed dolls.

Comic characters. Dolls made in the image of popular comic characters such as the Yellow Kid, Maggie and Jiggs, Felix the Cat, Snow White and the Seven Dwarfs.

Flirting eyes. Dolls that have eyes that move from side to side.

Foreign costume. Dolls dressed in the traditional costume of a region or country.

Frozen Charlotte. An unjointed solid-china baby doll.

Mask face. A doll whose face is either printed or molded and then attached to a stuffed fabric head.

Mechanical dolls. Elaborate dolls made with clockwork motors, which perform an action. Also known as automatons.

Portrait dolls. Dolls that have heads and hairdos designed to look like celebrities. An example would be the Shirley Temple doll.

Rooted-hair. Dolls that have hair (sometimes human, otherwise animal or synthetic) that is implanted as opposed to being painted on.

Swivel Necks. A doll that has a head that turns in a socket.

Talking dolls. Dolls made with mechanisms that when activated (usually by a pull-cord) cause the doll to say something.

In addition to these categories, collectors also save dolls according to the type of human being they represent. For example, there are some collectors who save only baby dolls or actress dolls, and there are collectors who save just men, women, or boy dolls.

Regardless of whether you decide to collect by material, maker, or type, you should always look for dolls that epitomize quality in workmanship and beauty. A desirable doll is a piece of art; one should keep this in mind when buying.

Modern dolls, particularly those made of plastic, are generally unpopular with serious collectors. The exceptions are the #1 and #2 Barbie dolls, which are worth over $500 in mint condition because they are very scarce and mark the emergence of a new style of doll. The original #1 and #2 Barbies came in blond and brunette versions (the brunette is scarcer); and they can be identified by the following features: (1) their eyebrows will look like inverted V's; (2) they will have a painted white iris (later it became blue); and (3) there will be round holes in the bottoms of their feet (these were used to hold them on stands). Many collectors mistakenly think they have an original Barbie because Mattel used a torso marked with MCMLVIII for several years after the first two Barbies were made.

BOOKS

Bach, Jean. *The Warner Collector's Guide to Dolls.*
New York: Warner Books, 1982.

Lavitt, Wendy. *American Folk Dolls.*
New York: Alfred A. Knopf, 1983.

Theriault, Florence, ed. *The Doll Registry: A Guide to the Description and Value of Antique and Collectible Dolls.* Order from editor at: Box 151, Annapolis, MD 21404.

Westbrook and Ehrhardt. *Encyclopedia of American Collectible Dolls.*

Order from: Heart of America Press, Box 9808, Kansas City, MO 64134.

PERIODICALS

Bambini
Bernice Meyer
900 Eighth Street
Highland, IL 62249

1yr./10 issues/$9. A magazine for doll and miniature collectors.

Doll Castle News
Box 247
Washington, NJ 07882

1yr./6 issues/$9. Includes articles, information and ads on dolls, doll-houses, and miniatures. The same publisher also publishes, *The Doll-maker*, which is issued bimonthly at a cost of $12 per year. It features articles on making and repairing dolls, as well as general information and buy/sell ads.

Doll Talk
Box 495
Independence, MO 64051

1 yr./6 issues/$3. Small booklet-sized issue with general information and a for-sale section. The publisher also sells books on dolls. Write for a catalog.

Midwest Paper Dolls and Toys Quarterly
Box 131
Galesburg, KS 66740

1 yr./4 issues/$8. Thin newsletter of articles and information on paper doll cutouts and recent toy dolls like Barbie.

National Doll World
Box 337
Seabrook, NH 03874

1 yr./6 issues/$5. The magazine for doll collectors with articles, ads, and pictures.

CLUB

The International Rose O'Neill Club
Box 668
Branson, MO 65616

 1 yr./$5. For collectors of Kewpie dolls.

ENTERTAINMENT COLLECTIBLES

Value range: low—very high. Some movie posters, props, and costumes have sold for over $10,000. Mostly, however, one can obtain collectible items within the low-value range.

Most popular items: those featuring the legendary stars and movies. (See below for more specific information.)

Good sources: dealers of entertainment memorabilia, general collectible shows, and private connections.

THE FIELD OF ENTERTAINMENT collectibles is enormous, encompassing everything from tickets to vaudeville acts to the costumes of contemporary megastars. There are three major categories into which most entertainment collectibles fall. These are *Hollywood, theater and other live acts*, and *television*. Following is a look at each of these with primary emphasis given to Hollywood, since it has produced the greatest amount of memorabilia.

Hollywood

Beginning with the silent films of the early 20th century and continuing with the development of the motion picture industry, Hollywood has generated many stars and legends. Along with matinee idols, thousands of Hollywood items have been produced over the last 65 years to satisfy an adoring nation. Today, a growing number of collectors are saving Hollywood memorabilia, which is anything that has been produced relating either directly or indirectly to the movie industry. One usually collects from either the *silent film era* or the *major motion picture era*. Before a collector begins, however, it is necessary to decide which one of the major areas of items to pursue. The areas of movie memorabilia are *movie posters*, *paper ephemera*, *props/costumes*, and *star or movie-type collectibles*.

MOVIE POSTERS. From the earliest silent films to the present, movie posters have been produced to promote interest in and attract patrons to the movies. Movie companies often hired the best artists to create posters that would visually stun passersby. Posters came about during a time when there was no television and visual sensitivities were different. A vibrant and striking movie poster could go a long way toward luring a moviegoer back the following week. More than just advertising items, the best of the posters were works of art. Many people have come to realize this during the past 10 years, and the movie poster, long a pariah, has arrived. Many of the country's highest paid decorators create period looks using framed "one sheets" of such movies as *Casablanca*, *Tarzan*, and *Frankenstein*. A poster of Bogart in *The Maltese Falcon*, which in 1972 sold for $300, is now worth over $1,500. Similar gains have been achieved by other posters that feature famous movies and stars.

From 1915 to 1945 movie posters and other printed promotional material were produced and distributed to theaters by the film companies. Two weeks before a feature arrived, the theater manager would receive various-size posters and display items with directions on how to best post them. After the film had begun its run, these materials were supposed to be returned to the film company for re-use in other theaters. Fortunately for collectors, not all theater managers followed these instructions, and over the years many posters were held in storerooms, given to favored employees, and sold to prescient collectors. This situation continued even after 1945 when the National Screen Service was organized to take over the job of sending out and retrieving movie publicity materials.

Collectors of movie posters save all *original issue* materials used to promote films. The most popular of these materials is the "one sheet," a poster measuring 27" x 41". This is the standard-size poster people are used to seeing in theater lobbies. In addition to the one sheet there are *lobby cards*, thin announcements of up-coming features; *standees*, large stand-up displays (often in the form of one of the movie's stars); *three sheets*, which are three one-sheet-size pieces fitted together to create one large poster; *six sheets*, six sheets fitted together to make one poster; and the colossal *twenty-four sheets* (you'd need a castle to display this one). The one-sheet is most suitable for collecting purposes.

The factors that figure in the valuation of a movie poster are *age*, *visual appeal*, the *movie*, and the *stars*. Posters from before 1945 are much scarcer than those produced later. This is because many were destroyed in the paper drives of World War II. Visual appeal is a subjective factor, but generally a poster that has visual appeal will hold your attention because it has been artistically done and blends color, proportion, and form in an appealing way. Judge movie posters the way you would any piece of art.

The movie factor can be approached by thinking in terms of all films falling into one of three groups. At the top are the pictures that have been mythologized in this country, films like *Gone with the Wind*, *Citizen Kane*, *King Kong*, and *The Phantom of the Opera*. Posters featuring a film of this caliber bring top dollar.

The second group consists of films like *The African Queen, Dr. Jekyll and Mr. Hyde, Yankee Doodle Dandy*, and *The Little Foxes*. Posters featuring films like these are still very desirable but do not bring the stratospheric prices that posters from the first group do. Lastly, there is a group three, which consists of films like *An Ideal Husband, Moon Tide, Come on Cowboy, Mr. Big*, and *Because of Him*. Unless you are an old-movie buff or happened to see some of these films when they came out, it is unlikely that you will have heard of them. Posters of films from this group are not sought after the way posters of films from groups one and two are.

The appearance of a particular movie star in the credits or the illustration can turn a poster of otherwise limited appeal into a desirable item. A sample of the hot stars among movie poster collectors today are Valentino, Chaplin, Pickford, Gable, Grant, Grable, Garbo, Harlow, Monroe, Hepburn (Katharine), Bogart, Flynn.

Collector demand has made those posters that have a combination of the best of all the factors (age, visual appeal, the movie, the star) the most valuable. This is fortunate for many beginning collectors who want to buy posters that have some personal significance. For instance, I bought a friend a Bowery Boys poster that so pleased him that he framed it and hung it over his desk at work.

When buying posters there are two pitfalls the beginner must be careful to avoid. The first is the reissue. Reissue posters are not worth nearly as much as original issue. The former can be identified by looking for an *R* or *r* printed on the bottom margin of the poster. Be leery of posters that appear to have had their lower margins cut off.

The second pitfall is the reproduction. These are not difficult to spot if you have handled enough posters. A reproduction will not have the same feel as an original, and the paper will look different. In the case of a reproduction of an early vintage poster, you may be able to see pinholes or crease lines on the poster that are actually not there. Seeing either would tell you that you were looking at a photo-mechanical reproduction. Often the people who make the repros are unable to get a hold of a top-condition example to reproduce. They have to settle for posters with defects, and the copies then yield up the truth.

The best place to look for old movie posters are the theaters themselves. Even though most of the movie houses in and around the larger cities in the U.S. have been checked, there are still collectors discovering caches of old posters or other movie material in many out-of-the-way or shut-down theaters. If you do go looking, don't confuse recent "made for the fan" posters, which come rolled instead of folded, with authentic movie posters. One beginner called me up excitedly to report that he had just purchased 200 *Rocky III* movie posters. He was heartbroken and out $300 when I told him what he had really bought. It served him right, however, for believing that any theater would have 200 of the same poster.

When buying posters, always try to obtain the best-condition examples. Rips and tears are almost inevitable but avoid posters that are brittle or missing pieces. The best way to store your posters is in their original folded position. If you decide to hang them, you may want to follow the example of other collectors who have their choicest pieces mounted on linen. A rather expensive proposition but one that assures the longevity of the poster.

PAPER. Paper Hollywood memorabilia ranges from the obscure to the popular, with items like Dixie Cup lids, sugar packets, and scripts as collectible as autographs, stills, and magazines. The qualities that make or break an item on the collector's market are *visual appeal* and the *popularity of the film or movie star featured.* Those who collect scripts, for instance, want the scripts of recognizable and, preferably, famous films. The script for *King Kong* is much more desirable than the script for *Beach Party.* Collectors of movie stills want the shots that feature the very best of the actors who have graced the screen. Collectors of movie magazines go for issues that feature their favorite stars and for issues that have irresistible covers. Any paper item featuring a legendary star like Humphrey Bogart, Lauren Bacall, John Wayne, Greta Garbo, Charlie Chaplin, Marilyn Monroe, Clark Gable, or Jean Harlow is going to be desirable. Similarly, any item related to a classic movie is worth picking up if the price is reasonable.

In addition to knowing the desirable stars and movies, you have to develop an "eye," that indispensable skill discussed in Part One, to effectively collect Hollywood paper items. The marketplace offers thousands of different paper collectibles featuring movie stars, motion pictures, film companies, and the like. Some of these pieces are wonderful, really "sexy" as dealers say. Others are prosaic and unexciting. Unless you are blessed with a natural eye, spend a few afternoons at collectible shows observing the variety of paper items for sale before you begin spending. A friend of mine, who followed this advice, startled me one day by finding a "super" item at, of all places, a men's clothing store. I was looking at shirts when he, who had been trying on pants, came running over to me and said, "Wait until you see what I've found." We proceeded to the changing stalls, which were located in the rear of the store, and there I did a double take when I saw what he had found: a life-size stand-up advertising piece of Ronald Reagan selling Arrow shirts. It was superb. We contained our excitement and bargained with the manager of the store. Reagan now stands greeting guests to my friend's den.

PROPS AND COSTUMES. During the last three years, news of the selling of costumes and props from major motion pictures has been disseminated by the media, which has fallen in love with stories about the ruby red slippers Judy Garland wore in *The Wizard of Oz* selling for $12,000 and, even more remarkably, Steven Spielberg's paying $60,500, also at auction, for a balsa wood sled ("Rosebud") from the movie *Citizen Kane*. While these and other stories are true, they are not representative of the costume and prop market which, for top items, is very thin and supported by only a few collectors who are willing to pay top dollar only for items of special significance.

The kind of pleasure some collectors get from owning a costume once worn by a famous performer can be likened to the pleasure an autograph collector gets from owning something that was penned by a personal hero or heroine. Some collectors say that in owning something once worn or held by a famous star they feel closer to that star. In the same vein there are collectors who feel that in owning something once touched by a star they own a little bit of that person. Of course, there are many other collectors who don't view it that personally but want a costume because it symbolizes a bit of motion picture history. In any event, the costumes most coveted are those once worn by legendary stars in great films. The most desirable props are those that are symbolic of an event in film making.

Collecting desirable props and costumes is difficult for the average collector because most of the best pieces are snatched up by those who work in the industry. Some of the better items that do reach the marketplace pose a problem in terms of legality. By law, all props and costumes usually belong to the film company. When a costume or prop is removed from a storage vault, often by a disgruntled or avaricious employee, and sold to a collector, there is no change of title since the seller did not own the piece. Those desiring to collect Hollywood props and costumes must protect themselves when buying. Always require the seller to produce a bill of sale or authorization, proving he owns the piece. Not only will this paper protect you in the event there is a problem, but it can also serve as documentation of the object. Collectors must also be wary of fakes. Many imaginative sellers find items that resemble props used in famous movies and then try to pass them off as the real thing.

The safest way to begin collecting is to contact other collectors who advertise in general collectibles publications. A friendly collector can help you get started and teach you the ropes. Those collectors who live in Hollywood have an added advantage as many connections can be made with film people.

STAR OR MOVIE-TYPE COLLECTIBLES. This category embraces all the miscellany that has been produced relating to Hollywood. Lunch pails, serving trays, plastic mugs, buttons, candy boxes, rings, figurines, towels, and jigsaw puzzles are but a few of the hundreds of different items available. The way to classify this material is by star or film type. The types of film are *Westerns, romances, science fiction, horror, thrillers, war*, and *historical.* If you decide to collect items by film type, say science fiction, your collection would consist of items, similar to the ones mentioned above, that tie in or relate to science fiction movies. On the other hand, if you decided to collect by star, you would pursue only those items that featured that particular star. Since collectibles relating to Westerns and their stars are very popular today, let's use them as an illustration of the possible approaches for collecting.

Following are lists of individuals and fictional characters who were made famous in Westerns and of collectible items that feature Westerns and their stars:

STARS

Men
Gene Autry
Hopalong Cassidy
Gary Cooper
Destry
Hoot Gibson
Tim Holt
Buck Jones
Alan Ladd
Lash LaRue
Lone Ranger
Tom Mix
Roy Rogers

John Wayne
Women
Dale Evans
Annie Oakley
Sidekicks
Gabby Hayes
Tonto
Animals
Black Jack
Champion
Silver
Trigger

ITEMS PRODUCED FEATURING WESTERN STARS
AND WESTERN THEMES

badges	magazines	posters
books	mugs	premiums
capguns	napkins	puzzles
clothes	pencil cases	rings
comics	photos	sports equipment
figurines	pistols	toys
guitars	plates	wallets
hair cremes	playing cards	watches

A collector may choose to collect (1) anything from the items list that has anything to do with Westerns; (2) anything to do with a particular Western star; or (3) all of a particular item that relates to Westerns or Western stars, e.g., only cereal boxes or toys. Of these the most popular is number two because it effectively narrows the field of pursuit. There are, however, collectors who like Westerns, period, and are anxious to own anything ever made that relates to them. There are also people who fall in love with a particular kind of item, say a radio premium, and then pursue all examples that are Westerns-related.

I prefer collecting by star and have seen a number of beautiful collections built this way. For example, I met a man who had a whole den filled with items that featured or directly related to Hopalong Cassidy. He had everything ever made, including paper ice cream containers with photos of Hopalong as well as candy wrappers, gum cards, and toothbrush boxes. Collecting by star, whether the star is known for Westerns, horror films, or romances (or all three), is very popular because it satisfies the need many of us have to worship a hero. (Beyond movie stars I've also seen collections formed around politicians, scientists, explorers, and even criminals.)

If you decide to collect Hollywood memorabilia by movie star or film type, I recommend making up a business card that states your interest. I still have a card given to me by a Jean Harlow collector seven years ago. Over the last several years I've bought collections in which there were Harlow-related items, and because I had this collector's card, she was able to purchase them from me. Having the card made up is the best investment one can make. It is amazing how word of one's specific interest gets around if one has a card.

For a while I was exhibiting at comic book shows, and I'll never forget one man who came to every show looking for *Sergeant Preston of the Yukon* comics and related items. All the dealers knew him and had his card, and we would joke about his fanatical devotion to the character. The last time I saw him he had been featured on a television show about collectors and was in the process of negotiating the establishment of a Sergeant Preston museum.

Movie-type and star-related collectibles can be found any-where, and all of the forums are recommended. Except for es-pecially rare or desirable items, nice pieces can be bought within the low value range.

Theater and Other Live Arts

Hollywood revolutionized stardom. Before the film industry be-gan producing overnight stars, most actors had to labor long years performing five times (and more) a week and often traveling all over the country, hoping to become well known. Each time a performer took the stage he had to "turn on" and give the au-dience (or crowd) their money's worth. Many great actors and actresses performed their whole lives without ever receiving more than regional celebrity. Hollywood changed all this. It took un-knowns and made them, often after only one appealing perform-ance before the camera, overnight matinee idols. Many performers who began as stage actors and actresses achieved fame beyond their wildest dreams once they journeyed to Hollywood. It is this fame or national celebrity that led to the manufacture of so many Hollywood-related collectibles. As the motion picture industry grew, the practice of endorsements became more and more popular, and pictures of screen stars could be seen everywhere promoting cars, food, medicine, etc. At the same time, very few of our stage stars ever made the big time by just staying in the theater, and consequently there are much fewer theater-related items for today's collector.

The most popular theater collectibles are *autographs, programs (Playbills), photographs*, and *announcement posters*. These items can often be found at general shows and paper shows. Classification is usually by period or type of play. The periods most popular now are *1900–1916, 1920–1940, The American Musical from 1941– 1965*, and *modern theater*, including early plays in the existential and absurdist tradition. The types of plays include *classical* (Shakespeare, etc.), *tragedy, comedy, romance, thriller, serious theater*, and the *musical*. Because Hollywood and television have so thoroughly eclipsed the stage on the national level, there are far fewer collectors of theater memorabilia than there are of Hollywood items. This had been fortunate for those who have Broadway on their minds. Many wonderful early programs, photographs, and posters can be purchased for well within the low-value range.

In addition to the theater, other live acts included vaudeville magicians, stuntmen, dancers, singers, and burlesque performers. In many cases the only proof that some vaudeville performers even existed are the colorful, often primitive broadsides and posters they used to publicize themselves. Here, too, is a collectible area that has not as yet attracted too much attention. For those collectors fascinated by the itinerant performers who used to tour the United States, the best place to look for items is the collectible paper show. Recently at such a show I bought a magnificent broadside advertising a vaudeville magician, an obvious charlatan, who claimed to be able to bring the dead back to life and change lead to gold.

Television

Early television-related collectibles will become infinitely more valuable once we have moved on to the next technological wonder of communication, the computer information and entertainment center. Most of us are too close to television to realize how profound its effect has been even though it has been in wide use only since the early 50's. Prescient collectors, however, have already begun to save 50's *television program guides, premiums, related toys, records, books, clothing*, and *advertising*. Nostalgia clubs have been formed to celebrate such television series as *The Man from U.N.C.L.E.*, *Star Trek*, and *Dragnet*. The eventual mass recognition of the historical importance of early television-related items will probably not occur until the next form of mass entertainment, mentioned above is well entrenched.

If you decide to collect "T.V.bilia," I strongly recommend that you pursue items related to early live shows. These items are quite scarce, but when they are encountered they can usually, like just about all T.V.bilia today, be picked up for under $15. If you have difficulty locating early items, write to The T.V. Guide Specialists at Box 90, Rockville, MD. They buy and sell paper T.V.bilia and will be glad to send you a list of the items they sell.

BOOKS

Dietz, James S., Jr. *Price Guide and Introduction to Movie Posters and Movie Memorabilia*. Order from: Baja Press, 2829 Nipoma Street, San Diego, CA 92106

Hake, Theodore and Robert D. Cauler. *Sixgun Heroes: A Price Guide to Movie Cowboy Collectibles*. Des Moines, IO: Wallace Homestead Books, 1976.

PERIODICALS

Film Collector's World
700 E. State Street
Iola, WI 54990

1 yr./24 issues/$15. A tabloid devoted to collectibles of the film and Hollywood. Mostly buy sell/trade ads of dealers and collectors.

Nostalgia World
Box 231
North Haven, CT 06473

1 yr./6 issues/$12; sample, $2. Geared toward collectors and fans of the world of entertainment. Features articles and plenty of buy/sell ads for collectibles.

The T.V. Collector
588 Hogy-Memorial Drive
Whitman, MA 02382

>   1 yr./6 issues/$12; sample $2. For people interested in news, gossip, and information about television programs. Some ads for T.V.bilia.

SOCIETIES

Gone with the Wind
6047 Oakland Mills Road
Sykesville, MD 21784

>   1 yr./$8, includes a membership card, certificate, and 4 issues of their newsletter. For collectors of *G.W.T.W.* memorabilia.

The International Al Jolson Society
2981 Westmoor Drive
Columbus, OH 43204

>   1 yr./$7.50, includes photos of Al Jolson and periodic bulletins and publications.

Movie Still Collectors Club
Box 191 Cooper Station
New York, NY 10276

>   Publishes a journal, *Movie Star News*. Send $1 for sample.

EPHEMERA

Value range: low–very high. The majority of ephemera presently collected sells for under $20. Only very rare items from one of the more established groups like trade cards, advertising, posters, etc., sell for prices into the very high value range.

Most popular items: 19th century ephemera that exemplifies an artistic quality unparalleled since—many examples of letterheads, billheads, greeting cards, bonds, etc., are of this quality.

Good sources: New ephemera can be obtained for nothing by collectors who make a point of saving the common items everyone else is throwing away. Older ephemera is best purchased through private connections, which can often yield finds. Paper collectible shows are good sources for purchasing rare or unusual items.

IF I TOLD YOU that I know of a man who collected examples of toilet paper from all over the world, you probably would not believe me. You would be right not to since in truth I know of no such person. However, I do know people who collect items like gum and candy wrappers, empty cereal boxes, airline baggage tickets, and bus schedules. These people are called ephemerists.

Ephemera is a term used today among collectors to describe a broad range of printed paper items originally produced for use in all sectors of life. Following is a list of the categories of ephemera.

advertising
aerial leaflets
auction catalogs
bank notes
betting slips
bill heads
bills of lading
birth certificates
board games
bonds
bookmarks
bookplates
broadsides
business cards
calendars
calling cards
car stickers
certificates
checks
coupons

dance cards
death warrants
deeds
draft cards
election badges
final demands
food stamps
game cards
greeting cards
grocery stamps
indentures
instruction sheets
insurance policies
invitations
junk mail
labels
laundry lists
letterheads
library labels
licenses

lottery tickets
magazines
membership cards
menus
mobilization papers
mourning cards
music covers
newspapers
notices
notices to quit
packaging
parking tickets
passports
permits
playing cards
police records

posters
price tags
proclamations
ration cards
receipts
scraps
stationery
stock certificates
summonses
tax forms
tickets
timetables
trade cards
valentines
wanted posters
wrappers

As can be gathered from this list, billions of items of ephemera are produced each year and have been for some time. Most ephemerists collect because they see historical importance in what some consider to be rather mundane artifacts of past life. It is the very fact that most ephemera is mundane that makes it so perfect for providing an insight into the everyday life of our ancestors. A collection of greeting cards, for instance, reveals how different speech patterns and phraseology were 100 years ago. More exotic ephemera like 18th century bills of sale for slaves and pauper's bread-line coupons serve as proof of past events most of us have only read about. Printed ephemera tells us a lot about the way life was. It is a written record of prices, products, customs, and practices. Fifty years from now much of the ephemera being produced today will be collected by those who want an insight into life during the 1980's.

Collectors divide ephemera into three types: (1) *those items originally intended to be used once and then discarded*, like train tickets and coupons; (2) *those items intended to be of service for a set duration*, such as calendars, stock and certificates; and (3) *those items meant to be saved for a lifetime*, e.g., birth certificates, marriage licenses.

The most popular ways of collecting ephemera are by *theme* and *category*. Collecting by theme means choosing an area of interest and then acquiring different kinds of ephemera that relate to the area. Examples of themes are law, banking, fashion, aircraft, and hotels (for a more complete list see end of chapter). Say you chose to collect law as a theme, items of ephemera you might then pursue would include "wanted" posters, traffic tickets, police handouts, pamphlets on the CIA, etc. If you chose hotels as a theme, you might look for hotel receipts, postcards, matchbooks, room menus, and tourist information sheets.

Theme collections are often very interesting as they bring together a large number of things bearing sometimes only the slightest association. If you collected aircraft, for instance, a circular for the U.S. Air Force could be just as much at home in your collection as a United Airlines' emergency instruction sheet. It is sometimes good to set the parameters of a theme collection so that you don't end up with too disparate a grouping.

Collecting by category means choosing one of the categories listed (or inventing your own) and then pursuing items that belong to it. Many of the categories are in their incipiency as collectibles. This is fortunate for beginners, who can still build fine collections without spending a great deal of money. It also requires, though, that you work extra hard at finding out information about the particular item you are interested in. In many cases you will actually have to design your own rules for collecting based on an item's nature. For instance, if you decide to collect greeting cards, you will find that there is no set of rules for collecting them (as there are for more established collectible groups) and that you must create your own criteria according to the general attributes of greeting cards.

Following is a look at the main features of stock and bond collecting. It is included to serve as an example of how an ephemera category can be broken down according to its main components.

STOCK CERTIFICATES AND BONDS. The hobby of collecting stocks and bonds is known in the trade as scripophily. It has grown tremendously because of the collectibles boom. Many pieces that were only a few dollars 10 years ago now sell for over $100. To become a scripophilist you must become familiar with the main features of every stock and bond and how these features affect value and desirability. Every *issued* stock and bond has the following identifying characteristics: *date, decoration, signatures, state of issuance, company name,* and *number.* These characteristics affect desirability and value as follows.

Collectible stocks and bonds are ones that date from between 1830 and 1935, the older the better. Decoration can vary from none at all (which is rare) to an elaborate vignette. A vignette is an engraving of a scene, animal, ship, etc., and is present on 90 percent of all stocks and bonds. Vignettes vary from simple to complex. They were incorporated into the document to make it difficult to counterfeit. Other elements of decoration include embellishments along the border or margins of the paper. Collectors most want examples with interesting or artistic decoration.

Issued stocks and bonds were signed by government and company officials. Generally, the signatures encountered are not significant; however, there have been cases where collectors have done some sleuthing and identified important signers. Such identification would obviously enhance value.

State of issuance simply identifies the state in which the document is authorized and registered. Generally, stocks and bonds issued by western states during the 1800's are desirable because the territory was young and there were fewer companies in business.

Company name, which is always printed prominently on the paper, is only significant if it is a known company. For example, early shares of General Motors and Standard Oil are especially popular with collectors. Ninety-eight percent of the shares one encounters will be of anonymous and long-defunct companies.

Each stock and bond has an issue number that identifies it. Issue number is not very important in determining desirability, but some collectors like to save low-numbered pieces.

In addition to issued stocks and bonds, collectors also save *unissued* examples. These differ in that they lack signatures, date, and, in some cases, a number. They also appear brand new because they have remained in folders or booklets over the years.

Just as scripophilists have organized the pursuit of stocks and bonds according to the main features of every stock and bond, you, too, can organize an approach according to the printed information included on the items you are interested in. Contacting other collectors can be helpful and can be accomplished by joining the Ephemera Society of America. Members are sent a list of the names and addresses of other members and their specific collecting interests.

As with all paper collectibles, condition is very important, and you should always try to obtain high-grade examples. For best results follow the guidelines for handling and storing paper covered in Part One.

EPHEMERA THEMES

agriculture
aircraft
animals
auctioneering
banking
busses
canals
cars
charity
church
cinema
circuses
conjuring
cooking
cosmetics
cotton
crime
cutlery
dancing
dentistry
drink
drugs
education
electricity
employment
fairs
fashion

footwear
funerals
gambling
gaming
gardening
gas
glass
horses
hospitals
hotels
hygiene
insurance
law
libraries
medicine
music
navy
needlework
nostrums
oil
optics
palmistry
perfume
phrenology
police
printing
prisons

Prohibition
public health
radio
railways
restaurants
shipping
shops
silk
slavery
space

sports
steam
taxation
theater
travel
turnpikes
vaccination
warfare
workhouses

BOOKS

Connolly, Robert, D. *Paper Collectibles.*
    Florence, AL: Books Americana, 1981.

Criswell, Grover C. *Confederate and Southern State Bonds.*
    Ft. McCoy, FL: Criswell's and Criswell's Publications, 1980.

Hargrave, Catherine Perry. *A History of Playing Cards.*
    New York: Dover Press, 1966.

Kaplan, Stuart R. *The Encyclopedia of Tarot.*
    New York: U.S. Games Systems, 1978.

Theofiles, George, *American Posters of World War I.*
    New York: Dafran House Publications, 1981.

PERIODICAL

Dime Novel Round Up
Edward T. LeBlanc
87 School Street
Fall River, MA 02720

    1 yr./6 issues/$10. Includes articles and information on late 19th
    century and early 20th century dime novels. Also has a buy/sell
    section.

CLUBS

The Ephemera Society of America
124 Elm Street
Bennington, VT 05201

>1 yr./$20, includes a subscription to *Ephemera News*, the society's quarterly newsletter; a directory of members and their collecting interests; and the right to discounts on ephemera books.

International Seal, Label, and Cigar Band Society
Myron H. Freedman
8915 E. Bellevue Street
Tucson, AZ 85715

>1 yr./$6.50, includes a year's worth of issues of their bulletin. For collectors of any kinds of seals or labels, including travel, steamship, beer, wine, liquor, etc., as well as trading stamps, matchbook covers, charity stamps, seals, and cigar bands and labels.

National Valentine Collectors Association
Box 1404
Santa Anna, CA 92702

>1 yr./$8, includes a subscription to their quarterly newsletter, which contains information on different kinds of valentines.

DEALERS

Distinctive Documents
Box 1475
Orem, UT 84057

>Send $1 for two catalogs of stocks, bonds, autographs, and early western documents. Also sells reference books on stocks and bonds.

William Frost Mobley
Box 333
551 Mountain Road
Wilbraham, MA 01095

>Sells beautifully illustrated catalogs covering all kinds of American ephemera. Write for information.

U.S. Games Systems, Inc.
Dept HB
38 E. Thirty-second Street
New York, NY 10016

Send $1 for their full-color catalog picturing beautiful decks of reproduction cards for sale. They are also sellers of books on playing cards and tarot cards.

FIREFIGHTING COLLECTIBLES

Value range: low—very high.

Most popular items: pre-1850 equipment, badges, and uniforms.

Good sources: flea markets and from the families of firefighters.

THERE ARE SEVERAL million Americans who are connected in some way to the firehouse. Many are volunteer firemen in small municipalities and towns throughout the nation. Others are paid employees in the big city stations. From their ranks come many of the collectors who are interested in items from the colonial period to the present related to firefighting. The things they collect are

uniforms
speaking trumpets
trophies
trade cards
toys
torches
statues
photographs
stamps

signs
shaving mugs
rule books
ribbons
rattles
patches
nozzles
extinguishers
models

lanterns   buttons
helmets   buckles
horses   badges
gongs   belts
gauges   axes
alarm boxes   salvage bags
capes

The best way to explain what some of these bizarre-sounding items are is to briefly trace the history of firefighting in the United States.

HISTORY. In the beginning there were no big red fire engines to come barreling up to a fire, sirens screaming, to put it out. A colonist's greatest fear after the Indians was fire. He had little control over a major blaze and was at the mercy of fickle mother nature. A rainstorm could put out a blaze eventually, but a shifting wind could fan it into a conflagration. When the cry "fire" was heard friends, neighbors, and everyone within earshot would grab anything that could hold water and head for the blaze. These early volunteer firefighters would spread out and form a bucket brigade between a water source and the flames.

It was not until the mid-1700's that horse-drawn fire engines were made that, utilizing steam pressure, could pump water to the blaze. Even then though the bucket brigades were necessary to keep the engines's water tanks full. Buckets remained the primary way of conveying water to the fire scene until the early 19th century. Early examples of buckets commissioned by fire marshals for sale to individuals, stores, and fire stations are prized by collectors today who save them as artifacts of the early period. Many of these leather containers still have their original owner's name hand lettered on them.

One of the most difficult problems at the scene of a fire is crowd control. During the early times there was often rowdyism and looting at the scene of a blaze. To combat this, and also to facilitate order and purpose, the role of fire warden was created. A fire warden was required to bear a staff signifying his office. He organized the bucket brigade, directed the volunteers, and arrested looters. When not firefighting or pursuing his occupation (his, too, was a volunteer position), the fire warden inspected chimneys for soot accumulation. He had the power to fine any household that had a dirty chimney. His was an extremely important position, and only a known leader, a man strong of will and body, was chosen for this august position. Today, the warden's staff is an extremely rare and valuable collectible. Most are now in private hands. Besides the staff, the early wardens owned other objects related to firefighting that bore their seal and family name. Any of these are rare and special for collectors.

Because of the confusion at a fire scene, a method had to be developed to distinguish between those who were actually volunteer firefighters and those who were simply in the way. One of the earliest ways this was accomplished was through the use of helmets. The first fire helmets were made in the early 1700's. Since that time the helmet has assumed hundreds of different shapes, sizes, and compositions. Some of the early varieties had small oil lanterns attached to them and are highly sought after today. Others were elaborately decorated. Helmets of any era are extremely popular with fire collectors. This is also true of uniforms, buttons, ribbons, badges, patches, and medals. Badges were first introduced in the 1850's as another way of identifying firemen. As the service developed, special commendations and awards were created to honor the brave volunteers.

Before the utilization of electricity, gas, and oil torches and lanterns were used to light the way to and at the fire scene. Any of this hardware is very popular among collectors. Especially desirable are the elaborate silver and brass lanterns that were attached to the engines themselves. The engine has a mystique, and anything that was once attached to one (hoses, axes, nozzles, gauges, and i.d. plates) is special.

COLLECTING. The best way to begin collecting is by showing up at your town, village, or city fire station and looking around. It is usually fairly easy to endear oneself to the "fellas" that will be standing around "shooting the bull." Should they seem suspicious of your motives for being there, tell them you are interested in becoming a volunteer. This should thaw them. If it doesn't, just tell them that you are studying the history of firefighting equipment and are interested in learning about the modern apparatus. Just about every modern piece of equipment has some forerunner. If you are lucky, some knowledgeable old-timer will give you a guided tour of the firehouse.

Two other places to learn about firefighting equipment, techniques, and uniforms are the "muster" and the "drill." A muster is a big social event where firemen and their families from one town meet with their counterparts from other towns. At the muster there are competitions involving equipment and men. Awards are given out to the winners, and there is a big barbeque. Musters are usually only for firepeople, so if you are not a volunteer you may need to be invited.

Drills are not as exclusive, and the budding collector who attends one will be fascinated watching the deployment of equipment. Call your local station to find out when and where the next drill will be held.

For buying fire collectibles, the usual sources are recommended, with flea markets being perhaps the best places to find a bargain. Occasionally one can find such rare items as an original fire rattle from the 1800's (used to summon townsfolk to the blaze); a speaking trumpet (essentially an antique [usually brass] megaphone used for shouting directions); and clockwork indicators, which were boxed mechanical devices (sometimes still used) hooked up in the firehouse to indicate in which zone a fire was located. The nice thing about this collectible group is that it is still rather undeveloped, and one can often pick up bargains from dealers who do not know what they are selling.

BOOK

Piatti, Mary Jane and James. *Firehouse Collectibles*.
   Published in 1980 by The Engine House, Box 666, Middletown, NY 10940.

CLUBS

Glenn Hartley, Sr.
Fire Mark Circle of the Americas
2859 Marlin Drive
Chamblee, GA 30341

Annual dues/$20, includes periodic bulletins, newsletters, and journals about fire marks and other reminders of the early days of fire insurance. Object of the club is to bring together people interested in all aspects of early firefighting as it pertains to fire insurance.

Society for the Preservation and Appreciation of Antique
Motor Fire Apparatus in America (S.P.A.A.M.F.A.A.)
Box 450
Syracuse, NY 13206

1 yr/$12.50, includes 4 issues of *Engine!-Engine!* magazine, a card, and a roster of all members.

FUTURE COLLECTIBLES

WHEN THE DEMAND for an item is greater than the existing supply, the market price goes up. Similarly, when enough collectors begin pursuing a group of items that formerly had only functional value, these items will increase in price. Demand ultimately creates a collectible category.

When too many people attempt to capitalize on the same ideas, no one makes money. An example: During the 1930's people began noticing that many of the postage stamps issued by the United States from 1890 to 1910 were becoming worth many times their value. Believing that the current stamps being issued would also become valuable in time, people all over the country began buying sheets of stamps to put away. This buying continued especially as the economy improved and people had more disposable income.

The facts: Except for a few scattered issues, United States postage stamps issued since 1940 are available from stamp dealers for only slightly over their face value. There are also many stamp dealers who routinely wholesale thousands of sheets of three, four, and five cent commemorative stamps (30's, 40's, 50's, and 60's vintage) at 10 percent under their face value. This is done because these stamps are so common that dealers will not buy them in quantity unless they get an edge.

To determine which things will become future collectibles, one must figure out what most people are *not* saving today. This is not an easy task because the collectibles boom has called everyone's attention to the fact that anything is potentially valuable, and the same people who laughed at collectibles 10 years ago are now hoarding beer cans, newspapers, magazines, bottle caps, current baseball cards and comic books, hoping that in 15 or 20 years these items will be valuable. So many people are saving the same items, however, that a situation similar to the one described for stamps is developing.

Following is a look at several categories of items that I feel may become desirable in the future. If you decide to collect some of these items, your decision should not be motivated solely by the potential profits. Collecting should always be fun.

ADVERTISING. While 19th and early 20th century tin, glass, and wood advertising pieces are popular and already very collectible, their plastic counterparts from the last 40 years are considered unappealing and are hardly collected. I think that one day people are going to realize that plastic promotional pieces for alcoholic beverages, cigarettes, and automobiles are rare and historically important.

CHARACTER COLLECTIBLES. Anything that has a picture of Mickey Mouse or any other of the Walt Disney characters on it is a collectible. I believe that in the future items that depict the Peanuts characters, E.T., and many other of the recognizable mass-merchandised animals, cartoon characters, and superheroes will become popular collectibles. The key for collectors is saving the items that feature a property that is bound to still be around 20 years from now.

COMPUTER MEMORABILIA. Computers are in the vanguard of modern technology, and yet 30 years ago the science hardly existed. A good bet for collectibles of tomorrow are items that have anything to do with computers. Such things would include pamphlets, books, advertising in newspapers and magazines, games, toys, postcards, computer watches, and hand-held calculators.

EPHEMERA. Ephemera is covered in its own chapter, but it is included here to call attention to a few items I feel will be particularly desirable in coming years. These items are (1) mutuel tickets from racetracks (dog and horse); (2) state lottery tickets; (3) personal business cards; (4) menus; and (5) leaflets issued by the government warning about the dangers of drug use. The best ephemera has information which dates and places it.

PLASTIC COLLECTIBLES. Plastic is not popular among collectors. For this reason I think that certain plastic things like cereal premiums, toys, figurines, banks, Halloween and Christmas novelties, dolls, and models will become valuable when people become aware of how rare they are. The trick is to buy the plastic items that are appealing in design, color, action, and purpose. A perfect example of such a plastic item is the "snow baby." Snow babies are those little plastic globes filled with water and some sort of scene. When the globe is shaken it appears to be snowing inside.

RADIOS. Except for the early "cathedral" and "breadboard" type radios from the 20's and 30's, which in some cases are worth over $500, many pre-1940 radios are available for prices within the low value range. I think that in 20 years any of the old tube sets, which have now been entirely supplanted by transistorized models, will be worth money. If you decide to buy old radios, don't worry if many seem to be broken. Often all they need is a tube.

SPACE COLLECTIBLES. In the 60's it was the race to put man on the moon; in the 70's *Voyager* took incredible photos of Mars; and now in the 80's the space shuttles have become big news. Space-related items, particularly those from the 50's and 60's, can still be obtained for very little. Now is the time to pick these up before a trend for collecting "spaceiana" develops. Space items include toys, pamphlets, books, stamps, postcards, novelty items, amateur photographs (of moon shots), and autographs of astronauts and space scientists.

T-SHIRTS. During the 60's the "advertising T-shirt" boom began, and by the 70's everyone was wearing illustrated T-shirts, which indicated their favorite rock band, liquor, cigarettes, state, political candidate, drug, activity, college, sport, cartoon character, movie, or food. How many of these T-shirts have been saved? I had dozens of them, all of which are now lost, having suffered the ignominy of becoming cleaning rags once they developed a rip or a hole. I feel that silk-screened, hand-lettered, heat-transferred, and lithographed T-shirts will become the clothing collectibles of tomorrow.

VIDEO COLLECTIBLES. The video fever is upon us, and few people have had, or are having, the perspicacity to save items such as posters, novelties, toys, games, and stickers that depict video-related characters and motifs. Most of these items are available for only a few dollars, and it seems likely that within 20 years they will be very desirable.

There are two last pieces of advice for those seeking to determine which items are likely to become valuable in the future: (1) find out what children are playing with or talking about today and then buy these items because in all likelihood they will be desirable in 25 years when the kids have become adults and want to buy back a piece of their childhood; (2) look for items that relate to national scandals (Watergate), assassination attempts, national movements (feminism, ban the bomb), and national events (the first artificial heart, the first test-tube baby).

HOLIDAY COLLECTIBLES

OVER THE YEARS thousands of different items have been produced for use by celebrants of the following holidays:

April Fool's Day	Groundhog Day
Christmas	Halloween
Columbus Day	Hanukkah
Easter	Independence Day
Election Day	Labor Day
Father's Day	Leap Year
Flag Day	Memorial Day

Mother's Day	Thanksgiving
New Year's Day	Valentine's Day
Presidents' birthdays	Veteran's Day
St. Patrick's Day	

Today many collectors are beginning to save the things discarded by the rest of us once a holiday has ended. For example, New Year's Day collectors are saving noisemakers, novelties, signs, advertising, paper party hats, and anything else they can find that relates to New Year celebrations; Halloween collectors have begun looking for old costumes, masks, jack-o'-lanterns, and UNICEF boxes; Valentine's Day collectors are saving cards, candy boxes, buttons, and heart-shaped objects; Thanksgiving collectors are out hunting down plastic turkeys, paper Indians, models of the *Mayflower*, and Thanksgiving advertising; and St. Patrick's Day collectors are saving anything painted with shamrocks or four-leaf clovers, as well as leprechaun items, cards, novelties, and plastic horseshoes.

There are no limitations as to what one can collect if it relates in some way to a particular holiday. The more visually appealing the piece, the better. Holiday collectors also like items that have dates or other identifying marks on them. This enhances the item from an historical standpoint.

In addition to building their collections, many people like to read up on the history behind the holiday they are collecting. For some of the holidays there are few collectibles available, and one must use one's imagination and creativity to think of things to save. For instance, I know one Fourth of July collector who has spent most of his free time in the last six years tracking down firecracker labels. Similarly, I know an April Fool collector who saves practical jokes (he loves to demonstrate his "squirting rose," hand buzzer, and electric shock cards).

Most holiday-related items are affordable and can be obtained for prices within the low value range. The exceptions are items that cross over from more developed hobbies. For example, some holiday postcards sell for over $20, Christmas ornaments and Father Christmas figurines can go into the hundreds, and glass Halloween candy containers have sold for over $200. Locating inexpensive items requires time, patience, and a little luck. Collectors who have been at holiday collecting for a number of years advise beginners to advertise in the classified sections of the collectibles publications, attend as many garage, estate, and tag sales as possible, and to hand out cards that indicate collecting interests.

HUMMELS

Value range: low–medium. Most in the higher end of the low value range.

Most popular items: early "full bee" pieces that are not currently produced.

Good sources: wholesale mail dealers for the new product. Antique and collectible dealers for the older varieties.

BECAUSE HUMMEL CERAMIC figurines are currently produced in Rodental, West Germany, they would not seem at first to qualify as an American collectible. However, their great popularity in the United States, combined with the fact that the first Hummels were produced long before the collectibles explosion, justifies their presence in this book.

HISTORY. Sister Maria Innocentia of the Siesen Convent in the German Alps was the creator of the artwork that was used to produce the original Hummel figurines. She was born in 1909 to parents who encouraged her artistic talents. After graduating from an art academy in Munich, she joined the convent in 1933. It was there that she drew the pictures that were later to become the famous figurines. Her vision was of innocent children engaged in play, study, or work. Her world was free of the corruption, deceit, and wickedness that often mark adult life. Initially she used the pictures to make beautiful hand-painted postcards, which were sold to raise money for the sisterhood. These attracted the attention of the Goebel Art Company, and in 1935 an agreement was reached whereby the convent would receive royalties on the sale of figurines made using the designs of Sister Maria.

These early creations were very popular in Germany because of their high quality. Each figure was (and is) put through a rigid manufacturing process with much of the production hand done. Hummels are made of clay that is fired, hand painted and glazed, and fired again. Hummels were produced until the late 30's. At this time the energies of the German people were being channeled into the war effort, and production ceased, not to begin again until after 1946. At that time soldiers of the American occupation force began buying the attractive little figures as gifts for their wives and girlfriends. They brought back thousands of them and are responsible for the initial popularization of Hummels in this country. The Goebel Company has produced figurines and related goods ever since. Many of the modern statues are cast from the same master molds as the originals.

COLLECTING. The best place to begin is at the local gift or specialty shop that carries the Goebel line. There one can examine the new product and decide which items are appealing. Some favor the very religious themes, others like the characters related to music. Try to obtain a catalog of what is presently being offered. The best place to buy the new issues is from one of the wholesale mail order houses that advertise in the national collectibles publications. Buying from them can save you up to 30 percent off the list prices. In addition to authentic Hummel figurines (which always have the M.I. Hummel signature incised somewhere in the base of the sculpture), the Goebel Co. produces limited editions and non-Hummel figurines (statues made from artwork of other artists). Like many other companies, Goebel jumped on the instant collectibles bandwagon in the early 70's, producing plates, plaques, and bells. These and the non-Hummel figurines should not be bought for investment since collectors favor original Hummel pieces that are produced for decoration and not collector speculation.

Collectible Hummels are priced according to their age, which can be determined by becoming familiar with the various "bee" trademarks stamped on the underside of the base. An original piece from the 40's with a "full bee" trademark is worth several times what its contemporary counterpart is. To receive information about the many nuances of trademark identification, write to one of the Goebel or Hummel clubs listed at the end of this chapter.

The second most important value factor is condition. A repaired piece is worth far less than an undamaged one. This benefits those collectors who do not mind owning a figurine that has a crack or chip. Expect to buy damaged pieces at up to 80 percent off the perfect-condition price. If you have a figure with a missing part, you may be able to obtain it from one of the clubs' "repair banks." Fortunately, no really convincing fakes have been made of Hummel pieces. Japanese attempts can be distinguised by the absence of the M.I. Hummel signature.

BOOKS

Luckey, Carl F. *Hummel Figurines and Plates*.
  Florence, AL: Books Americana, 1982.

Miller, Robert L. and Eric Ehrmann. *Hummel, the Complete Collector's Guide and Illustrated Reference*.
  Huntington, NY: Portfolio Press, 1979.

CLUBS

Hummel Collector's Club, Inc.
Box 257
Yardley, PA 19067

  1 yr./$20, includes a quarterly newsletter pertaining to M.I. Hummel figurines, plates, and bells. The club offers opportunities for members to buy Hummel items at a discount.

Goebel Collectors Club
105 White Plains Road
Tarrytown, NY 10591

1 yr./$17.50, includes the quarterly publication *Insights*, featuring profiles on Goebel artists, articles on collecting, and general information. A bisque plaque, calendar, and membership card are also included.

JUKEBOXES

Value range: high–very high. Most popular Wurlitzer models sell for $3,000 plus in restored condition.

Most popular items: Wurlitzer models designed by Paul Fuller and manufactured between 1936 and 1948. These feature colored lights and sculpted plastics in art deco designs.

Good sources: from dealers who sell restored models.

IN THE LAST TEN YEARS jukebox collecting has grown tremendously. The Wurlitzer model 1015 that could not be sold for $300 in 1971 regularly brings $6,000 in restored condition today. All over the country Americans are becoming re-enchanted with the colorful "light-up" jukeboxes of their youth. The pleasure of watching the dramatic light show and listening to Crosby, Sinatra, or Jerry Lee Lewis, out of an old Wurlitzer is somewhat lost if the same records are played on a modern hi-fi.

HISTORY. The first jukebox (of sorts) was created in 1889 when an Edison Speaking Phono was rigged with a coin slot. For a penny a customer, after cranking the machine, could start the phonograph's "wax cylinder" turning and listen through a "speaking tube" held to his ear. In the next 15 years many variations of primitive jukeboxes were produced. All played only one selection though and required the listener to listen through a tube or earphone. It was not until 1906 that the John Gabel Company manufactured the Gabel Automatic Entertainer, which could play more than one selection and be heard by a group of people. This model played ten-inch discs (instead of cylinders) and employed a large metal horn to amplify the signal picked up by the stylus. In 1926 the Automatic Music Company (AMI) brought out the first electronically amplified phonograph. For a nickel AMI's machine could be turned up loud enough to be heard in a crowded room. The jukebox had arrived.

The mid-30's marked the beginning of what was to become the classic period of jukebox production. At this time a young designer named Paul Fuller joined the Wurlitzer Company, which was trying to break into the jukebox market in a big way. His innovative designs, which melded art deco lines with the current mechanical technology resulted in the production of light-up machines that were not only functional but fun to watch. Between 1935 and 1948 Fuller designed "boxes" that set the standard for the industry and put Wurlitzer at the top of their game.

One of the company's famous advertising campaigns used the phrase, "Wurlitzer is jukebox." Although Wurlitzer, because of their beautiful machines, dominated the market, other companies produced boxes and contributed to the technological advancement of the jukebox. Some of these companies were Rock-Ola, Seeburg, AMI, and Mills.

The classic design period of light-up jukeboxes ended in the late 40's, to be replaced by machines that were larger and could play more tunes. Boxes stayed extremely popular in diners, drugstores, and restaurants through the 50's and late 60's. In 1973 the Wurlitzer Company, plagued by years of poor sales and faced with a dismal future, closed its doors. Today only a few companies still produce large jukeboxes.

COLLECTING. Jukeboxes are collected because of their visual appeal. Light-up Wurlitzers from the 30's and 40's, with their "bubble tops," fluorescent-colored plastics, brilliant chrome, and smooth woods are among the most beautiful mass-produced items ever made. They were and are far more than merely functional. In a dimly lit or darkened room they drew patrons with their hypnotic light shows created by rotating circles of colored acetate and illuminated "bubble tubes" with slowly moving droplets of oil. Today, collectors want the old Wurlitzer models designed by Paul Fuller between 1935 and 1948. Wurlitzer models like the 750, 850 (known as the Peacock because of two peacocks on the front lit up by two rotating discs), 1100, and, of course, the most popular jukebox of all, the 1015 are considered by collectors the most beautiful light-ups ever produced. Other companies tried to imitate them, but none ever came out with as appealing machines. During the last 10 years, the prices for these desirable jukeboxes has steadily increased. Stores have opened in New York and Los Angeles that exclusively deal in restored jukeboxes. There is a mail order company that sells only replacement parts, and everywhere distributors and repairers of automatic mechanical devices have begun to buy, sell, and fix old classic boxes.

Collecting desirable jukeboxes is an expensive hobby. Most collectors own a few models, and some only own one, which they make the centerpiece of their living room or den. There are two ways to buy a box. You can go to a dealer and purchase one that has already been restored; or you can try to find one decaying in the basement of an old bar, drugstore, or candy shop, purchase it, and then have it restored.

This second approach has drawbacks. Restoration on an old Wurlitzer can run as high as $3,000, and often the people who do restoration do not pick up or deliver. Unless you happen to be an expert at working with antique electrical parts and refinishing and restoring wood, chrome, and plastic, it is wise to either pass up broken or damaged machines or to pay very little for them.

While Wurlitzer boxes are the most sought after, other companies produced models that, because of a design implementing sculpted plastics and colored lights, are also desirable. Rock-Ola for instance, made the Spectravox and the Commando; Seeburg made the 9800 and S-148, and *AMI* produced the Singing Towers and the Model A. Always appraise a box based on its visual appeal. Beginning collectors who are not sure about spending thousands of dollars on a prime Wurlitzer or other box can start by purchasing one of the simpler models made by one of the companies other than Wurlitzer. A small machine from the 50's can be obtained for under $1,000 in fully restored condition.

BOOKS

The Official Victory Glass Price Guide to Antique Jukeboxes.
   Order from: Box 119, Des Moines, IA 50301

A Pictorial Guide of Collectible Jukeboxes.
   Order from: Jukebox Junction, Box 1081, Des Moines, IA 50311

PERIODICALS

The Coin Slot
Box 612
Wheatridge, CO 80034

   1 yr./12 issues/$25; sample, $3. A magazine with articles, ads, and features on all coin-operated machines. (Slot machines are emphasized over others, however.)

Coin Machine Trader
Box 602
Huron, SD 57350

   1 yr./12 issues/$18; sample, $3. Calls itself a newsletter and is printed like one but features articles, buy/sell ads, and information on all kinds of coin-operated machines. Jukeboxes are included.

NEWSLETTERS

Jukebox Collector
2545 Southeast 16th Court
Des Moines, IA 50317

   Send for information.

Nickel a Tune
9514–9 Reseda Boulevard #613
North Ridge, CA 91324

   1 yr. 12/issues/$25; sample, $3.

DEALERS

Jukebox Junction
Box 1081
Des Moines, IA 50311

The world's largest mail order seller of replacement jukebox parts. Send for their catalog illustrating parts for sale, as well as literature and related items.

KITCHEN COLLECTIBLES

Value Range: low–high. The majority of pieces available sell for under $25.

Most popular items: *antique* (in this case those items made before 1900): cookbooks, corkscrews, molds, and utensils. *Modern era* (1900–present): early electrical appliances and anything that is better made than its contemporary counterpart.

Good sources: estate, garage, and rummage sales, flea markets and antique shows.

TODAY A GROWING NUMBER of collectors are pursuing the virtually thousands of items produced during the last 200 years for use in the kitchen. The list of desirable items includes cookbooks, catalogs, stoves, pot scrapers, toasters, egg beaters, mixing machines, teapots, coffee grinders, fruit dryers, ice boxes, matchbox holders, dinner pails, corkscrews, bottle openers, minute glasses, scales, and cherry pitters, as well as hundreds of varieties of utensils for molding, chopping, slicing, grinding, peeling, dispensing, canning, freezing, drying, cleaning, decorating, containing, preparing, and cooking food. With the exception of certain items that cross into the domain of more established collectible groups, like books and advertising, most kitchen collectibles are still affordable for the collector on a budget. Prices seldom go above $50, and a majority of the desirable items are available for under $25.

The most popular categories of collecting are *era*, *purpose*, and *personal appeal*. The era category is divided into pre-1900 and post-

1900. Generally, the most available items date from the second era. The purpose category breaks down into the 14 groups mentioned above. These groups provide a way of intelligently organizing one's collecting pursuit. Below is a list of the most popularly collected kitchen items. Each one of them falls into one of the 14 purpose groups.

apple: corers, parers, roasters
baskets
basting tools
batter pitchers
bean pots
biscuit cutters
bottle openers
bread: boards, boxes, knives, molds, pans
butcher knives
butter: boxes, molds, stamps
can openers
candy molds
cake: knives, mixers, pans
carving sets
cheese: bins, molds
cherry: pitters, stoners
chocolate molds
chopping: bowls, knives
churns
cleavers
coal tongs
coffee: bins, grinders, makers
colanders
cookie: cutters, jars
corers
corkscrews
corn bread: molds, pans
corn poppers
cream whippers

cutlery boxes
dish: cleaners, drainers, scrapers
dishes
dough: kneaders, mixers
doughnut cutters
dredgers
dryers
electrical appliances
egg: baskets, beaters, cookers
egg: separators, scales, slicers
fire kindlers
flour sifters
fritter bakers
frosting tubes
fruit jars
frying pans
funnels
grape presses
graters
gravy strainers
hooks (meat)
hot plates
ice: boxes, hooks, makers, picks
ice cream: makers, molds, scoops
jar openers
Jell-o molds
jelly molds

juicers
kettles
knife sharpeners
knives
lemon: reamers, squeezers
matchboxes
measuring devices
meat: choppers, cleavers,
    cutters
meat: grinders, juicers,
    mashers
milk: pails, jugs
mixing: machines, spoons
molds
morter and pestle
nut crackers
nutmeg graters
pancake makers
pans
pastry: brushes, molds
pea shellers
peelers
percolators
pie: crimpers, stands
pitchers
potato: mashers, peelers
pot scrapers
pots

preserve kettles
pressure cookers
pudding molds
racks
raisin seeders
roasting: pans, racks
rolling pins
salt: boxes, crocks
sausage: grinders, stuffers
sieves
skimmers
spice: boxes, cabinets, mills
stoves
strainers
strawberry hullers
sugar containers
tea: caddies, holders, pots
thermometers
tins
toasters
toy kitchenware
trivets
turners (meat, pancake)
utensil packs
vegetable: choppers, graters
vegetable: peelers, slicers
waffle irons

Collecting by purpose provides order. If you choose to collect items that contain food, you would pursue things like tins, baskets, boxes, etc. Similarly, if you decide to collect items used for molding, you will try to obtain butter, chocolate, and gelatin molds, and bundt pans.

Deciding to collect kitchen items by purpose category also means choosing, where applicable, an era to concentrate on. Some of the more interesting collections contain examples of a particular utensil, say an eggbeater, from the beginning of its invention to the present.

The third category, personal appeal, is the most popular because it allows a collector to indulge his fancy whenever he encounters a piece that strikes a respondent chord in him. Many gourmets, for instance, like to assemble an eclectic ramble of antique kitchen tools and then decorate their kitchens with them. The criterion they use in selecting pieces is simply personal taste.

With the exception of certain quasi kitchen collectibles like antique advertising, books, and trade catalogs, collectors do not require mint condition for the items they save. In fact, the only real demand collectors make is that the item still be serviceable. This requirement is especially important for the collector who uses his collection to prepare, cook, or serve food. A leaking cake tin or a recalcitrant apple parer simply will not do. When buying, always check to see if the piece works. Stains, dents, and scratches are acceptable and, unless they detract from its aesthetic appeal, usually add to the history of the piece. Rust, holes, and missing parts are another story, however, and pieces with these defects should be avoided.

The best place to buy is at flea markets, and estate and garage sales. Prices are still very low for most items, but the public is beginning to catch on, and already the individuals who conduct professional estate sales are charging $5 for the teakettle they used to sell for 75¢. One thing they do not know about, though, is the electrical appliance. Often, very early (1900–1930) toasters, mixers, juicers, and coffee makers are sold for only a few dollars. These are fantastic bargains when one considers how truly rare these early examples of the electric era are.

BOOKS

Franklin, Linda Campbell. *300 Years of Kitchen Collectibles*.
    Florence, AL: Books Americana, 1981.

Lantz, Louise K. *Dictionary and Price Guide to Kitchen Collectibles*.
    Order from: Pegasus Ltd., 1981 Moreland Parkway, Bldg. 4A, Annapolis, MD 21401

CLUB

American Graniteware Association
Box 605
Downers Grove, IL 60515

Write for information.

RELATED COLLECTIBLES

APPLIANCES

Fredgant, Don. *Electrical Collectibles: Relics of the*
Electrical Age. Published by and available from Padre Productions,
Box 1275, San Luis Obispo, CA 93406.

This book covers the era of early kitchen appliances.

SPOONS

American Spoon Collectors
Box 260
Warrensburg, MO 64093

They publish a monthly newsletter called *Spooners Forum*, which includes information on and buy/sell/trade ads for spoons.

MAGICANA

Value range: low—very high. The majority of magic items can be obtained for prices between $10 and $250. Only the very elaborate or special items like posters drawn by Alphonse Mucha or Toulouse-Lautrec bring prices into the thousands.

Most popular items: anything related to Houdini or any of the late 19th century/early 20th century vaudeville stage magicians.

Good sources: *modern magic and books*: from one of the dealers
(listed at the end of the chapter) who issue catalogs; *antique
magic memorabilia*: at auction and antique shows.

BEFORE THE COLLECTIBLES boom of the 70's prompted
everyone to begin looking for new "things" to make into collectibles, most of the people who collected magicana were magicians.
Today, however, the popularity of the new breed of magic performers has combined with the appeal of colorful magic items to
create the hobby of magicana. Many fledgling magicians and non-
magicians are getting into the act so quickly that the most popular
items seem to be disappearing into thin air.

While many students of magic feel that its long history (which
goes back centuries before 1900) was more glorious and real than
today's brand of stage illusionism in a predominantly rational (and
disbelieving) atmosphere, the fact is that collectors most want artifacts from the late 19th and early 20th century.

Some of the most popular magic items are tricks, mementos,
and letters once owned by the famous vaudeville magicians. Houdini tops this list, and even a small signed photo of his brings a
couple of hundred dollars. Other magicians from this era are
Keller, Thurston, Carter, Raymond, and Blackstone. Many stories
circulate about these men, stories that describe events that (if they
occurred) bordered on the supernatural.

Houdini, for instance, had been preoccupied during his lifetime with making contact with the spirit world. He is said to have
told his closest friends that upon his death he would make every
possible effort to contact them. He died on October 31, 1926, and
on every Halloween since, magicians, spiritualists, and mediums
have tried to contact him. Anything once owned by one of the
famous magicians is believed to still hold psychic residues of that
magician. For this reason, these items are especially desirable.

Another popular category of magicana is posters. Colorful and
large, these depicted illustrations of magicians preparing to perform dangerous tricks and listed the amazing and wondrous feats
an audience could hope to see live before their eyes. Posters were
distributed throughout a town or city by advance men several days

before the magician arrived. Today they are considered master-pieces of advertising art with their brilliant colors (the result of chromo-lithography), weird pictures, and chilling promises. Some are very large (4' x 8') and if done by a great artist/illustrator like Mucha or Toulouse-Lautrec can bring over $15,000 at auction. Smaller posters and ones not done by the big names can be obtained for as little as $300.

A less expensive (and possibly more rewarding) area of magicana collecting is the magic trick. While there are some elaborate and extremely well-made tricks from the turn of the century and later that cost thousands, the average modern trick can be bought for between $15 and $100. In Manhattan, two of the largest magic shops in the world sell thousands of tricks to neophytes as well as to experienced magicians. According to these store owners, many of the popular current stage magicians like David Copperfield, Doug Henning, and Mark Wilson began as children playing with the tricks in the showroom and spending time with older magicians. The nice thing about collecting tricks is that you can do more than just look at them.

BOOK

Milbourne, Christopher. *The Illustrated History of Magic*.
New York: Thomas Y. Crowell and Co., 1973.

CLUBS

International Brotherhood of Magicians
Kenton, OH

Write for information. Members receive a magazine called *Linking Rings*, but to become a member you must pass a magic test.

Society of American Magic
3616 Henry Hudson Parkway
Bronx, NY

Write for information

DEALERS

Abbots Magic Manufacturing Company
Colon, MI 49040

Write requesting catalog of books and tricks.

Hornmann Magic Store
304 West 34th Street
New York, NY 10001

Sells tricks, books on magic, and memorabilia; issues a catalog. Drop into the showroom if you are in New York, otherwise send $5 for catalog.

Louis Tannen Magic Store
1540 Broadway
New York, NY 10036

Sells tricks, books, and memorabilia; runs a summer magic camp and hosts a magic jubilee every October at Brown's Hotel in the Catskills. Send $7 plus postage for an 800-page, profusely illustrated, hardbound catalog, or drop in when visiting the city.

MAPS

Value range: low–very high. Desirable maps in collectible condition can be obtained for $250–$500. Rarer or very popular folio-size examples will cost between $600 and $6,000.

Most popular items: folio-size maps of the New World (North America) executed by "name" cartographers working between the 16th and 19th centuries.

Good sources: from reputable map dealers who guarantee the age and attribution of their maps; private connections.

MAPS HAVE BEEN COLLECTED for hundreds of years, but during the last 10 years the collectibles boom has made many people realize just how beautiful and historically important many maps are, and consequently there has been a dramatic increase in price. Certain maps that sold for $300 in 1968 are now worth over $5,000.

HISTORY. From the earliest times man has made maps. Babylonian city plans have survived that date back to around 2100 B.C. Maps have always been necessary for being able to work with the land, the sea, or people. The history of the maps that are the most collectible today begins in the 16th century.

In the 1500's maps were drawn, engraved, printed, and then colored by a master craftsman. He sold his product through a store, which was also his workshop. Many early mapmakers were subsidized and encouraged by book dealers and publishers, who saw great potential in printed maps. As the trade grew, apprentices were taken on and production increased. Surplus maps were sold to wholesalers, who dealt at the great book fairs in Europe. Eventually the business of mapmaking divided into three divisions: engraving, printing, and coloring. This division of labor encouraged uniformity and organization. A publisher would place an order for a map with a cartographer (draftsman) whose job it was to draw the map. When he was done, the engraver (sometimes the cartographer) engraved the map on a plate and then turned it over to the printer. The printer made impressions of the map, which were then given to a colorist for final work. The publisher then sold the maps.

Before 1820 printed maps were made through two processes: the woodcut and the copperplate. The woodcut process was used mostly during the early days of mapmaking, because although it was inexpensive it did not produce as high a quality impression as the copperplate process. Copperplate printing predominated from the mid-16th century on.

In 1510 the first books of maps were already being published and sold by book dealers. These early collections were of uneven quality. The publication of *Theatrum* in 1570 by the Flemish cartographer Abraham Ortelius marks the first appearance of a map-book with consistent standards. *Theatrum*, along with *prospect*, *speculum*, and *tabularum*, means collection of maps.

The first man to use the term *atlas* to describe a collection of maps was the famous Flemish cartographer Gerard Mercator, who lived between 1512 and 1594. He began as an apprentice, and by the time he was 25 was already drawing his own maps. His most famous work is his atlas, the first part of which was published in 1585 and consisted of 51 maps of France, Belgium, and Germany. In 1590 part two was published and was made up of 23 maps of Italy and Greece. The third part was published a year after Mercator's death and consisted of 36 maps. The same year the three parts were also issued together as a comprehensive work. Over the next 40 years more than 50 editions of the atlas were published.

Between the 16th and 19th centuries many countries had cartographers turning out beautiful representations of the known world. The countries that most dominated map production were Italy, Belgium/Holland, France, and England. Austrian, German, and Swiss cartographers also produced maps.

COLLECTING. The five factors that determine the desirability of a map are its *maker, date, area depicted, size,* and *execution.*

The maker, or cartographer, is very important. A map done by Mercator, for instance, even if it were lacking in appeal would still be valuable as an example of the Flemish master's work. The book *Maps and Map-Makers* by R. V. Tooley lists the names and a brief biography of all the important cartographers. A beginning map collector should become familiar with this text.

The age of a map becomes more important if its maker is not known. The most collectible maps are those made before the 19th century, although in the case of maps that depict North America, many 19th century examples are also desirable. Each century had a particular style regarding map design. While dating is not easy (since most makers purposefully did not date their work so that it might seem current even if it were years old), some dating clues can be garnered by observing the style of the map. Sixteenth century maps, for instance, were often not colored, and their makers favored the use of architectural designs in decorating them. Seventeenth century maps were far more elaborately decorated with colorful figures, flowers, and family crests. Eighteenth century maps were less elaborate and often only the titlepiece was ornamented. The 19th century saw maps that varied from extremely romantic, with depictions of natural settings and castles, to simply utilitarian, with no ornamentation at all.

When purchasing an antique map from a dealer, you should always ask for an attribution and dating, which should be included on the bill of sale. This information will be important if you intend to resell the map at some point.

Presently, the most popular maps with American collectors are those that depict the North American continent (or parts of it) while it was still under exploration. Many of these depictions of the New World are charming with respect to the naiveté of the cartographer. Nineteenth century maps of the Western territory, New England, and Texas are also very popular. Besides America, collectors actively pursue maps of the world, the Holy Land, and Africa.

The size of a map is extremely important in determining its desirability and value. The most expensive maps are folio size, which usually means they are 24" x 24" or larger. The term *folio* refers to the largest-size books produced during the past 400 years. A folio-size book was made from sheets of paper that were folded only once. An *octavo* refers to a book made up of printer's sheets folded into eight leaves. Folio-size maps are the most popular because they are the largest and therefore usually the most impressive. On the back of most folio- and quarto-size maps, you can see traces of the hinge that was affixed down their center to hold them into atlases or other collections.

Many collectors have been drawn to maps because of their visual appeal. For this reason, execution is one of the most important qualities to look for. A gorgeous Mercator will bring several times the price of an average one. An unattributed world map will still sell for quite a bit if it has artistic merit. When buying, judge a map like a piece of art. Is it balanced? Does the color scheme work? Is there too much or too little ornamentation? Remember, you will probably have to look at any map you purchase for many years. If you have trouble discerning desirable maps from undesirable ones, seek the aid of a knowledgeable dealer.

Condition is particularly important with antique maps. One does not usually have to worry about brittleness as all pre-20th century maps were printed on rag, but there are other factors like foxing (little brown patches caused by mold or contact with other corrosive materials) and trimming that can detract from a map's appeal and value. Many maps were "lain down" (dry- or wet-mounted to cardboard) during the 20th century, before collectors learned that the acids in the cardboard would eventually migrate to the map and brown it. While a lain-down map looks neat and flat when displayed, it is seldom worth the price of a similar un-mounted example.

Beginning buyers should frequent reputable dealers and auctions. They can usually be found by checking under the rare book dealer section of the Yellow Pages. Most maps originally came out of atlases and hence fall under the domain of booksellers.

BOOK

Tooley, R.V. *Maps and Map-Makers.*
New York: Crown Publishers, 1982.

CLUB

The Chicago Map Society
60 W. Walton Street
Chicago, IL 60610

1 yr./$10, includes a copy of the *World Directory of Dealers in Antiquarian Maps* and a subscription to the quarterly newsletter *Mapline*.

MATCHCOVERS

Value range: low–medium. The majority of covers that change hands in the hobby are traded. A relatively small number of covers sell for more than $5.

Most popular items: covers from the early period (1920–1940), covers that are especially attractive, and covers from interesting or esoteric businesses.

Good sources: By joining one or more of the clubs (listed at the end of the chapter), one can trade via the mail with collectors from all over the country. This is the best way to build a collection.

ACCORDING TO PHILLUMENISTS (matchcover collectors) theirs is the second largest hobby in the world (behind stamps). This claim is surely true if all of us who have accumulations of matchbooks taken from stores, restaurants, and bars over the years are counted. To be a real phillumenist, however, requires that one take his assorted books and "shuck" them, "press" them, and then categorize them according to *subject, era, size,* and *maker*. Clearly, there are many of us who are not matchcover collectors even if we do have bowls, trays, and even drawers full of matchbooks.

HISTORY. The first matchbooks began to appear in this country in the 1880's and were sold along with cigarettes and tobacco. By the 1920's the cost of producing matches had greatly decreased. This fact, along with the proven efficacy of advertising, led to the national distribution of matchbooks with covers promoting popular consumer products. Free matches were an instant success, and many companies began allocating funds to put their products on the cover of matchbooks. Between 1920 and 1945 thousands of different kinds of books were produced. These varied in size, number of "strikes," design, and quality. Novelty matchbooks, which held complimentary razor blades, candy, and charms, were popular for several years. More than 100 match producers competed with one another for the business of the advertisers.

The largest companies were Diamond, Lion, and Ohio Match. During the war many of the companies went out of business or merged with one another. Today, fewer than 20 companies produce all the matches used in the United States. Book sizes and appearance have become uniform as a result of several safety laws enacted over the last 20 years. Although there has been a decline in the number of smoking Americans, the matchbook as an advertising medium for restaurants, bars, and stores has never been more popular.

COLLECTING. Phillumenists, as you have already seen, have a jargon that includes specific words to identify things most of us have never thought to name. To "shuck" a matchbook means to remove the matches after carefully prying open the binding staple. Phillumenists don't collect matchbooks, they collect matchcovers.

After removing the matches, one "presses" the matchcover under books to flatten it out. A "regular" describes a book of matches that holds 20 "stems" or "sticks." If it is on the front of the book, the strip of flint is known as the "striker." If it is on the back of the book (as has been required by law since 1977), it is called a "reverse striker" or S.O.B. A "used book" describes a matchbook that has a "bitten," "struck," or "hit" striker (or reverse striker). The top ridge of the book between the front and back cover is called the "saddle." An "MM" refers to the maker mark, which usually appears somewhere on the book. A "bobtailed" book is one without a striker (or reverse striker). Lastly, a "caddy" describes a full box of matchbooks. These are just some of the expressions phillumenists have chosen to organize their hobby. Armed with this new vocabulary, let's look at how matchcovers are collected.

There are over 125 different categories of matchcovers. Following is a list of the most popular of these:

airlines	military
auto dealers	patriotics
banks	personalities
Christmas	politicals
clubs	railroads
colleges	restaurants
fairs	ship lines
foreign	sports
full lengths	transportation
hotels	

Most of these categories describe a particular kind of business or endeavor. Several describe phillumenistic terms. A "full length" is a matchcover with advertising or decoration that runs the full length of its back and front. A "patriotic" describes matchbooks issued during World War II that had patriotic mottos like "We Must Win," "Crush the Axis," and "Loose Lips Sink Ships." "Personality" covers are ones that feature pictures of famous actors and actresses, politicians, and sports figures.

Each of the categories can be divided according to the MM, number of strikes, date, size, and region. A beginning collector must make sure to tailor the category he is interested in to a manageable size. For instance, restaurants is much too large a category to pursue. A collector would have to choose to collect a particular type of restaurant. This choice, however, might have to be tailored, as in the case of Chinese restaurants. One might tailor down to include only Chinese restaurant covers from a particular state or of a certain size or a specific era. There are over 5,000 Chinese restaurants in the United States. Each year hundreds of new ones open and hundreds more close. Only a person with a Sisyphus complex would try to assemble a complete collection of Chinese restaurant matchcovers. Tailoring is very important.

Phillumenists obtain covers primarily by trading among themselves through the mail. To join the network of collectors, one must first join one or more of the many clubs located throughout the country. By joining, one's name, address, and collecting interests are added to the lists that circulate among members. Collectors contact one another by using the lists as a starting point. Acquiring examples for your collection begins with the acquisition of "trading stock." Collectors pick up their trading stock from stores, restaurants, shops, bars, gas stations, hotels, etc. The object is to amass as many different types of covers as possible so that you will have something to offer the collectors you want to trade with. You should begin by making the rounds in the area where you live. Whenever you encounter an exceptional matchcover, it is your duty to try to acquire a caddy so that other collectors will also benefit from the find. Obtaining a caddy is not always easy, and collectors recommend that the best approach is to explain to the owner or manager of the business that you are a collector and are willing to pay the cost of the box.

The main qualities to look for in a cover are *visual appeal, subject matter*, and *how well it is identified*. Like any other collectors, phillumenists go for the "look." "Girlies" (covers that depict attractive women in cheesecake poses) are very popular, as are covers that feature pictures of ocean liners, railroads, and aircraft.

Regarding subject matter, the esoteric is always desirable. If you live in a city that has a Vietnamese restaurant, try to get as many of the restaurant's matchbooks as you can because midwestern collectors will be happy to trade you five to one in your favor. Identification of matchcovers as to age, maker, and region is important. For this reason the more descriptive information a cover has, the better. Anonymous American covers are referred to as "nationals" and are generally not very popular among collectors.

While the collectibles boom affected the value of older matchcovers (some worth only $2 in 1970 are now worth over $50), beginning collectors can still choose to collect current issue examples where they will only have to pay for postage, stationery, and an occasional few dollars for caddies. If you decide later to go into older material (1920's–1940's), expect to pay as much as $50 for certain rarities. 1945 to 1960's covers, however, generally cost under $5.

Besides matchcovers, phillumenists have recently begun to save matchboxes. Five years ago, the boxes were considered pariahs in the hobby; today they are sought after and have even been given a name, "skillets." Since there are fewer boxes than covers, collectors do not have to be as strict about tailoring.

CLUBS

Following is a list of the three largest clubs in the United States. Each one issues several bulletins a year, which contain hundreds of names and addresses of other collectors. By writing to the Rathkamp Society, you can obtain a list of various smaller clubs located throughout the country. Write to each regarding current membership, dues, etc.

Garden State Matchcover Club
18 Hemlock Street
Clifton, NJ 07013

Golden Orange Matchcover Club
1457 Westmont Drive
Anaheim, CA 92801

Rathkamp Matchcover Society
13321 Kenwood
Oak Park, MI 48237

MECHANICAL BANKS

Value range: medium–very high. Few desirable banks in collectible condition sell for under $500. Many sell for thousands, and several have sold for over $25,000.

Most popular items: In this hobby, popularity varies according to a particular collector's income bracket. Collectors of means often pursue very scarce and expensive banks. Average collectors go after more common and affordable varieties. All collectors, however, try to buy banks that have retained a majority of their original paint.

Good sources: from reputable dealers at toy and antique shows who will warrant the authenticity of the banks they are selling.

MANY AMERICANS HAVE vivid memories of the fascinating mechanical banks that helped them save their pennies as children. Few who had banks have forgotten the excitement of watching their coins disappear when the clever action of the bank was triggered. Between 1870 and 1930 tens of thousands of colorfully painted banks were produced and sold. More than 250 different banks are known today, most of which were sold originally between 75¢ and $1.25 retail. Today some of these same banks sell for over $25,000.

HISTORY. Mechanical banks are a testimony to Yankee ingenuity and the American craftsman's mastery of iron casting. The first banks were made during the years following the Civil War, when skilled iron casters were available (having recently lost their jobs as war needs ended), labor was cheap, and iron ore plentiful. The original inventor remains anonymous, but it is known that John Hall is the man who designed the first patented mechanical bank. It is appropriately named Hall's Excelsior, and was produced by the Stevens Company of Cromwell, Connecticut. This bank was produced and sold early in 1870 and was an instant success with the thrift-minded inhabitants of the Northeast who lived by the Protestant ethic. The bank is in the shape of a house, and when the doorbell is pulled, the roof of what looks like a chimney lifts up, revealing a small wooden monkey (in some varieties a man) holding a platter onto which one is supposed to place a coin.

The Stevens Company was soon joined by others who saw potential in selling banks. No company ever formed specifically for the manufacture of mechanical banks. Rather, companies already producing iron toys or tools equipped themselves to produce the banks, which they then sold directly to the public or to middlemen such as novelty and toy companies.

The producers employed in-house designers or else bought the patterns for banks from outside inventors. After a patent was applied for, the banks were cast in pieces and then assembled and hand painted. What amazes collectors today is how inexpensive the banks were. Invoices and advertising cards have survived, which reveal that many banks were sold wholesale for only a quarter. Some banks sold for even less, and it was only the extremely complicated or fragile banks that cost more than 50¢ on the wholesale level.

Between 1870 and 1930 over 250 different banks were produced. Three of the most prolific designers were John Hall, Charles A. Bailey, and James H. Bowen. Each is known for a particular talent in bank design: Hall for his imagination, Bailey for his attention to minute detail and colorful scenery, and Bowen for his complicated designs.

Most banks can be placed into one of nine genres. These are *animal, circus, ethnic, historical, patriotic, political, religious, sports*, and *technological*. Following is the name and description of a bank that is representative of each genre.

Animal: The Elephant Bank. It came in many varieties, the most common of which is an elephant with a place at the end of his trunk for a coin, which is thrown over the animal's head and into an opening between the shoulders when the tail is pressed down.

Circus: The Circus Bank. When a lever is pressed, a clown driving a pony cart makes a quick revolution around a ring and knocks a coin into the box with his outstretched hand.

Ethnic: The Jolly Nigger Bank. Many varieties are known, the most common of which is the bust and upper torso of a Negro who lifts his hand to his mouth, feeding himself a coin and rolling his eyes, when a lever is pressed down.

Historical: The Ferris Wheel Bank. Meant to replicate the famous wheel at the Chicago World's Fair of 1893, this is one of the largest mechanical banks, standing 22 inches. A mechanism is wound up, which produces the force necessary to make the wheel rotate when a coin is inserted. There are six chairs on the wheel and in each sit two figures.

Patriotic: The Uncle Sam Bank. Uncle Sam stands on a platform with an umbrella in one hand and a satchel near the other hand. A coin is placed in the hand near the satchel and when a lever is pushed, the hand drops, causing the coin to fall into the bag, which opens.

Political: The Tammany Bank. The figure of a fat man meant to be the infamous politician Boss Tweed sits in a chair waiting for you to place a coin in his right hand, which when placed immediately drops into his coat pocket, triggering his head into nodding an acknowledgment.

Religious: The Jonah and the Whale Bank. Features Jonah in a boat about to be pushed into the whale's gaping maw by a Moses-like man. The whale has to settle for a coin, which is tossed from a plate held by Jonah when a lever is pushed. The whale's lower mouth shakes in gratitude.

Sports: The Calamity Bank. Three football players revolve into a quick huddle when a coin is inserted and a lever pressed.

Technological: The Camera Bank. When a coin is inserted, a picture pops out of the top of what looks like an old-fashioned box camera on a tripod.

In addition to the banks that fall easily into one of the genres, other banks were made into the shapes of buildings, furniture, and people. Bank designers had a vast reservoir of motifs to use from goods produced as a result of the rapidly expanding Industrial Revolution.

COLLECTING. The range of value for mechanical banks is enormous. A common bank that has lost most of its original paint over the years may command only $100, while an extremely rare bank in poor condition may bring $10,000. The two factors that determine value are *condition* and *rarity*.

Condition is always important, but in this hobby it is extreme rarity that propels certain banks, regardless of condition, into the tens of thousands of dollars. One collector has a standing offer out to buy a Woman in the Shoe bank for $55,000. Not one, in any condition, has been brought to him yet. Certain banks are extremely rare today because they did not sell well when they were first produced. A bank that did not catch on because it was considered ugly or unexciting would eventually be sent back to the factory to be melted down in the iron pots. Paradoxically, it is banks like this, many of which are indeed ugly, that bring the most money today because of great rarity.

There are some banks, for instance, of which there are no known examples, although it is known, through patent papers and company records, that they were produced. There are also some banks of which there is only one known example. To the list of banks that are expensive because of rarity, one can add banks that are highly valuable because few have survived in working or complete condition. Two such banks are The Girl Skipping Rope and The Bread Winner, both of which have complicated mechanisms and fragile appendages. Neither one is easy to locate in working order.

Condition plays a much greater role where banks that are considered "common" are involved. A common bank is often one that was so popular in its time that many were sold and have thus survived until today. Common banks are judged by their condition. The criterion for condition is paint. For a common bank to be desirable, it should still retain from between 50 to 85 percent of its original paint.

Original paint refers to that paint applied by hand at the factory. A subsequent paint job, no matter how artfully done, detracts significantly from the value of a bank. Every common bank has a paint "reputation," which collectors have established through years of comparing notes. Some banks, for instance, "come nice," referring to the way their paint survives the ravages of time, while others are "tough," which usually means that they are difficult to find with a majority of their original paint still intact. A bank that is known to come nice must therefore be in "good paint" (or better) if it is to command the usual price. Conversely, a bank known to be tough will sell for much more than usual if it appears in especially good paint. Beyond paint, all banks are expected to be complete regarding their parts. A common bank that is missing a part will be devalued substantially.

Reproductions are the bane of all beginning collectors. There are an enormous number of banks for sale at antique and collectible shows that are in fact partial or complete fakes. The most common fakes have been created by disreputable individuals who take Book of Knowledge castings (a company that legitimately reproduced banks) and file off the markings on the base that indicate the bank is a reproduction.

Some of the fakes are insidious because they are conditioned through various processes to look old. Advanced collectors are never fooled. Beginners often are. The best way for you to protect yourself is to handle a number of "good" banks. Fakes never have the same smooth feel and well-put-together look. In addition to physical observations, one is advised to use the book *Toy Bank, Reproductions and Fakes* (listed at the end of this chapter). It helps one to determine if a bank is authentic by comparing its base size to a tracing in the book. Reproductions usually have smaller bases.

Deciding what to collect in banks is dependent on one's financial situation. Many more banks sell for over $1,000 than for under this figure. Few banks in desirable condition are available for less than $500. Serious bank collectors are generally individuals of means who regularly travel great distances in the pursuit of desirable banks. Money is usually no object when an extremely rare bank comes along. At one recent sale of several rare banks, a Texan spent $85,000 for three banks. What to buy, therefore, is going to depend on how large or deep your purse is.

For the average collector, my recommendation is to go after those banks that can still be obtained in high grade for under $500. A collection of even three or four such banks can become an impressive display in a den or living room. Remember, many of the nicest banks are also the least expensive (because more were sold originally and therefore more have survived).

Reputable dealers at toy and antique shows are your best sources for mechanical banks. Besides being able to buy at the shows, you can see what the banks should look like and obtain useful information through talking with the dealers. Collectors are also a good source for buying banks, as they are usually not as profit hungry as the dealers. Auctions can sometimes be a good source, but be careful if you are a beginner to make sure that the auctioneer will guarantee the authenticity of the bank. Auctions are sometimes the places where mistakes are disposed of. In addition to banks, some collectors pursue trade cards that depict advertisements for them. These colorful cards are becoming very popular and nicely complement a bank collection (see chapter on trade cards).

BOOK

McCumber, Robert L. *Toy Bank, Reproductions and Fakes*.
　　Available from author: 201 Carriage Drive, Glastonbury, CT 06033.

COMPANIES THAT PRODUCED MECHANICAL BANKS

Barton J. Smith Company of Philadelphia
Berger and Medau Manufacturing
Enterprise Manufacturing Company of Philadelphia
Greg Iron Casting Company
Hubley Manufacturing Company
Ives Company
J. & E. Stevens of Cromwell, CT
Jerome Secor Manufacturing
Judd Manufacturing Company
Kilgore Manufacturing Company of Westerville, OH
Proctor-Raymond Company of Buffalo, NY
Richard Elliott Company of Chicago
Selchow & Righter of NY
Shepard Hardware Company of Buffalo, NY
Strauss Manufacturing Company of NY
Wrightsville Hardware Company of Mount Joy, PA

CLUBS

Mechanical Bank Collectors of America
Bill Norman
2601 Empire Avenue
Burbank, CA 91504

Write for information.

RELATED COLLECTIBLES

STILL BANKS

Also made of cast iron (in most cases), still banks are very popular. Some mechanical bank collectors also save them.

CLUB

Still Bank Collectors Club of America
Kenneth E. Dersey
1181 Dewey Street
Plymouth, MI 48170

Write for information and newsletter.

MILITARY COLLECTIBLES

Value range: Most popularly collected items fall in the low value range, with exceptionally rare or larger pieces bringing into the high range.

Most popular items: artifacts from the Nazi regime.

Good sources: dealers of militaria and private connections.

THE WORD *MILITARIA* REFERS to anything that is in any way related to the military or martial arts of a country. The following are the more popular items of militaria: ammunition, badges, banners, bayonets, coins, daggers, decorations, flags, helmets, headdresses, insignia, jeeps, medals, muskets, pistols, posters, rations, regimental steins, revolvers, rifles, stamps, swords, and uniforms.

Some collectors of militaria have developed their interest through serving in a war. Others developed an appreciation for the design and craftsmanship of the superbly made pieces. Still others collect out of an interest in the history of war. And there are those who use the hobby as a way of extending their fantasy world.

The best way to begin collecting militaria is by attending one of the shows devoted entirely to the hobby. The larger ones are generally advertised in the major antiques newspapers. One can find out about smaller local shows by calling the area gun club. Many people who collect militaria also own and shoot pistols. It is likely that someone at the local range will know when the next show is. Going to a show should be augmented with trips to the library and museums. Some items like samurai swords, Roman helmets, and old suits of armor are very rare, and the museum trip affords an opportunity to see the very best items.

Most collectors collect items by *war*, *era*, or *country*. At this time the most sought-after items are those produced in Imperial Germany and during Hitler's reign. Unfortunately, the hobby has received some bad press because of this. Certain rare incidents have stimulated the popular imagination to believe that those who collect German militaria also dress up in Nazi uniforms and are members of secret societies. This is hardly the case. The popularity of Nazi military items stems from their historical importance as artifacts from the most nefarious regime ever. Within most of us there is a fascination for the bizarre, the grotesque, the extreme. The impulse to collect Nazi memorabilia stems from the same perverse interest that prompts people to rubberneck at an accident.

The collector must be wary of reproductions of military artifacts being sold as genuine. Many items have been recast and produced in quantity. If you are not sure of an object's provenance or have any reason to suspect that it is not authentic, stay away from it. Of course, there are certain instances where one knows he is buying a genuine piece, even if it is not from a dealer. An example would be buying from a family friend who served in the war and brought back several battlefield souvenirs. Friends can be good sources for obtaining material since in every family there is usually someone who has served in the military.

The condition factor is a little different with militaria. A dent in a helmet could have been the result of shrapnel from a grenade. Thus, it can enhance the item instead of detracting from it. Many collectors like buying goods that have battle scars. Dealers know this, however, and often come up with the most creative stories. I was once offered a dagger that was said to have been owned by Göring. When I asked for proof, all the man could offer was a story about being the nephew of one of Göring's mistresses. Imagination is fine as long as you don't end up paying for someone's flight of fancy.

BOOKS

Hartline, David L. *Military Dealers Directory and Collectors Handbook.* Order from: Haas Publications, Box 775, Worthington, OH 43085.

Rankin, Robert. *Official Price Guide to Military Collectibles.* Orlando, FL: House of Collectibles, 1981.

PERIODICALS

Military Collector News
Box 7582
Tulsa, OK 74105
   Sample, 50¢.

Military Images
706 Mickley Road
Whitehall, PA 18052

   1 yr./$16. For collectors of antique American military photography. Also includes biographies of soldiers, articles on regimental history, and detailed analysis of uniforms and insignia.

CLUBS

American Military Society
Frank G. Frisella
1528 El Camino Real
San Carlos, CA 94070

> Publishes a quarterly magazine designed to connect military history to the collection of militaria.

Imperial German Military Collector's Association
Dr. Eric Johanson
Box 651
Shawnee Mission, KS 66201

> Publishes a quarterly journal designed to study the artifacts of Wilhelmine Germany pre-1918. Has a for-sale and trade section.

Japanese Sword Society of the U.S.
Ron Hartmann
5907 Deerwood Drive
St. Louis, MO 63123

> Publishes bimonthly newsletter and annual bulletin. Purpose is to study the art of Japanese swordmaking.

RELATED COLLECTIBLES

GUNS

Flayderman, Norm. *Flayderman's Guide to Antique American Firearms and Their Values*. Order from: DBI Books, One Northfield Plaza, Northfield, IL 60093.

Madaas, Michael. *American Longarms*.
New York: Warner Books, 1981.

Quertermous, Russel and Steve. *Modern Guns: I.D. and Value*.
Paducah, KY: Collector Books, 1981.

INSIGNIA

Police Insignia Collectors Association, Inc.
James J. Fahy
15 Pond Place
Cos Cob, CT 06807

1 yr. membership/$12, includes 6 issues of the *Newsletter*, a shoulder patch, membership card, etc. Club is for people interested in collecting police and law memorabilia.

KNIVES

De Riaz, Yvan A. *The Book of Knives*.
New York: Crown Publishers, 1981.

Ehrhardt, Roy. *Encyclopedia of Old Pocket Knives*.
Order from: Heart of America Press, Box 9808, Kansas City, MO 64134.

National Knife Collectors Association
Box 21070
Chattanooga, TN 37421

1 yr./$15 dues, includes subscription to *National Knife Collector*, published every month, and free admission to 6 knife shows a year.

NAUTICAL COLLECTIBLES

Value range: low–very high. A majority of the collectible items encountered can be obtained within the low to medium range.

Most popular items: varies according to classification (see below) but generally items that were on a famous ship (military, commercial, or exploratory), e.g., the *Titanic*, are very desirable.

Good sources: general antique and collectible shows, specialized dealers, and private connections.

HISTORY. While the history of man on the high seas can be traced back thousands of years, the modern era of navigation began only a little over 500 years ago when the Portuguese sent out their first explorers. Most of the relics from the first 300 years of modern sea voyage are long lost or decayed. Those items that have survived reside in museums and the collections of the rich. The subject of this chapter will therefore be the nautical collectibles from the last 180 years and the way collectors classify and save them.

COLLECTING. The following is a list of the nautical items collectors pursue:

bathometers
belt buckles
bills of lading
binoculars
blowers (speaking tubes)
boarding axes
boarding tools
boatswains' whistles
bone carvings
branding irons
buttons
caulking tools
charts
clocks
coins
compasses
crossing the Line certificates
cutlasses
depth thermometers
epaulettes
figureheads
fire buckets
flags
galley items
globes
gyro-compasses

half-block models
handbills
harpoons
instruments
jack knives
lamps
lanterns
log books
loggerheads
logs
maps
marine seals
medals
nautical almanacs
nautical prints
oil lamps
paintings
paper ephemera
pennants
photographs
plans
postcards
posters
powder horns
quadrants
rutters

sailing cards
sailors' clothes
sand glasses
scrimshaw items
seamen's paybooks
sextants
shells
ship letters
ship models
ships in bottles
ships' bells

signal flags
stern lights
tableware
telescopes
trade tokens
trophies
uniforms
whalebone items
whaling tools
wheels

Before one can begin collecting these items, one must decide which of the 14 nautical genres to specialize in. These genres are:

commercial ships
excursion boats (day liners and
tourist vessels)
ferries
fishing boats
luxury power boats
luxury yachts
military vessels

motor boats
ocean liners
racing yachts
sailboats
tankers (oil)
whaling ships
work boats (tugs)

Once one determines which genre to pursue, one can set about locating the particular collectibles that relate to each category. Certain genres, like motor boats and sailboats, offer a collector only a few choices of things to collect. Other genres, like military vessels and whaling ships, offer a very large number of choices, and a collector must be careful once again to specialize.

The surest way to gather background material on the genre you are interested in is to go to the library. Most aspects of our nautical history have been documented. Acquiring knowledge of the history of the ferry boat or racing yacht creates the proper foundation on which to build a collection.

In addition to the usual forums for buying items, I recommend that the motivated collector advertise in some of the small newspapers that publish weekly editions in many of the small towns that dot the eastern seaboard. It is in and around these towns that many of the descendants of 19th century sailors still live. By advertising in the local paper, a collector places himself in a strategic position should an estate or collection of early nautical items come up. (See Part One for how to place buy ads.)

Currently, the hottest nautical genre is ocean liners. Collectors compete to obtain items that once sailed on the *Titanic*, the *Lusitania*, the *Queen Mary*. The ocean liner has always been associated with romance, adventure, and excitement. Collectors want anything in any way associated with the great ocean liners of past and present. This includes dining room china, napkins, ashtrays, pins, postcards, souvenirs, spoons, and towels. The more illustrious the liner, the better. When buying, always choose the item that bears the boldest identifying mark; for example, an ashtray that bears the enameled seal or mark of an ocean liner.

BOOK

Major, Alan. *Maritime Antiques: An Illustrated Dictionary.*
  San Diego: A. S. Barnes and Co., 1981.

NON-SPORTS CARDS

Value range: low—medium.

Most popular items: high graphic quality cards from the 1890–1900 period, comic character cards from the 30's, modern sets featuring popular characters.

Good sources: paper collectible shows, flea markets, and through the mail.

THE TITLE NON-SPORTS card refers to the hundreds of trading card series issued and placed in cigarette and candy packs during the period from 1880 to the present. These cards are called non-sports to distinguish them from their baseball, football, boxing, and hockey counterparts issued during the same period. Non-sports cards of actors, actresses, bathing beauties, college men, magic, automobiles, sailing ships, early aircraft, famous men, agriculture, and animals are very popular collectibles today because they are inexpensive and beautiful.

HISTORY.   The precursor of the trading (non-sports) card was the trade card. Trade cards were used originally as a receipt between merchant and buyer (later they became promotional). As printing processes developed during the Industrial Revolution, it became possible to inexpensively imprint logos and advertising on the trade cards. Businessmen saw the advantage of handing out such cards and began ordering them with simple line drawings, woodcuts, and sketches. During this same period the processes of lithography and photography were making technological leaps, and it was becoming affordable to print photos for use in advertising.

Tobacco companies were responsible for the first trading cards, when in the late 1870's thick little cards were issued featuring photos of famous people of the day and tobacco advertising. These cards were inserted into packs of cigarettes as a promotion and also as a backing to protect the cigarettes. They became popular as children began collecting them and trying to complete sets.

As color lithography came more into use, these cards were improved and began featuring color illustrations from the worlds of art, entertainment, and science. Because cigarettes were essentially a luxury item, the companies did not spare expense in producing these cards. The 1880's saw the issuance of several large and significant series of trading cards by such companies as Allen & Ginter, Kinney, Duke, and Goodwin. Some of their brand names were Sweet Capporal, Mecca, and Turkey Reds.

Between 1895 and 1908 very few trading cards were produced. The American Tobacco Company had come to monopolize the industry, and there was no longer a need to include a promotion in cigarette packs. It was not until 1909 that cards were issued once again. This happened at the time right before the American Tobacco Company was forced to allow competition from other companies. A new and intense period of trading card production began, and many large and beautiful sets were produced. Children and adults alike avidly sought to have complete sets of these cards and would often search the gutter and sidewalks for discarded cards. During World War I card production was stopped again, and the era of the tobacco card came to an abrupt end.

Because the viability of the trading card as a promotional tool and an inexpensive form of advertising had been demonstrated, it did not die. Rather, it was picked up and used following the war by candy, gum, and bread companies. Many of the traditional designs were resurrected, and new ideas were developed by card creators and artists. Unfortunately, the economics of selling penny gum did not allow for the same high-quality production methods that the tobacco companies had employed, and these new cards were not nearly as attractive as their ancestors.

It was not until 1936 and the issuance of the G-men and Heroes of the Law series by a newcomer, the Gum Inc., Company, that the quality of the trading card improved. Gum Inc., was very successful, and by 1938 had come out with several very popular series, among which were the Mickey Mouse, Horrors of War, and Wild West series. In addition to producing some of the finest cards ever, Gum Inc., made a very tasty gum.

During and following World War II there were no trading card series issued. Paper drives were on, and it would have been frivolous to produce cards. In 1948 a new company called Bowman issued the first post-war series. In 1949 they were joined by other companies, and the modern period of card production had begun. Television was already making its way into households across the country, and just as the old cards had reflected the popular themes and people of their time, the new ones would do the same using television stars.

Today, trading card production has become big business, with the residual rights to popular television programs and movies selling for big money. Topps, Fleer, and Donruss are the companies that presently dominate the market, providing an endless number of series to satisfy the popular demand. Cards are a high-profit item, and most packs of 10 currently sell for 25¢.

Millions of each series are produced. Some companies no longer even include the customary slab of gum. Kids who are able to put together complete sets of series often sell them to others at twice what they cost. With the plethora of comic-book-type character cards coming out each year (E.T., Superman), the trading card business has never been better.

COLLECTING. Given the continuity of card production over the last 100 years, it becomes clear why they are becoming so desirable as collectibles. They are reflective of the time period in which they are produced, have graphic appeal, and are issued in series.

The beginning collector should start by going to the local drug, stationery, or candy shop to look at the different series of trading cards now being produced. Perhaps one will catch your fancy and you will buy it. Or, try buying several. By reading the information contained on the cards, you can find out how many cards constitute the series. Compare the graphics on each card. Some will be better than others. What do the cards depict? By becoming familiar with today's trading cards, you can develop an understanding of the hobby and be better prepared to begin collecting the older series.

The best place to look for the older trading cards is at a paper collectibles show, where you will see dozens of different series represented. The most desirable cards are ones that are very colorful and depict popular characters like Mickey Mouse, Superman, Buck Rogers, the Lone Ranger, and Hopalong Cassidy.

Collectors save cards by *series, type, era,* and *company.* I favor saving them by type because it is far less costly and difficult to obtain one example each from 50 different series than it is to complete a series of one issue that could number 100 cards. Condition is important, and you should always try to obtain cards closest to being perfect (no pieces missing, rips, foreign matter, or creases).

In addition to buying at the paper shows, you may want to try some of the mail order companies that advertise. Most sell new series by the set at wholesale as well as selling the older issues. They are able to do this because they buy cases of cards directly from the manufacturer and then assemble sets from them.

BOOKS

Benjamin, Christopher and Denny Eckes. *The Sports Americana Price Guide to Non-Sports Cards.* 1981. Published by Den's Collector's Den, Box 606, Laurel, MD 20810.

PERIODICAL

The Wrapper
309 Iowa Court
Carol Stream, IL 60187

> 1 yr./8 issues/$13; sample, $2. For collectors of gum cards and wrappers, a pamphlet of buy/sell ads and some articles.

PAPERBACK BOOKS

> Value range: low. Most collectible books can be bought from paperback dealers for less than $20. Some exceptional books bring up to $100.
>
> Most popular items: paperbacks from the 40's and 50's with covers picturing women in provocative and seductive poses. Early science fiction, fantasy, and crime books.
>
> Good sources: secondhand bookstores, garage, estate, and library sales.

MOST PEOPLE TREAT paperbacks as poor relations to the hardback. They read them and then pile them into boxes in their basements or attics. Eventually the books are thrown away when their owner discovers that they have become yellowed and decrepit. It is for this reason that, despite the vast number often produced, first-edition paperbacks from 1939 to 1959 are becoming more difficult to find and more popular with collectors.

HISTORY. The first paperbacks of the modern era were issued by Pocket Books in 1938–1939. These included issues of *The Good Earth* by Pearl S. Buck, *Lost Horizon* by James Hilton, and *Enough Rope* by Dorothy Parker. These early editions (which were an experiment) were limited to 10,000 copies printed and distributed in New York City. Pocket Books wanted to see if they could make it as a low-cost alternative to the hardcover. The experiment was an enormous success, and Pocket Books was soon joined by Avon, Bantam, Dell, and others in producing hundreds of thousands of paperbacks. Today, paperbacks account for a large percentage of book publishers' revenues.

COLLECTING. The most popular paperbacks with collectors are ones issued between 1939 and 1959 and feature especially attractive cover art. Paperbacks have always attracted readers because of their visual appeal. Their covers usually sell them. In many cases their contents do not even match their suggestive covers. Many have been chagrined to find the density of Faulkner when they expected a romance.

The literary genres best suited for the alluring or exciting covers are *science fiction, fantasy, horror,* and *crime.* Most collectible paperbacks fall into one of these categories. The most appealing covers for collectors are ones that feature *"good girl art," futuristic science fiction art, women being tortured or abused,* and *women in provocative poses.*

Some of the early exploitive covers from the 40's were considered sensational, and efforts were made to have them banned. One can read the mood of the times by looking through a collection of covers stemming from the 1939–59 period. The provocative covers that were cathartic during the war were toned down during the puritanical 50's. Through this entire period, however, artists continued producing what is today known as good girl art. This work features beautifully proportioned women in a variety of seductive and alluring poses. Surprisingly, as many female readers as male were drawn to buying these editions.

Paperbacks that have a popular author in addition to having an appealing cover are very desirable. In the crime and mystery genre the most popular authors are Irish (a.k.a. Cornell Woolrich), Chandler, Spillane, Christie, Hammett, Sayers, and Stout. In the science fiction and fantasy genre some of the popular authors are Merrit, Lovecraft, Howard, Bradbury, and C.L. Moore.

Serious collectors will only buy first-edition paperbacks. This is particularly true of books where the first edition is either the first appearance of an author or the book was done only in paper. A first edition copy of *Junkie* by William Lee (pseudonym for William Burroughs) is particularly valuable because it is the first appearance of Burroughs' work in print.

Many fiction writers can only get paperback deals for a book, which is therefore the first edition since there is no hardcover edition. Jack Kerouac and Kurt Vonnegut have written novels of which the first editions were paperbacks.

To tell whether a copy is a first or a later edition, open it to the copyright page and look for the words "First printing" or "First edition." If you decide to collect only for the appeal of the cover art, I recommend that you buy subsequent editions as opposed to firsts. The difference in price for two books that are identical in everything but their edition number can be as much as three or four times. Don't pay $10 if you can acquire a book that will serve just as well for $2.

Condition is important with paperbacks. Almost no collector ever reads his collection, but this does not stop him from desiring books that are *clean, unmarked*, and *free from acid deterioration*. The condition problem one most often encounters is browning. The paper used in manufacturing paperbacks is very cheap and laced with acids, which begin to break down. Eventually all paperbacks will turn brittle if they are not stored properly or treated with deacidifying compounds. Of course, if one is able to buy copies inexpensively enough, the condition factor is not so important.

The best places to pick up old paperbacks are estate, library, and garage sales, at which you should never have to pay more than a quarter a copy. Most of the time sellers only charge a dime. Secondhand bookstores are good places to look, but sometimes owners will be familiar with the market and attempt to get catalog prices. Before paying dealers anywhere from $5 to $50 for desirable copies, try digging up some yourself.

The most popular ways of collecting are by *literary genre, publisher*, and *cover art*. The first and last ways are usually the most practical, since collecting by publisher can mean having to acquire thousands of books if you go after Bantams, Pocket Books, or Avons. There are many smaller publishing houses that went out of business in the 50's, and their entire lines can be collected more easily.

BOOKS

Bonn, Thomas L. *Undercover*.
New York: Penguin Books, 1982.

Hancer, Kevin, *The Paperback Price Guide*.
Published in 1982 by Overstreet Publications, 780 Hunt Cliff Dr. N.W., Cleveland, TN 37311.

Schreuders, Piet, *Paperbacks, U.S.A. A Graphic History 1939–1959*.
San Diego: Blue Dolphin, 1981.

PERIODICALS

The Comics Buyers Guide
700 E. State Street
Iola, WI 54990

26 issues/$10; sample, $1. A tabloid issued weekly with some advertisements for paperback books and related materials.

Paperback Quarterly
1710 Vincent Street
Brownwood, TX 76801

A journal of mass-market paperback history. 1 yr./$10; sample, $3.50.

PHOTOGRAPHICA

Value range: low–very high. There is a vast range of values within this collectible group. Check below for specific price ranges.

Most popular items: images, cameras, and photography books.

Good sources: For cameras and photographic equipment, out-of-the-way camera shops in small towns can be a good source. For common 19th century images any of the general collectible forums are good, and for quality 19th and 20th century images, photo galleries and dealers and auction houses are best.

THE TERM *PHOTOGRAPHICA* describes a broad range of items all of which share a direct, or in some cases slight, association with photography. The most popular categories of photographica are *images, cameras,* and *photography books*; however, there are an enormous number of collectors who save only those items that feature a picture of a camera or photographer. Examples of such items are magazines, sheet music, trade cards, postcards, and advertising pieces. There are also collectors who only save darkroom equipment, posing chairs, antique lenses, and photographer's tools.

HISTORY. Louis Jacques Mandé Daguerre invented the first camera in 1837. Working from processes begun by Joseph Niépce, a scientist and fellow Frenchman, Daguerre worked out a way of fixing the image seen through a camera obscura (a darkened box in which the image of an object, received through a small aperture, is projected on a plane surface) onto a silver-coated copper plate through the reaction of mercury fumes on the plate's surface. Daguerre's process was presented to the French Academy of Sciences on August 19, 1839. A month later he gave a public demonstration at which he produced an image using a camera obscura. Prior to that time the only images that existed were those created by hand.

This was a process that seemingly bordered on magic. Many religious men spoke out against it, claiming that it was sacrilegious. The initial reaction of most was not unlike the fear and astonishment exhibited by African tribesmen when they first had their pictures taken.

In deference to their inventor, photographs produced using Daguerre's method were called *daguerreotypes.* The camera obscura was soon replaced by the daguerreotype camera, which at first consisted of two boxes constructed so that one could slide in and out of the other for focusing. When taking a daguerreotype, the photographer would uncover an aperture for several moments, allowing the image to fall on the plate inside the camera and "fix." The aperture was then closed, and chemicals were applied to develop the photograph. Early picture taking relied to a great extent on trial and error. An exposure could take 5 to 45 minutes, depending on how light the day was.

In 1851 the "wet-collodion" process was invented, which fixed the image coming through the aperture of the camera onto a piece of glass or sheet iron. Images fixed on glass in this manner were called *ambrotypes*. Images fixed on sheet iron were called *tintypes*. "Ambros" and tintypes were only two of the more popular new developments in photography. Once Daguerre's process became known, inventors and scientists all over the world began working at creating new types of images and inventing better processes. One early development was the stereo camera, which was used to produce a double image of a particular scene. This double image photograph is called a *stereograph* (or *stereoview*) and when viewed through a *stereoptican* appears to be three-dimensional.

The Civil War was the first major war to be recorded by photography. Professional photographers followed the troops, producing thousands of images. Paper photographs, known as *albumens* because of the egg whites used in producing them, and tintypes became very popular with servicemen who would have pictures taken for their loved ones back home. Many full-size battlefield photos were taken and have survived to provide us with a sense of what the war was really like.

By 1880 dry photographic plates were rapidly replacing the wet-plate process. Cameras were becoming smaller, more compact, and many amateurs began experimenting. The new emulsions (used to fix an image on the plate or negative) were becoming more sensitive, and exposure time was reduced. This led to the development of the shutter, which could be set to allow a measured amount of light in.

During the 1880's there were hundreds of patents for cameras as inventors thought up all kinds of housings and designs. Many of these were of a kind now called "detective" cameras because their inventors disguised them as books, briefcases, watches, canes, and so on.

In 1888 the first Kodak camera was developed and produced by George Eastman. It came factory loaded with a 100-exposure film pack, which users would send in to the company for development. This was the first camera to use roll film, and it paved the road for Eastman Kodak's tremendous success. Their slogan at the time became, "You press the button and we do the rest." The early Kodaks were made of wood and resembled small boxes. They represented one more stage in the evolution of the camera, which was continually becoming more convenient and suitable for general use.

By 1912 the folding camera had replaced the box shape, and with Kodak leading the way the country became camera mad. At this time two German inventors, Oskar Barnak and Ernst Leitz, developed an even smaller camera that became the first commercially successful camera to use 35mm film. This camera, called a Leica, was the first of a line that would eventually be considered the Rolls-Royce of cameras.

Throughout the 20th century the science of photography continued to develop with new high-speed films permitting picture taking in dim environments, the introduction of a commercially successful instant camera (the Polaroid), and, recently, the debut of pictures that develop before ones eyes.

The most significant photographic development in the 20th century, however, has been the final acceptance of photography as an art form. Major museums now house collections of the work of great American and European photographers, colleges offer degree programs for photography as a fine art, and books of photographs are popular as gifts for the aesthetically minded.

COLLECTING. Photographica is an enormous field, and the best way to begin is to go to the library. General reading can be augmented with trips to museums, photographic shows, and photo galleries. It is essential that one sample the field before beginning to collect.

Following is a look at the two main categories of photographica—*images* and *cameras*.

Images

In collecting photographic images, one has to choose between the earlier forms like the daguerreotype, ambrotype, tintype, and albumen, which are collected primarily for their historical importance and subject matter, and modern images taken by such masters as Stieglitz, Steichen, Strand, Weston, and Adams, which are collected as art.

THE EARLY IMAGES. Of the earlier types of images, the daguerreotype is the most popular. Daguerreotypes are easy to identify—they look like a silver mirror onto which an image has been etched. Because they are extremely sensitive to light and moisture, many daguerreotypes have faded over the years.

Ambrotypes are sometimes confused with daguerreotypes. This is because both were made in the same size range and sold in decorative dark brown cases made from coal, ground sawdust, and shellac (often called gutta-percha cases). An ambrotype, however, is made of glass (daguerreotypes are metal) and will appear (even if it is in a case, as most are) to be backed by a piece of dark cloth or paper. Because it is a "negative image," it will appear faint to beginners who are familiar with contemporary photos.

Tintypes are easier to recognize as they appear more vivid. Albumen photographs are made of paper, so there is no mistaking them.

The main criteria for value, though, are *size* and *subject matter*. Two-by-three-inch daguerreotypes, ambrotypes, and tintypes of studio poses are common and are worth only between $5 and $15, depending on condition and the quality of the case they are in.

In 1855 there were over 90 portrait galleries in New York City. These galleries churned out tens of thousands of small studio shots for individuals eager to have their images preserved. Larger images (6½" x 8½" and up) are worth more than the smaller ones.

Subject matter is the most important criterion for value. Desirable subjects are: Civil War battlefield scenes and any other interesting or historically important outdoor scenes like shots of slaves, carriages, towns, city streets, and workers with their tools. Because the exposure time for early photographs, particularly the daguerreotype, was long, outdoor scenes are the least common and hence the most valuable. For years it was thought that no daguerreotype existed depicting a recognizable street in Manhattan. In 1981 such an image was found and brought over $6,000 at auction.

The more interesting or unusual the image, the more desirable it is. For instance, an ambro of an undertaker standing next to his carriage, which has "G. Hall Undertaker" stencilled on it, or an albumen of slaves carrying cotton bales across a field with a plantation house in the background are both unusual and therefore very desirable images.

Stock studio shots of men, women, and children are the least desirable. Unfortunately, these are the images one most often encounters when poking through collections at tag and garage sales. Every family at one time or another went to a studio photographer, and thousands of images were produced.

In addition to the early photographs discussed, there were several other types like the *calotype* and the *ferrotype*. These are fairly rare, and the average collector will not encounter them. *Cartes de visite*, which are small ($2^1/_2$" x 4") paper photographs were very popular and were produced in the millions during the Civil War (and after). "CDV's", unless they depict a rare view, are worth only a dollar or two.

For buying quality early images, a photographica dealer is best. One must be careful to avoid buying fakes and damaged pieces. There have been several recent instances of vintage cameras being used to photograph ersatz Civil War battlefield scenes. This is not that difficult when one considers that vintage clothing is available and that many historic locations look the same as they did during the Civil War. Buying from a reputable dealer protects you should there later be some question as to an item's authenticity. Damage can often be subtle, and the beginner must always make sure to carefully check an image for cracks, stains, tears, creases, scratches, and retouching. Like all other collectibles, photographs in top grade bring far more than their damaged or low-grade counterparts. For buying inexpensive examples of early images, the flea market, garage sale and other secondhand forums are fine.

20TH CENTURY PRINTS. Collecting modern images requires a very different set of skills. One must develop an eye for detecting the qualities that make one photograph a piece of art and another just an interesting shot. These qualities are not dependent solely on subject matter. One of the greatest Edward Weston images, is a photograph of a vegetable, a green bell pepper. This image is a product of the artistic vision of the photographer both in shooting and then in printing. As Weston's student Ansel Adams said, "The negative is the score, the print is the performance."

Clearly, one must learn the criteria for judging photographs before one begins to buy. The best way is by looking through photography books featuring the works of great modern photographers. Some of the names you might look for, in addition to the ones already mentioned, are Man Ray, Sudek, Cartier-Bresson, Avedon, Atget, Strand, Kertesz, Evans, Frank, Coburn, Steichen, and Stieglitz. These photographers have produced images that run the gamut of the photographic genres—landscape, portrait, fashion, documentary, surrealism.

You might also consider taking a basic photography course at an adult education program. Some collectors feel that you must know what goes into printing an image in the darkroom before you can really understand the qualities that make a great print. Going to photo galleries and museums is a good way to see the work of the masters up close.

Collecting: 20th century images are usually collected by *photographer* or *genre.* As you become familiar with the work of different photographers, you may decide to pursue the prints of one or more of them. The genres of photography are similar to those in painting and include portrait, landscape, documentary (journalistic), fashion, surrealism. Many image collectors prefer to collect by genre since this enables them to acquire the work of many different photographers while still maintaining a central theme.

The best source for obtaining the work of modern photographers is an image dealer. The larger cities like New York, Los Angeles, Chicago, all have photo galleries, which function in the same way as traditional art galleries. They exhibit the work of promising new talent and keep inventories of the work of established photographers. If you do not live close enough to visit such a gallery, your best sources are dealers who sell through the mail and auction houses, both of which issue catalogs.

The Market: The market for quality 20th century images has been erratic in the last five years as a result of investor speculation. Prices for desirable images range from $40 up to thousands of dollars for the work of masters. When buying images, documentation is very important, as there have been instances of unauthorized prints being sold. Often an image will be sold with the signature of the photographer.

Cameras

Cameras are collected by *type, company, age,* and *country.* Type describes the kind of camera. Daguerreotype, stereo, 35mm, instant, movie, and miniature are types of cameras. Some collectors save a type, like 35mm, they can still use. Others collect a type, like a stereo camera, solely for its historical importance. Of the many companies that have produced cameras, some of the more popular ones are Leica, Kodak, Zeiss, Nikon, Graflex, Alpa, and Voigtlander.

Collecting by company is popular because it presents a collector with a finite goal, even if, in the case of a Kodak collector, that goal might mean acquiring over 100 different cameras.

Early cameras (1839–1900) can be extremely expensive. The average daguerreotype camera, for instance, sells for over $3,000 on the collectors' market (with some examples bringing up to $10,000). With the exception of a few cameras like the gold-plated Leica Luxus made in 1929, which sells for over $12,000 today, 20th century cameras are generally less expensive. This is due in great degree to the fact that as the camera became viable as a consumer product, millions were made to meet the demands of the general public.

Beginning in the early part of this century, tens of thousands of inexpensive Kodak Brownie, Folding Pocket, Autographic, Special, and Cartridge cameras were produced. Many of these have survived and are available today for prices within the low value range. As the century progressed, Kodak was joined by many other smaller companies that produced inexpensive cameras for the masses. The major camera-producing countries are Japan, France, Germany, England, Switzerland, and the United States. Collecting by country is far too large a field for the average collector and one must usually set some kind of parameters to narrow the field.

COLLECTING. One should follow the usual steps of familiarization before beginning to buy antique cameras. There are several good guide books, and these can be used in conjunction with visual appraisal at photographica shows. Beginners are advised to make contact with other collectors as a way of learning about the hobby. Collectors often trade among themselves and help each other in locating specific cameras. *Shutterbug Ads* (listed at the end of the chapter) is a very good publication and can be used as a source for buying and selling.

Once you have become familiar with the field, the best places to look for old cameras are camera shops that have been in business for a number of years and are off the beaten track; Salvation Army and thrift stores; consignment shops; tag, estate, and church sales; and flea markets. A *patient*, knowledgeable collector will find many bargains. He must be willing, however, to look through a large number of undesirable Polaroids, Instamatics, and anonymous plastic box cameras to find the quality cameras.

Condition varies from mint in the box all the way down to damaged/poor. Collectors want a camera that is operable or at least, restorable. A missing leather strap is not a serious defect, a broken shutter or a cracked lens is. When buying cameras always ask the seller to explain how it works. Unless one is a mechanical wizard, certain older models are very difficult to figure out.

BOOKS

Darrah, William C. *Cartes de Visite* and *The World of Stereographs*. Order from author at: R.D.1, Gettysburg, PA 17325

Gernsheim, Helmut and Alison. *L.J.M. Daguerre: The History of the Diorama and the Daguerreotype*. New York: Dover, 1968.

Gilbert, George. *Collecting Photographica*. New York: Hawthorn Books, 1976.

McCulloch, Lou W. *Card Photographs: A Guide to Their History and Value*. Exton, PA: Schiffer Publishing, 1978.

McKeown, James M. and Joan C., eds. *Price Guide to Antique and Classic Still Cameras*. Grantsburg, WI: Centennial Photo Service, 1981.

Newhall, Beaumont. *The History of Photography*. New York: Museum of Modern Art Publications, 1964.

Sharbrough, David. *American Premium Guide to Olde Cameras*. Florence, AL: Books Americana, 1983.

Welling, William. *Collecting Guide to 19th Century Photographs.*
New York: Macmillan, 1976.

Wolf, Myron S. *Blue Book: Illustrated Price Guide to
Collectible Cameras.* Order from: Photographic Memorabilia, Box 351,
Lexington, MA 02173.

PERIODICAL

Shutterbug Ads
Box F
Titusville, FL 32780

> 1 yr./12 issues/$8. The national marketplace for old and new pho-
> tographic items. Thousands of classified ads each issue. Subscribers
> can place ads at a discount.

CLUB

The Western Photographic Collectors Association
Box 4294
Whittier, CA 90607

POLITICAL COLLECTIBLES

Value range: low–very high. Twentieth century items are generally less expensive than 19th century items. The majority
of pieces in the market fall into the low–medium range.

Most popular items: presidential campaign items, the most popular of which are buttons, badges, and 19th century novelty
items.

Good sources: from dealers who specialize in political items and
are willing to warrant the authenticity of what they sell.

REMEMBER THOSE BUTTONS you wore advertising your choice for president? How about those bumper stickers you put on your car? Well, today, both are considered political collectibles and, depending on the candidate and campaign they featured, may be valuable to collectors. Political collectibles are things like ashtrays, autographs, badges, banners, buttons, bottles, china, novelties, paper ephemera, photos, pins, silk ribbons, and tokens, all designed and produced to promote a particular candidate in a particular election.

Today these items are collected for their historical importance and for their visual appeal. The presidential campaigns have always generated the most memorabilia and interest. For this reason, the majority of political collectibles pursued are items relating to a president, a presidential campaign, or a runner-up in a presidential campaign.

HISTORY. Although the first presidential election was held in 1789, Washington had no need for a campaign; in fact, his loyal supporters wanted to make him king. Presidential campaign items began appearing in the early 1800's. By 1840 the number of these items had increased dramatically as publicity men began to see their importance in the promotion of a candidate. Industrial developments led to the production of inexpensive silk ribbons, banners, medalets, and photo cards, all of which either depicted a likeness of the candidate, or a motto, and his name. Many of these items were given away at rallies, train depots, and village squares. In 1896 the first celluloid buttons appeared in time for the presidential campaign. They immediately became popular as a novelty and a way of showing political affiliation.

The 20th century has seen the development of mass communication mediums, which have revolutionized the strategies of election publicity. Publicity men now have the responsibility of making sure that their candidates appear regularly on television, radio, and the front pages. Buttons and other political items are still produced, but they have lost some of the quality, visual appeal, and much of the importance that their earlier counterparts had. Following is a look at the most popular area of political collectibles—campaign buttons.

Buttons

HISTORY. The buttons we are familiar with today were first made in 1896. Celluloid, a relatively new product, was used to cover a round piece of printed paper that lay on a metal disc with a curled-up rim. The button was held together by a steel ring that snapped into place in the disc's rim. A heat process was used to make the celluloid shrink and become taut over the paper. Thousands of colorful celluloid buttons were produced for the McKinley/Bryan election of 1896, and they were immediately popular with the people who regarded them as novelties. The 1920 election saw the first major use of lithographed tin buttons. These were simple (in comparison with celluloids) buttons stamped out of sheets of tin that had been lithographed with hundreds of the same pattern. These "lithos" became very popular with publicists because they cost very little to produce and could be manufactured quickly.

COLLECTING. The celluloid button is far more popular than the tin litho button. Tin lithography becomes very expensive if more than three or four colors or a complex design are used. Hence, manufacturers had much less artistic latitude in producing these buttons. Celluloid buttons, on the other hand, have images produced on printed paper, allowing a designer or artist many colors and complexity of design. Celluloid buttons are nearly always more appealing from a visual standpoint than tin lithos.

Collectors pursue four different types of buttons. These are the *jugate, slogan, name,* and *picture* button. A jugate features a picture of the presidential candidate next to his running mate. Jugates are very popular with collectors and generally bring more than other types of buttons. The slogan button features a slogan, e.g., "I Like Ike." A name button depicts only the candidate's name, and a picture button features a photo or likeness sometimes accompanied by words.

Value usually depends upon *scarcity, condition,* and *visual appeal.* Some of the most beautiful buttons were made in large quantities and are relatively inexpensive today. A case in point are buttons from the 1896 McKinley/Bryan election. Because it was the first election featuring celluloid buttons and they immediately became a novelty, tens of thousands were produced, distributed, and, most importantly, saved. Beautiful examples from this campaign are available for prices within the low value range.

Condition is, as usual, very important. The most common defect to look for in a celluloid button is "foxing," which is a term used to describe brown stain marks that appear on paper as a result of exposure to mold or moisture. Other possible defects include scratches, dents, cracks, or peeling of the celluloid. Celluloids suffering from these defects and tin lithos that are rusty or scratched are worth as much as 80 percent less than similar high-grade condition buttons.

Some collectors prefer large tin buttons of recent vintage, while other collectors prefer early 20th century celluloid jugates with art nouveau designs. Generally, however, a desirable button will have an artistic balance. It will be an appealing miniature work of art.

The greatest danger for collectors is the "brummagen," a term describing a reproduction button or political item. Brummagens are quite common, and the best way for you to avoid getting stuck with one is to buy only from dealers who will warrant, in writing, the authenticity of the item that they are selling. Of course, this approach is not necessary when you are purchasing inexpensive items. To reach the level of knowledge where you will know on your own whether a button is good or not requires handling and reading. There are several good books on buttons and general political memorabilia. In addition to reading those books, you should read up on the particular president or campaign you are collecting. This will greatly enhance your enjoyment of the hobby.

One branch of political collectibles that has been becoming popular over the last three years is Watergate items. These are anything related to the scandal, including newspapers, magazines, Tricky Dick rubber dolls, buttons that say "Impeach the Bum", etc. Some dealers are bullish on the Watergate collectibles market and feel that within 10 years many of these items will be very valuable. My own feeling is that if you like them and find them historically interesting, buy them; otherwise avoid them.

BOOKS

Frank, Beryl. *The Pictorial History of the Democratic Party*
and *The Pictoral History of the Republican Party.* Each book features
hundreds of photos of presidential campaign items. Order from:
Campaign Collectibles, 315 Oak Lane, Hightstown, NJ 08520.

Hake, Ted. *Encyclopedia of Political Buttons.*
Mr. Hake is the acknowledged expert in the field of political buttons
and has published three volumes of his encyclopedia. Write to him
at: Box 1444, York, PA 17405 for copies or information.

Sullivan, Ed. *Collecting Political Americana* and *American
Political Badges and Medalets.* Order from: Charles McSorley, Box 21,
Closter, NJ 07624.

PERIODICAL

The Political Collector Newspaper
444 Lincoln Street
York, PA 17404

1 yr./12 issues/$7.50; sample, $1. Features articles and photos as well
as classified ads for all items of political collecting.

CLUB

American Political Items Collectors
Box 340339
San Antonio, TX 78234

1 yr./$16, includes membership card, APIC handbook, and a year of
their quarterly journal, *The Keynoter,* which features news and articles
on the hobby.

POSTCARDS

Value range: low–high. The great bulk of cards collected sell for between $2 and $15. Exceptional art nouveau cards have brought over $1000.

Most popular items: artist-signed; coin and stamp; early aviation, ship, and fire engine; and U.S. Exposition (1873–1903) postcards.

Good sources: on approval from mail order dealers, at postcard shows, and through private connections.

POSTCARD COLLECTORS are known as *deltiologists*, their hobby *deltiology*. In the past ten years their ranks have grown tremendously owing to the collectibles boom and the attractions of postcard collecting.

HISTORY. The first postcards were far different from the slick photo cards one presently sends to relatives and friends. They looked like our postal cards today, which are blank on both sides except for an imprinted stamp and directions for use. In 1869 the first such card was produced in Austria. Within four years most of Europe was using and producing them. The U.S. Postal Service inaugurated the use of postal cards on May 13, 1873. Businesses were quick to realize how these cards could be used for advertising. They began printing their product's name (and address of sales locations) on the blank side and mailing the cards in large numbers to prospective customers.

In the mid-1870's the first pictures began appearing on cards. These were mostly primitive engravings of buildings and lithographed pictures of ships, animals, and figures. During the 1870's the cards became extremely popular in this country, and upwards of several million a year were sold. The real explosion, however, came during the 1890's when the first cards printed by private enterprises were permitted to be sold in the U.S. (called private mailing cards). By this time improvements in the offset color lithographic process had made it possible to reliably produce beautifully colored cards. Prior to 1907 the Post Office did not permit a written message on the back of private mailing cards. As a result, many of the early cards found today have messages scrawled on the picture side. The period between 1900 and 1920 is considered the Golden Era of postcard production. During these years beautiful and well-made cards were imported from Germany and England.

COLLECTING.   There is no set cutoff year beyond which postcards are not collected. Some people save only current cards; others want 1950's vintage; however, the most desirable cards were made before 1930. Dating cards takes experience. The most definitive clue to a card's age is the cancellation (if it has one, since many cards were bought to be saved unused). If the date of the cancellation were August 1891, the card would have to be at least that old. Another way to determine age is by the amount of postage. Between 1873 and 1928 the cost of mailing a card was one or two cents. After 1928 the penny postcard never returned. Therefore, any cards stamped with a penny (whether they are cancelled or not) should be before 1928. Two-cent cards are trickier because they existed as late as 1952. Of course, the most reliable index of a card's age is your experience. Once you begin handling cards, determining their age will become second nature.

The most popular genres in postcard collecting are *advertising, art deco, art nouveau, children, Christmas, coins and stamps, comic, company, Easter, early airplane* (1905–1930), *early exposition* (1873–1903), *Halloween, hold-to-light, horse-drawn fire-fighting equipment, signed artist, trains, Thanksgiving, Valentine,* and *women.*

The particular "look" collectors go after varies among genres. Generally, though, the most desirable cards are ones that are colorful and have been well drawn or painted. Within the category of signed artist cards there are dozens of artists and illustrators who are popular among collectors (a list of the best known of them is included at the end of this chapter). Artists drew and painted cards in all the genres, and collectors often choose to save cards done by a particular artist or several different ones.

Most of the genres can be broken down into categories. Because so many cards were produced and are available today, a collector must be selective or else end up with an impossible task. For example, if you choose to collect advertising cards, you may want to save only the ones that advertise tobacco or breakfast cereal; if you decide you like cards that picture children, you may want only the ones done by a certain artist; if you want to collect Halloween cards, you may determine that only those with a black cat are of interest to you. The possibilities are endless.

Some collectors save only those cards made by a particular company. The most popular are Albertypes, American Souvenir Card Company, Detroits, International Art Company, Edward H. Mitchell, Raphael Tuck, and Ullman Company. Not all of the cards these companies produced are considered special today. For example, I once made the mistake of purchasing 500 Tuck cards because I had been told that Tuck postcards are the most beautiful ever produced. Many of them are, but the examples I had purchased were not. In fact, they were so awful looking that I ended up giving them away. Trust your eye and buy only when it tells you to.

Cards can be broken into two value classifications. The first consists of those that fall into one of the desirable genres; the second, of those cards that are not desired and end up (or should end up) in nickel and dime boxes. Of this latter group, the most familiar are museum cards (cards that feature photos of paintings, sculpture, and pieces of furniture) and tourist view cards (those prosaic depictions of landscapes and attractions). *Of the billions of cards produced during the past 115 years, only a small percentage are actually desirable to collectors.*

Condition is very important. Postcard collectors have a grading scale that includes poor, good, fine, and mint. Except in the case of an extremely rare card, serious collectors buy only those cards that are in at least fine condition. A fine-condition card is only slightly worn and has no tears, creases, stray words, missing corners, or water damage. Writing on the image side of a card detracts from the overall grade. Be particularly wary of dealers who wishfully overgrade their better cards.

The best place to buy and learn is the postcard show or convention. Dates and locations of shows are publicized in most of the general antiques and collectibles publications. Another good way to learn is to subscribe to *Barr's Post Card News*. Many dealers who advertise in this publication are willing to send approvals. Many also conduct auctions. For beginners, the best advice is to stick with cards selling in the $2 to $5 range.

MOST POPULAR POSTCARD ARTISTS. (90 percent of the time the card will be signed)

Asti	Gunn	Reynolds
Brill	Harber	Russell
Brown	Harmony	Sager
Brundage	Humphreys	Schmucker
Christy	King	Sherie
Clapsaddle	Klein	Shinn
Dirks	Knox	Spargin
Ditzler	Marco	Swinnerton
Dwig	Mucha	Thackeray
Fisher	O'Neil	Wain
Golag	Platt	Wall
Greenaway	Powell	Weiss

BOOKS

Carver, Sally S. *The American Postcard Guide to Tuck.*
  Available from author: 179 South Street, Chestnut Hill, MA 02167.
  Write to Ms. Carver for titles of other postcard books by her.

Ryan, Dorothy B. *Picture Postcards in the United States 1893–1918.*
  New York: Clarkson N. Potter, 1982.

PERIODICALS

Barr's Postcard News
Lansing, IA 52151

  1 yr./24 issues/$12.50. Features articles and ads, especially those of dealers conducting mail auctions.

The Postcard Dealer
Box 1765
Manassas, VA 22110

   1 yr./6 issues/$15. Features articles on collecting, buying, and selling postcards, as well as collector and dealer ads. The publisher will also send you a free directory of over 200 accredited postcard dealers in the United States.

CLUBS

Deltiologists of America
10 Felton Avenue
Ridley Park, PA 19078

   1 yr./$10, includes 6 issues of *Deltiology* and a free advertisement in same. The club also publishes books on postcards.

Golden Gate Postcard Club
Karl Heuer
3315 Sweet Drive
Lafayette, CA 94549

   1 yr./$5.

Metropolitan Post Card Collectors Club
Mrs. Rose Shiffrin
16–08 212th Street
Bayside, NY 11360

   1 yr./$7, includes subscription to their bimonthly bulletin.

National All States Hobby Club
Mrs. Leta Crogg
Route 2 Box 158
Mountain Burg, AK 72946

   Write for information.

Rhode Island Postcard Club (RIPC)
Miss Evelyn M. Marshall
37 Ryder Avenue Apt. 2
Cranston, RI 02920

   Write for information.

The Triviall Group
Henry Kamphuis
4601–101 Street
Oak Lawn, IL 60453

1 yr./$3, includes 6 issues of their newsletter.

RADIO PREMIUMS AND CEREAL GIVEAWAYS

Value range: low—medium. There are a few extremely rare items that have brought over $1,000.

Most popular items: 30's, 40's, and 50's radio premium rings that work as secret decoders; magnifying glasses, telescopes; direction finders—all of which feature a picture or the name of a popular hero.

Good sources: dealers who auction and sell through the mail; collectible shows.

BEFORE THE TIME when most households had televisions, children came home from school to be thrilled by the adventures of their favorite radio heroes. Between four and six o'clock they could listen to the exploits of the Lone Ranger, Terry and the Pirates, Superman, Captain Midnight, Little Orphan Annie, and a host of other do-gooders. At the end of each program an announcer would usually give information about how one could obtain secret decoder rings, viewing scopes, identification bracelets, and dozens of other imaginative premiums. Since sponsors of the adventure radio shows were mostly cereal producers, many of the same items were also offered on the backs of breakfast cereals. Today, premiums obtained for a boxtop and a dime (or quarter) during the 30's, 40's, and early 50's have become very desirable to collectors, and some bring hundreds of dollars each.

HISTORY. Cereal and radio premiums and giveaways were produced and sold beginning in the late 30's. They enjoyed immediate and fantastic success as young listeners everywhere rushed to send in for these magical devices that would bring them closer to their radio heroes. Radio premiums faded in the mid-50's as television usurped radio's reign in the lives of youngsters, but cereal premiums continued to be produced and are still made today.

The companies that offered the most radio premiums were Ralston and Ovaltine. They sold and gave away hundreds of different items, the most popular of which were (and are) the cleverly designed rings that could do everything from lighting up and making sounds to acting as telescopes, compasses, magnifying glasses, and secret decoders. Who can forget the ring that displayed an image that seemed to move as you rocked your finger back and forth slightly? Or the famous secret compartment? In addition to the rings, a variety of other premiums were produced. These included belts, beltbuckles adorned with the picture or logo of the hero, spy scopes, pedometers, ray guns, badges, and buttons. By today's standards the composition and design of all these items are astonishing. One could not imagine a modern producer being able to make identical items without having to charge several dollars a piece for them.

COLLECTING. Because of their size (most being ring size or only slightly larger) and purpose, most premiums were (and are) lost, destroyed, or discarded. The typical item enjoyed a week or a month of adoration and was then relegated to the bottom of the toy chest, where it remained until a diligent spring cleaner threw it away. Premiums from the 30's through the 50's are difficult to come by today. The only individuals who have major collections (over 500 pieces) are people who by quirk or fate happened to save them as young adults or who have spent thousands of dollars acquiring them.

For the beginner, obtaining vintage premiums is going to require patience and money. The best place to buy them is from one of the mail order dealers who run quarterly mail auctions in which radio and cereal premiums are offered (two are listed at the end of the chapter). A method that will be less successful is to look for them at general antique and collectible shows. Occasionally dealers there may have acquired an odd piece or two. Prices range from a minimum of $5 to $10 for a common vintage premium to upwards of $1,000 for unique or extremely rare examples. The great bulk of collectible premiums sell in the $40 to $80 range.

As an alternative to collecting hard-to-find older premiums, many collectors begin by saving the items currently being offered by cereal producers. To see what is available, go to your local supermarket and examine the back of cereal boxes for offers (pick a time when the aisle is not crowded). Although most of the current plastic premiums don't equal their ancestors in quality and imagination, there are some that are unusual and bound to become desirable in the coming years.

BOOK

Sugar, Bert Randolph. *The Nostalgia Collector's Bible*.
    New York: Quick Fox, 1981.

MAIL AUCTION DEALERS

Hake's Americana and Collectibles
Box 1444
York, PA 17405

   Subscription $8 for 4 well-illustrated catalogs that feature radio premiums in addition to many other collectibles.

Historicana
1632 Robert Road
Lancaster, PA 17601

   Small company that issues a mail order auction catalog 3 times a year and sends it free to interested parties. Some premiums.

RAILROADIANA

Value range: low–high. A majority of the items collected can be purchased for prices within the low value range.

Most popular items: things that feature an image of a steam engine, preferably identifiable, or that are marked with the logo or name of a famous railroad line.

Good sources: railroadiana conventions (advertised in the collectibles and antiques publications as well as the specialized magazines listed at the end of this chapter) and from mail order dealers.

DURING THE LAST 130 YEARS over 200 railroad lines have operated routes throughout the United States. Among the more famous of these are the Union Pacific, Rock Island, New York Central, B and O, Norfolk and Western, Penn Central, Pennsylvania, Northern Pacific, and Southern Pacific railway lines. From the days of the early steam locomotives, which puffed slowly across the country, to today's modern diesels, which sometimes look like rocket ships, a tremendous amount of train equipment, souvenirs, and operating goods have been produced. Collectors call it *railroadiana*. Below is a list of the items and categories they pursue:

advertising items
artwork
breast badges
brotherhood items
buttons
caps
cloth insignia
date nails
dining car items
emblem pins
keys

lamps
lanterns
loco maker plates
medals
models
paper items
telegraph items
tools
watches
wax sealers
wood tokens

Following the historical background is a look at paper railroadiana, locks and keys, and date nails. Each has been selected
because it reflects a different kind of collecting, from the general
to the esoteric. For those interested in pursuing any of the other
items listed, please follow the guidelines for desirability given under the section on paper railroadiana.

HISTORY. Our first experimental steam engines were imported from England during the 1820's. In the early period, people were not convinced that steam-powered vehicles could generate
enough horsepower to move loads. Many early trials involved
racing horse-drawn loads against steam-engine-drawn loads. In
the beginning the horses always won! By the early 1830's the
engines had been improved enough to convince several wealthy
businessmen to begin constructing small rail lines.

As the decade wore on, more and more investors entered the
new field, and between 1840 and 1854 railroad expansion and
development exploded. During this time the government was not
actively involved, and rail lines were being laid by competing privately owned companies. Because of a lack of organization and
rules, it was common for rival lines to lay track parallel to one
another. Some towns had as many as four different railroad lines
serving them. This wasteful and counterproductive situation worsened as more and more companies entered the field.

There are many accounts of sabotage and deceit. Many train
wrecks and disasters were caused by hired vandals who laid ob-
structions on the rails or diverted trains onto the wrong track.
Ironically, it was the Civil War that brought order to railroading,
when the respective northern and southern governments stepped
in and took control of the rails in order to convey troops and war
supplies.

During the war, track size and rolling stock axle widths became
uniform, so that any train could travel on any track. By the end
of the war there was no longer any question about the importance
of the railroad. The government began encouraging the construction of track through land grants and subsidies. 1870 is generally
thought of as the beginning of the Golden Age of railroading.

ERAS. The era of the steam engine continued until the early
1950's. At this time steam engines, many of which had been in

service for over 30 years, were finally phased out and replaced by the gasoline diesel engine, which had been growing in popularity since the early 1930's. The diesel was stronger and did not require the antediluvian practice of coal burning. Many mourned the passing of steam.

In addition to the steam and diesel engines, both used primarily for long-distance freight and passenger transport, the electric engine made its first appearance in the early 1900's and is still used today for passenger service along suburban routes.

COLLECTING. Regarding the relative popularity of collectibles from one of the three kinds of engines—steam, electric, and gasoline—artifacts of the steam era are far and away the most popular, with diesel memorabilia and electric train items a distant second and third. The romance and the adventures of the steam engine chugging west to the new frontier, and the excitement of various Civil War stories where engines played a crucial role in the outcome of a battle, have succeeded in mythicizing the steam locomotive. Following is a look at three categories of railroad collecting:

PAPER RAILROADIANA. More railroadiana collectibles are made of paper than of any other composition. Following is a list of the specific paper items collectors pursue. The more popular ones are indicated with an asterisk.

*advertising paper
 baggage claims
*bonds
 books
*calendars
 drawings
 engravings
 etchings
 magazines
*maps
 matches
*passes
*photos
 playing cards

*postcards
 posters
*railroad postmarks
 sheet music
 signs
 stationery
*stereo views
*stocks
 tickets
*timetables
 tourist guides
 woodcuts

In addition to these items some collectors save things like menus, sugar packets, fans, and napkins. One can save anything made of paper as long as it somehow bears some printed relationship to the railroad. This printing can be in the form of words, logo, or picture. A fan, for instance, would qualify as railroadiana if it bore the logo of the B & O R.R., a picture of a steam engine, or the words "Courtesy of the Baltimore and Ohio R.R."

Generally, the most popular items are those that date from and relate to the steam era (c.1850–1950). *Visual appeal, the name of the railroad line*, and *the relative importance of the object* (is it merely a matchbook or is it a large poster?) are the specific factors that determine the desirability and value of a piece. Examples of choice items are, a calendar from 1889 featuring a large colorful chromo-lithograph of a steam engine and the name of the railroad line; a timetable from 1856 indicating arrival and departure times for the New York and New Haven Railroad; a railroad exchange pass elaborately decorated with a labeled steam engine and block letter instructions for use; and a stock certificate with an engraving of a steam engine and information pertaining to a now-defunct line.

From these examples one can see that the identification of the item is very important. So much of the pleasure of the hobby comes from being able to identify the railroad line. An anonymous piece of memorabilia may be nice to look at, but it can't provide access to the romance or excitement of a specific rail line or period. To learn which rail lines had a colorful past, one need only begin reading generally on the history and development of the railroad in the United States.

RAILROAD KEYS AND LOCKS

History. During the early days of railroads the controls used to hold a train on course or divert it to another track were kept in the switch box that lay beside the tracks. When competition between rail lines and discord between farmer and railroad led to the sabotage of these controls, the rail companies had to devise a way to safeguard them. The eventual solution, after years of experimentation with different locking systems, came in the form of strong padlocks made of bronze, brass, and galvanized steel, to which a short piece of chain was welded. This chain was placed through iron rings, which were welded on to the existing switch boxes. The padlocks were operated by barrel-type keys usually made of either brass or bronze (although steel, iron, and aluminum keys were also made). Locking the switch boxes put an end to most of the misadventures caused by vandals; however, it also put a tremendous burden on the railroad man whose job it was to unlock and operate the switch box. A lost key could (and did) lead to disaster. For this reason, the keys were a tremendous responsibility, and their importance and symbolism have grown over the years. Today, with manual switching a thing of the past, railroadiana collectors actively pursue the locks and keys once used to secure switch boxes as well as other railroad line property like the station house, the tool shed, the water tower, and the caboose of the freight trains.

Collecting. Prior to the collectibles boom, locks and keys were collected only by a small number of devoted collectors. Today, investors and dilettantes have entered this highly specialized field of collecting, and the resulting price increases have led to the production of fake keys and the sale of misattributed locks. Knowing whether a key is authentic or a lock correctly attributed requires a lot of experience, and beginners are strongly advised to be cautious in buying. I recommend that one begin by collecting the more common examples, which in the case of keys can be purchased for $10–$15, and in the case of locks for $25–$35. As one begins to handle the pieces and learn about them, one's ability to spot fakes or incorrectly identified items will develop.

Collectors can usually tell the particular railroad a key has come from by the type of bit cutting it has. A less reliable way of obtaining this information is looking at the initials that are usually stamped or embossed in the bow of the key. The initials are unreliable because over the years many lines have had the same initials. Also, many key forgers have purposefully used the initials of desirable railroads as a way of enticing customers. In identifying locks, one runs into the same problem of duplication of certain railroad initials. To truly know which railroad a lock has come from, one must be familiar with other identifying clues such as lock type, composition, and size.

The most popular railroad locks are those that have fancy-style lettering indicating the railroad line and those that resemble valentine hearts. The most popular keys are those from one of the smaller railroads that failed as the larger lines began to dominate. Much of the current appeal of locks and keys derives from their historical significance; so remember to always try and buy the piece from one of the lines with an exciting or romantic history.

The usual rules about condition don't apply to locks and keys. Railroad hardware was used and had to withstand extremes of weather and tampering. Expect to find pieces in well-used condition. Most collectors prefer the one with the dent or chips since their defects lend credibility and add to the romance.

DATE NAILS. A date nail is a small nail ($1\frac{1}{2}''$–$4''$) with a large head into or onto which has been stamped or embossed two digits indicating the year. Date nails were driven into railroad ties as they were laid. In this way the railroad lines could learn about tie longevity. Most date nails were made of steel, but some were made of copper, aluminum, and plastic. Collectors generally save them by type and year. The various types can be identified by the shape of the head and shaft. Head shapes are round, square, oval, and pentagonal. Shaft shapes are round, square, two pronged, and tapered. Collectors also save them by composition. Currently the price range is 50¢–$8.

BOOKS

Baker, Stanley L. *Railroad Collectibles.*
Paducah, Collector Books, 1981.

Lewis, Joseph W. *Date Nails Brought Up to Date.*
Order from: Lewis Enterprises, Box 4655 SFA Station, Nacogdoches, TX 75961.

Stewart, Don. *The Standard Guide to Key Collecting*
and *The Charles J. McQueen Collection of Railroad Switch Keys.* Available from the author: Box 9397, Phoenix, AZ 85068.

Wirwell, Glen and John Evans. *Date Nails Complete.*
  Order from: Wesis Publications, 29 Meadowbrook Lane, Cedar Grove,
  NJ 07009. Also publishes a catalog.

PERIODICAL

Key, Lock, and Lantern
Box 15
Spencerport, NY 14559
  A quarterly publication for collectors of locks, keys, and lanterns.

CLUBS—GENERAL

Railroad Enthusiasts
Box 133
West Townsend, MA 01474
  1 yr./$7. The club is for anyone interested in early railroading.

Railroadiana Collectors Association
405 Byron Avenue
Mobile, AL 36609
  Publishes a quarterly, *The Railroadiana Express.*

Railway and Locomotive Historical Society
Box 1194
Boston, MA 02103
  Publishes a quarterly, *The Railroad History Bulletin.*

CLUBS—SPECIFIC

Key Collectors International
Box 9397
Phoenix, AZ 85068
  For collectors of all kinds of keys. Write for information.

The National Association of Timetable Collectors
Tom Coval
21 East Robin Road
Holland, PA 18966

1 yr./$15. Membership includes *The First Edition*, which is a monthly newsletter, and a quarterly magazine, *The Timetable Collector*. Also good for collectors of trolley and bus timetables.

Texas Date Nail Collectors Association
Jerry Waits
501 West Horton
Brenham, TX 77833

1 yr./$10, includes 6 issues of *Nailer News*, a newsletter covering all aspects of date nail collecting.

RECORDS

Value range: low—medium. The majority of records one encounters will be of the quality that now commands $2–$8 in the collector's marketplace. Such records sell for much less however (25¢–$1.50) at garage, church, rummage, and tag sales.

Most popular items: early *original* recordings of individuals who were later to become stars, rare record labels, and *original issue* records of 50's and early 60's rock and roll stars and bands, e.g., Elvis Presley, Buddy Holly, The Beatles.

Good sources: As indicated above, the best place to buy records is at one of the non-collector forums. For obtaining rare or hard-to-find records, the best place to buy is at a record convention or from one of the dealers who advertise in *Goldmine* (see end of chapter).

HISTORY. Thomas Alva Edison invented the first phonograph in 1877. It was a primitive device able to reproduce sounds that had been recorded on a tinfoil-covered cylinder. Between 1889 and 1912 Edison's company produced what are called wax cylinder records. These were sold as blanks to offices for use in dictating machines as well as pre-recorded with popular music for use at home. The first disc records resembling the records we are familiar with today were produced in the 1890's by the Berliner Company. These caught on, and in the early 1900's the first major wave of disc records appeared in stores. The Victor Talking Machine Company of Camden, New Jersey, was responsible for most of the early production of records. By 1912 the wax cylinder was out, replaced by the disc record.

On innumerable occasions I have had the sorry task of informing people who believed they had a fortune in old Caruso records that in fact they had nothing more than an afternoon's entertainment, if they enjoyed opera. Records are not valuable merely because they feature a particular artist or are of a certain age. There are records from 1905 you can not give away, and then there are records from the early 1960's that command over $100.

Most of the records that are available today are valuable because they were originally produced in small supply for a limited audience and since have become popular with collectors. Examples of the kind of music that has undergone the transformation from limited appeal to major popularity include country western, blues, and jazz. Not all records from these categories are valuable. It is only the early recordings, *issued in small quantities*, that are valuable because they are scarce today. Once jazz had become popular, for instance, the public began buying tens of thousands of jazz recordings. Today, few of these later recordings are available. Common jazz records from the mid to late 1930's on are only worth a couple of dollars each.

I have also found that people believe certain popular singers to be valuable. Bing Crosby is the first name I hear when sellers are trying to impress me with the particulars of their collections. The truth is that except for his early recordings (before he began to record on Decca in 1934), Crosby 78's are a tough sell even at a buck. Because he was so popular in his day, hundreds of thousands of Crosby discs were pressed and most have survived until today.

The desirability and value of old records is also determined by the record label. There are over 1,000 different record labels known for all the 33's, 45's, and 78's produced during the last 80 years. Some of these labels are quite scarce, and a record bearing one of them will be valuable even if the music is not especially desirable. Familiarization with labels is unavoidable if one wants to become a knowledgeable record collector. Learning about labels is best accomplished by reading the books (see end of chapter) on collectible records and talking with other collectors.

COLLECTING. Discophiles, as record collectors call themselves, collect in many different ways. The most popular ways are by label, record speed (33,45,78), *performer*, and *musical genre*. I favor the last two ways because they encourage a collector to save what he enjoys listening to. I am continually amazed by the number of collectors who do not listen to their records and who are often more concerned with the fanatical goal of owning everything recorded on a particular label. Following is a list of the musical categories collectors pursue:

acid rock	foreign
big bands	hillbilly
bluegrass	jazz
blues	new wave
broadway musical	punk
celebrity	ragtime
classical	rhythm and blues
country western	rock and roll
dance band	string bands
fiddling	swing
folk	western swing

Depending upon which category(ies) you are interested in pursuing, you may want to think about narrowing your scope to focus on a particular artist or period. For example, rock and roll is far too large a category for the average collector. Most collectors of rock and roll choose to collect a few artists or records produced during a particular period. Determining which artists to pursue within a category requires sampling. Sampling means listening to the recordings of several different artists and reading about their lives. For instance, you might decide, after sampling blues artists, that you only want to collect Bessie Smith and Billy Holliday records. The library is a good source for sampling categories. City libraries often maintain large collections of 33's, many of which are rerecordings of classic jazz, swing, and ragtime, musicians.

Presently, records are one of the best collectible buys. At rummage, garage, church, and estate sales, one can always find several boxes of 45's, 33's, and 78's for sale in the 25¢–$2.00 range. I often think that the average person must believe that records are always scratched or incapable of producing a good sound once they have been used. This is untrue. Most of the records one finds for sale at the secondhand forums play 90 percent as well as they did when they were new. Often, they are also first pressings. Like serious book collectors who insist on buying the first edition, serious record collectors only want original issue records. An Elvis Presley original recording on the Sun label is worth many more times what a rerecording or reissue on a later, different, label is worth. Determining which label is the first pressing requires becoming familiar with the recording history of a particular artist. It can sometimes be a tricky business, and the guides and other collectors can be invaluable resources.

Record collectors are especially demanding when it comes to condition. A record that has lost its original sheen and is slightly scuffed is worth, even if it plays well, less than half what a mint record is worth. A cracked, chipped, or heavily warped record is valueless unless it is extremely rare. If you are buying records at a church sale or any other secondhand forum and the price is low, you don't have to be as careful about condition. If you buy 20 albums and find when you get home that 3 are slightly damaged, so what? At least you didn't risk losing any of the other 17 by taking the time to examine each record carefully. Reserve such close scrutiny for record shows or stores where you are paying collector prices. At these forums always examine each record in a well-lit area, moving the record into different angles so that all surfaces can be viewed. Dust or dirt alone is not a major problem, as either can be removed. A major defect like a gouge or crack, however, should prompt you not to buy the disc. Scratches are trickier. A light scratch that you can't feel when passing your index finger over it will probably not affect the play of the record. Deeper scratches you can feel will affect play.

Besides the record one must be conscious of the condition of the album cover (also called the slip jacket and illustrated cardboard sleeve). In the case of 50's and 60's rock and roll albums, the sleeve can be worth much more than the record. I remember once finding the album cover for the first American Beatles record. Years later when I reported my find to a record collector and asked him if it were possible to obtain the 33 that belonged in the sleeve, I was amazed to learn that the cover was worth $50, the record only $10. In some cases the little illustrated paper covers that protect 45's are also worth more than the record.

CARING FOR USING AND STORING RECORDS. Records should be stored in their sleeves in an upright position in a cool, dry area. Heat can melt records, and moisture can cause mold growth. Never store records in piles as this will warp them.

To clean records of dust use a soft, dry, lint-free cloth. Never use the silicone-impregnated cloths sold in record shops. If a record is particularly dirty, you can wash it under the tap using a mild soap and lukewarm water. When washing, always make sure to rinse the record well and avoid getting the label wet.

Never stack records on an automatic changer as this can damage them. If you wish to listen to your 78's on an antique wind-up machine (as many collectors do because of the authentic "old" sound produced), change the needle frequently. It is advisable to avoid playing records too often on an old wind-up as the weight of the stylus cutting into the record will eventually ruin it. I have made tapes of my favorite old records playing on a wind-up. In this way I can hear how the old machine reproduces the sound without ruining my 78's.

BOOKS

Docks, L.R. *1915–1965 American Premium Record Guide.*
     Florence, Al: Books Americana, 1982.

Koenigsberg, Allen. *Edison Cylinder Records 1889–1912.*
     Order from author at: 502 East 17th Street, Brooklyn, NY 11226.

Sorderbergh, Peter A. *Olde Records 1900–1947: Popular and Classical 78 rpms.* Des Moines: Wallace Homestead, 1980.

PERIODICAL

Goldmine Magazine
Box 187
Fraser, MI 48026

> 1 yr./12/issues $20; sample, $3. This is *the* publication for the record collector. Each issue features loads of buy/sell ads for all categories of music (on record) as well as articles and interviews.

CLUB

International Association of Jazz Record Collectors
Box 10208
Oakland, CA 94610

> 1 yr./$15, includes *IAJRC Journal*, which is issued quarterly, and the privilege of purchasing LP's at reduced rates. Club specializes in reproducing early jazz records and selling them inexpensively to members.

RELATED COLLECTIBLES—
PHONOGRAPHS AND RECORDED SOUND

Antique Phonograph Monthly
Allen Koenigsberg
502 East 17th Street
Brooklyn, NY 11226

> 1 yr./10 issues/$16. A newsletter with articles and buy/sell ads for phonographs, records, music boxes, player pianos, etc. Mr. Koenigsberg also sells reproduction phono catalogs, repair manuals, and other books for phonograph collectors. Send for catalog and information.

Association for Recorded Sound Collections
Les Waffen
Box 1643
Manassas, VA 22110

> 1 yr./$15, includes a quarterly newsletter and annual bulletin. The purpose of the association is "the preservation and study of historic recordings ranging across all fields of music from opera to rock."

Kastlemusick Inc.
901 Washington Street
Wilmington, DE 19801

Sample copy of their bulletin is $1. This club is for collectors of all recorded sound, with primary emphasis placed on early jazz and phonographic recordings. Write for more information.

The New Amberola Phonograph Co.
37 Caledonia Street
St. Johnsbury, VT 05819

2 yrs./8 issues/$5; sample, 75¢. A publication featuring articles and ads for record and phonograph collectors.

SPERDVAC

(Society to Preserve and Encourage Radio Drama, Variety, and Comedy)
J.A. Theodore
1175 Brockton Street
El Cajon, CA 92020

1 yr./$15, includes the use of the society's lending library of over 2,000 tapes of old radio programs, the monthly newsletter *Radiogram*, and opportunities to buy related items at a discount.

ROYAL DOULTON

Value range: low–high.

Most popular items: old and new character jugs (Toby jugs) and the older limited editions.

Good sources: For the currently issued Doulton products, buy from one of the wholesale mail order companies that advertise in the national collectibles publications.

THOUGH PRODUCED IN ENGLAND, Royal Doulton stoneware and ceramic figurines, jugs, and limited editions are so popular in America that it would be remiss not to include them in this book.

HISTORY. John Doulton began as an apprentice potter with the Fulham Pottery Company of London in 1805. By 1815 he had advanced sufficiently to become a partner with two others in a pothouse in Lambeth. For the first 10 years they produced mostly domestic stoneware such as flasks, bottles, jugs, and inkstands. Later they began to produce industrial containers. John Doulton's business prospered, and his two sons, Henry and John, Jr., eventually entered the ceramic production industry under their father's guidance.

During the 1840's each founded his own business. In 1853 John, Sr.'s sole remaining partner retired, and the two sons and their father merged their three companies to become Doulton and Company. The firm continued to do well by producing for the domestic and industrial market.

In 1873 John, Sr., died and Henry took charge. Under his direction the company acquired a Burslem pottery factory in 1882 and began to produce porcelain art pottery, lamps, and tableware. This was the beginning of what would become the line of art goods Royal Doulton is famous for today. In 1897 Henry died and was succeeded by his son, Lewis, who continued the development of the company's art line. It was Lewis who decided to concentrate on the manufacture of figurines, character and Toby jugs, and other artware. Royal Doulton collectors of today can thank him.

COLLECTING. Royal Doulton has produced and still produces figurines, character jugs (known as Toby jugs), tableware, animals, mugs, vases, tumblers, and limited editions. Of these, the most desirable for collectors are the older Toby jugs and the limited editions produced in the 30's in editions of around 600.

The early Toby jugs can usually be picked up in nice condition for somewhere near the high end of the medium value range. The limited editions are somewhat more expensive and often bring in the middle of the high value range. Be careful not to confuse the limited editions from the 30's with the later ones Doulton has put out. In the early 70's they began issuing limited-edition plates in enormous quantities (15,000 and up), and these, by dint of how many were made, are not good investments.

Doulton collectors have the option, not usually available to savers of collectibles, of collecting the old product or the one currently being produced. For the older stock, the usual sources for collectibles are fine. For the brand-new editions, however, I would suggest that you hook up with one of the mail order houses that wholesales Doulton items at up to 40 percent off the list price you will have to pay if you buy in a retail shop. These wholesale houses advertise in the national collectibles publications.

BOOKS

Kovel, Ralph and Terry. *Illustrated Price Guide to Royal Doulton*. New York: Crown, 1980.

Pollard, Ruth. *Official Price Guide to Royal Doulton*. Orlando, FL: House of Collectibles, 1980.

SODA CANS

Value range: low

Most popular items: early "cone top" cans produced in the late 30's and early 50's.

Good sources: for free at abandoned dump sites.

SODA CAN COLLECTING has been growing in popularity since 1975. Although millions of cans have been produced, most are discarded or recycled after they have been drained. For this reason many early examples of popular soft drink cans are scarce, and collectors will pay into the medium value range to obtain choice cans.

HISTORY. The use of the can for packaging did not catch on as quickly as it did for beer. The earliest trials were conducted by the Cliquot Club Company of Millis, Massachusetts, in 1938. They test marketed their Ginger Ale in a cone-top-type can, which resembles the kind of container brake fluid is sold in today. The experiment proved unsuccessful as the citric acid in the beverage ate through the can's lining. It was not until 1950 that any company seriously considered canning soda again. Canned beer had become extremely popular, and this fact led the Pepsi-Cola Company to test market a canned cola. This time the problem was that the cans were not strong enough to contain the carbonation. If slightly shaken they would explode. Another setback.

The eventual perfection and success of the soda can was to come as the result of the great potential market the major American can companies envisioned. They spent a fortune on research and development, knowing that if they succeeded in producing a good soda can, the market was there. In 1953 they came up with an improved metal container. This early model was a cone top like its predecessor. It sold for nearly twice as much as its glass counterpart but caught on anyway out of novelty and the ease of not having to return it for a deposit. As cans became popular they were modified to have flat tops so that they could be stacked. The onslaught had begun. Today, the wildest dreams of the can producers has come true with cans accounting for over 60 percent of the soda market.

COLLECTING. Soda can collecting is a relatively new hobby and is very easy to get into. Most collectors begin by acquiring all the different cans currently on the market. When they travel, they make a point of picking up regional varieties to add to their collection.

A special place for canaholics in search of rare cans is the village dump. There, particularly in the drier regions of the country, one may find old cone tops in collectible condition. Even with a little rust certain cans are a proud addition to any collection.

Another method employed to find cans is to ask at candy shops and soda fountains that have been in business for a number of years. Collectors often come across old cases of pop hidden under some rubbish in the basement of a store.

At present the hobby is rather undeveloped and there are no major clubs or conventions. Soda cans are usually sold at breweriana shows, though, and once in a while at general collectible shows. Regarding price, there have been some reports of cans selling for up to $100. In general, however, prices seem to be well within the low range, and one should not have to spend more than a few dollars a can in assembling a collection. For the future, it looks like the shift toward all-aluminum cans will result in a premium eventually being placed on steel and alloy containers.

BOOK

Toepfer, Betty. *Soda Cans Old and New*. Published privately
  in 1976 by L-W Promotions, Box 69, Gas City, IN 46933.

SPORTS CARDS

Value Range: low. A few exceptional cards featuring the most famous football players and boxers have brought into the medium value range.

Most popular items: sports cards featuring the superstar players of yesterday and today.

Good sources: new sets wholesale from mail order dealers; older cards at conventions and from private connections.

DURING THE LAST SEVERAL YEARS there has been an explosion of collector interest in baseball cards while other sports cards have been overlooked. Now, however, as certain baseball cards have become too expensive, collectors are beginning to pay greater attention to the cards produced from the 19th century to present that feature other sports. For this reason a separate chapter is devoted to boxing, football, hockey, and basketball cards.

HISTORY. The earliest sports cards produced were used as inserts in cigarette packs during the 1880's. They helped protect the fragile cigarettes as well as serving as promotions. Different series of champion boxers were among the early issues. The cards were beautiful, featuring a color lithograph of a boxer on the front and his fight record on the back. Of course, the requisite tobacco plug was also included somewhere on the card.

Pugilism was perhaps the most popular American sport prior to World War I, and the number and quality of boxing cards produced afterward would never match the early tobacco cards. In fact, since 1951 there has not been a single series of fight cards.

During the early T-card (for tobacco card) period on through the early 20's and 30's and the E-card (denoting candy cards), the only other sports that were featured prominently on cards were hockey and track. Occasionally a company would include a famous swimmer or strongman.

In 1933 the first sign of America's new fascination appeared on the Goudey Sports King series in the form of Knute Rockne. Two years later the National Chicle Company produced the first full series devoted strictly to football. It consisted of only 36 players and did not attract enough attention from the baseball-mad public. Lack of interest and the upcoming war years, which saw a lapse in all card production, combined to keep football cards off the market until 1948. In that year a newcomer in the field called the Bowman Gum Company issued a 108-player set. In addition, they also produced the first basketball card series. While the latter did not catch on, the football cards did and to date at least one company has produced a series each year.

Basketball cards were not resurrected until 1958 when the Topps Bubble Gum Company, of baseball-card fame, tried their hand at a series. The set was not successful. To date, basketball cards have been produced irregularly, never seeming to garner the popularity necessary to ensure their production.

Hockey's tremendous popularity in Canada led eventually to

the formation of American leagues and divisions. During the 50's, Topps and the Parkhurst Company began issuing series featuring American and Canadian players. By 1964 Parkhurst was out of business, but Topps continued to produce sets and has up until this day.

COLLECTING. The best place to begin collecting sports cards, regardless of one's age, is the local candy, stationery, or drugstore that stocks the current cards. At these stores you will be able to see the kinds of cards that are on the market today. You may want to buy a few packs to learn about such details as how many cards make up a series, their format, their design. Many collectors of older cards also save some of the newer series as a way of maintaining continuity between past and present.

To buy the older cards, you must go to one of the selling forums. Of these, the best place to buy old sports cards is at a baseball card convention. Dealers of baseball cards *always* stock other sports cards as well. This is also true of dealers who do mail order. Fortunately, sports cards are still available at a modest price. A 70-year-old tobacco card featuring a painted pose of Gentleman Jim Corbett or John L. Sullivan can be bought for as little as $3. Cards featuring popular football players from the 50's are plentiful at 75¢.

The most popular ways of collecting sports cards are by *sport*, *team*, *player*, *era*, and *type*. Select a category that is large enough to be interesting but not so large as to be impossible. To undertake to collect, for instance, all the boxing cards ever produced would be a monumental task. Choosing to collect all the boxing cards of a particular company would be more reasonable. Collecting by type can be fun and means that you try to obtain one example of all the different varieties of cards produced for a particular sport. I once saw a type collection of boxing cards that began in the 1880's and stopped with the last boxing card in the 50's.

People who buy for investment should try to obtain examples of the superstars in a particular sport. The yearly increase in value of cards featuring greats like Namath, Rockne, Dempsey, and Orr is much greater than the increase in cards featuring average players. Investors must make sure to buy only cards in superior condition. No matter how old the card is it must look the way it did when it emerged from its candy or cigarette pack to be considered high grade. Many collectors liked to glue the early cards into albums and so one finds that many cards offered today have glue stains and pieces of their backing removed. Avoid these cards unless you can buy them for very little (about 20 percent of the mint price) and do not mind owning them.

BOOK

Beckett, James and Dennis Eckes. *The Sport Americana Football, Hockey, Basketball, and Boxing Card Price Guide.* Published in 1981 by Den's Collectors Den, Box 606, Laurel, MD 20810.

PERIODICALS

Card Prices Update
Box 500
Seldon, NY 11784
   Issues a quarterly price update on the major football card series.

Sports Collectors Digest
Krause Publications
700 E. State Street
Iola, WI 54990
   1 yr./26 issues/$13.50. Features buy/sell ads and some articles.

SPORTS MEMORABILIA

Value range: low–very high. A majority of the items available fall within the low value range.

Most popular items: anything once owned or autographed by one of sport's greatest athletes, e.g., Ruth, Gehrig, Cobb, Rockne, Dempsey, Joe Louis, etc.

Good sources: sports collectible shows, mail order dealers, and private connections.

THE POPULARITY OF SPORTS memorabilia can be traced to the media, which throughout the 20th century has been more and more successful at creating and then apotheosizing sports celebrities. The devotion of many fans to their sports heroes is amazing: The country wants and needs heroes, and our spectator sports have long provided them. Today, fans have a new way to worship their heroes: sports memorabilia. Sports memorabilia describes thousands of items in some way related to one of over 25 different sports played in the United States. It can be something as prosaic as the back of a cereal box with a photograph of Babe Ruth to something as esoteric as the singlet worn by Eammon Coghlan when he broke the record for the indoor mile.

Sports memorabilia can be of a *personal nature*, meaning that an item was once owned, used, or touched by a famous athlete, or it can be of a *peripheral nature*, meaning that it relates to a particular sport or athlete but was never touched. Examples of items of a personal nature are uniforms, autographs, balls, equipment, personal effects, and jewelry. Examples of items of a peripheral nature include pennants, programs, yearbooks, scorecards, souvenirs, books, advertising pieces, and novelties.

The most popular sports memorabilia come from baseball and boxing. Football, hockey, and basketball items are the next most popular, followed by memorabilia from the following sports:

bobsledding	karate	surfing
bodybuilding	Olympic sports	swimming
bowling	Ping-Pong	track
car racing	pool	volleyball
golf	road racing	weight lifting
horse racing	sailboat racing	wrestling
judo	skiing	

To begin collecting, one must first determine which sport one is interested in. The popular sports mentioned earlier lend themselves very well to the collecting of memorabilia, whereas the more obscure sports, like pool or Ping-Pong, present a challenge. If you decide to collect items related to a major sport like baseball or football, you will have to find some way of narrowing down your field of pursuit. Most collectors choose a team, player, or manager to center their collections around.

Say you were interested in baseball and chose to collect items related to the New York Yankees baseball team. On the personal level you could spend a lot of money acquiring autographs, uniforms, balls and bats, personal effects, jewelry, and awards that relate to the team. On the peripheral level you could spend much less money accumulating Yankee programs, yearbooks, scorecards, souvenirs, newspaper clippings, magazine articles, books, and advertising pieces.

You might find, however, that collecting items related to the Yankees is too broad a category and that it is necessary to further narrow your scope by collecting only certain items or items related to a particular player or two. There are a number of possibilities, and you should decide in which direction your collection will develop according to personal desires. There are no rules. Following is a look at several categories of sports memorabilia.

AUTOGRAPHS. An autograph is anything, ranging from a mere signature to a long letter, written in the hand of a celebrity. Autographs are one of the most popular categories of sports memorabilia. Collectors save signed balls, programs, jerseys, bats, hats, uniforms, bank drafts, in short anything that has been autographed by the athlete. The autograph captures a "piece" of the person, and many collectors place special value on an item that has been signed by one of their heroes. Autographed sports items are available from many sources, the best of which are mail order dealers and dealers at sports collectible shows. You can purchase anything from an extremely rare signature of a 19th century boxer to a more common 1970's vintage signed baseball.

If you are interested in obtaining the autographs of living sports figures, I recommend the personal solicitation method. This involves sending an index card, a SASE, and a brief note to the person you are interested in, *care of* the team they play for. Whether they are retired or not, athletes who have team affiliation, as in the case of surfers, bowlers, roadrunners, etc., an address can probably be found for them by checking the *Who's Who in American Sports* at the library. If this fails, check through sports magazines. That obscure bobsledder who at first seems impossible to reach could be just a one-message-unit "information call" away if you find out, through reading an interview or article that he lives in Dublin, New Hampshire.

When writing to celebrities, try to draw them into responding with more than just a signature. This can often be accomplished by asking a question or two or by mentioning your own particular interest in the sport. Some collectors send programs, pictures, and other articles through the mail for the star to autograph. In the event that you are interested in a former athlete whose better days are behind him, there is a good chance that you will receive a nice letter in response to your solicitation.

Many collectors don't realize how happy most sports figures are to hear from the fans, particularly figures who have been out of the limelight for years. I know one collector of Olympic items who has even arranged visits with former Olympians and their families. A visit, besides providing the ecstasy of meeting one's hero in the flesh, can also be the means for acquiring a personal memento or two. In fact, much of the personal type material (autograph letters, medals, jewelry, trophies, etc.) that has reached the collector's market has been brought there by dealers and collectors who made contact with sports figures and then bought items they were willing to sell.

SPORTS PARAPHERNALIA AND PERSONAL EFFECTS. The paraphernalia and personal effects of famous athletes are collected for two reasons. One, having been owned and used by a star, an item is believed to retain some of the star's vibrational or spiritual energy, and so a collector who owns such an item is in the possession of a little part of his hero. Two, the item may have been part of an important event in sports history, e.g., the baseball hit by Hank Aaron on his 600th home run.

The value of paraphernalia and personal effects varies according to the popularity of the particular athlete or the magnitude of the event in which the item was featured. Collectors of items from offbeat sports are fortunate, because demand, even for relatively important pieces, is small. A baseball signed by Ruth can bring $200, while a cue autographed by Willie Mosconi (thought to be one of the greatest poolplayers ever) may not fetch $50.

To collectors interested in buying items from within this category, I strongly advise the following: Never buy unless proper documentation can be provided. Ersatz memorabilia is often offered by sellers with vivid imaginations. For instance, I was offered a baseball uniform supposedly worn by Ty Cobb. The uniform was "period" but bore no identifying marks. There were no accompanying papers and therefore no way of proving that the uniform was Ty Cobb's. Be careful. The best source for acquiring items is the family of the athlete or a dealer representing that family.

JEWELRY, TROPHIES, AND MEDALS. In certain sports, baseball and football for example, jewelry is created and distributed to the players on the winning team of the major event such as the World Series, or the Superbowl. This jewelry has come to collectors' marketplaces over the years as desperate, destitute, or angry players have sold their once-cherished rings, cufflinks, and other jewelry to fans and dealers. Sports jewelry can be quite expensive, as in the case of World Series rings, which are worth a minimum of $500. Again, the value of a particular piece will depend on the popularity of the sport and the stature of the player to whom the piece belonged. If a piece of Mantle sports jewelry came on the market, no price would be too high.

Sports trophies and medals, like sports jewelry, are items produced and distributed to winning team members or individual athletes. Value varies according to the popularity of the sport and the importance of the trophy or medal. There are many bargains available in the less popular sports. For instance, I have seen early 20th century sterling silver trophies from the Larchmont Yacht Club selling at slightly over the scrap value of the silver and third and fourth place Olympic medals from various Olympic games offered for under $20.

PROGRAMS, YEARBOOKS, AND OTHER SPORTS PAPER COLLECTIBLES. Except for early major league World Series programs (pre-1930), most sports programs, yearbooks, and other paper items (tickets, menus, magazines, newspaper clippings) can be obtained for relatively little money considering their scarcity and historical importance. I recently bought a beautifully printed

1893 program for a Harvard/Yale baseball game. It cost me only $6, and I think the dealer was happy to see it go. The point is that although there probably are not even a dozen of these programs still in existence, there is no real demand for college baseball items. A much more common 1903 World Series program, on the other hand, is worth $3,000, and there are several collectors anxiously looking to obtain a copy.

Interest in, and demand for, the sport are the determining factors in value. If college baseball becomes a hot collectible area, my Harvard/Yale program could be worth $500. Fortunately for collectors, most sports paper is still affordable. Tickets to boxing matches, for instance, can often be picked up for a few dollars. I bought a Dempsey vs. Gibbons ticket (ringside was $50 back then!). It cost only $5. Olympic programs are also relatively inexpensive, especially considering how interesting they are. I know a man who collects only Olympic sports paper and has items for every game back to the first modern event held in Athens in 1896.

Some collectors supplement their collections of other kinds of sports memorabilia by assembling scrapbooks of tie-in articles, magazines and newspaper clippings, and photos. The most complete Mickey Mantle collection I have ever seen included every article or sports blurb that appeared in the *New York Times* while the Mick was playing. Usually such a scrapbook will not have much monetary value; however, assembling this sort of a collection costs almost nothing and can provide hours of enjoyment.

A good source for obtaining copies of old newspaper or magazine clippings is the library. Most large branches have microfilms and microfiche of all the popular 20th century magazines and newspapers. One boxing collector I know spends his Saturdays searching day by day through microfiche of old New York newspapers. When he comes upon a fight story, he has a copy made. He has a gigantic scrapbook filled with articles and features and hopes one day to write a history of the sport. Other sources for clippings are copies of old *Life* and *Sports Illustrated* magazines. These can often be picked up for a quarter to 50¢.

SOUVENIRS. Sports souvenirs range from plastic soda cups, given away by McDonalds, depicting a likeness of a major league ballplayer to a key chain with an attached plastic Muhammad Ali doll. The best sports souvenirs feature a specific player or team, that is, they are *identifiable*. A plastic horse marked "Seattle Slew" is far more desirable than a similar, but unmarked, horse.

ADVERTISING PIECES. Sports advertising describes anything originally created to promote a product through sports. It can be a 19th century reverse painting on glass of a baseball player promoting a brand of tobacco, or it can be a recent cardboard counter display advertising free football cards in every box of Ring Dings.

Collectors buy advertising pieces to use as impressive wall hangings and decorations in their hobby rooms or dens and because they are historically interesting. A motivated collector can obtain current advertising pieces for free by becoming chummy with supermarket managers, deli owners, and bartenders. Most of these individuals throw the advertising away once the promotion has ended. A friendly word and regular patronage on your part can result in their saving desirable items for you.

PERIODICAL

Sports Collectors Digest
Krause Publications
700 E. State Street
Iola, WI 54990

1 yr./26 issues/$13.50; contains ads and articles for sports memorabilia.

STRAIGHT RAZORS

Value range: low.

Most popular items: elaborately etched blades of sailing ships, mottoes, and eagles. Attractive handles made of celluloid, sterling silver, ivory, and horn.

Good sources: old barbershops, flea markets.

MANY INDIVIDUALS UNDER the age of 40 have never used a straight razor, having grown up with Gillette razors and shaving cartridges. Often, the closest they have ever come to one of these ominous-looking tools is three feet, having observed it on the counter at a barbershop. The razor collectors are afoot, however, and given the way the hobby has been growing, it will be no time at all before the public is made well aware of antique straight razors.

HISTORY. Straight razors have been manufactured in some form for centuries. We will only concern ourselves here with the ones produced after 1800 either by or for the American trade.

For the first half of the 19th century, the United States depended mostly on the larger cutlery manufacturing cities of England, such as Sheffield, for straight razors. During this period only a handful of American firms produced razors. In the 1860's the famous German steel-producing city of Solingen began manufacturing razors for the American market. From this time on German and American razors began to edge out English razors. As mass production of blades became possible, the English product (which was expensive to produce) was priced out of the market. By 1930 the development of stainless steel 15 years earlier had led to the manufacture of safety razors, and the use of straight razors began to decline. Today, the straight razor is virtually extinct in American homes.

COLLECTING. There are four distinguishable elements to most straight razors produced after 1800. These are the tang, the blade, the shoulder, and the handle.

A collector learns to date any razor by examining the design and composition of these parts and observing any documentation that may be stamped into the blade or tang. For instance, early razors have little in the way of stamped information but can be identified by the absence of a distinct tang and shoulder.

The composition of the handle is very important in determining age. Prior to 1875 almost all razors had simple handles made of wood, horn, or ivory. Occasionally they were decorated with brass escutcheons or etched monograms. Handles did not become fancy, however, until the invention of celluloid in the late 1860's.

This inexpensive easily molded and colored material made it possible to mass produce brightly colored handles with intricate designs. Later, sterling silver handles were produced and were very
popular with the wealthy.

Another element of design is the etched blade. Beginning in
the 1830's companies began etching designs, scenes, and mottoes
on their blades. Some of these were beautifully done and featured
sailing ships, eagles, and early trains.

The most popular straight razors with collectors are not necessarily the oldest. Collectors pursue pieces that have the most
elaborately etched blades and attractive handles. Eye appeal is
most important, and an attractive art-deco-style handle will bring
a better price than a much rarer 19th century blade. Similarly, an
elaborately etched picture of an early sailing ship will appeal to
many more collectors than a crude 18th century razor.

Collectors will generally save by category. The most popular
ones are *age, size, country of origin, manufacturer, etched blade*, and
handle composition. The hobby is in its infancy, and most dealers
are only beginning to catch on. Watch out for overpriced pieces.

BOOK

Doyle, Robert A. *Straight Razor Collecting*.
Paducah, KY: Collector Books, 1980.

RELATED COLLECTIBLES

Powell, Robert Blake. *Occupational and Fraternal Shaving
Mugs of the U.S.* Order from author at: 1333 Kathryn Street, Box
833, Hurst, TX 76053

Organization of Shaving Mug Collectors
Mr. Deryl Clark
R.D. #6
Bedford, PA 15522

Write for information.

TEDDY BEARS

Value range: low–medium. A nice collection of new to old bears
can be assembled for between $10 and $35 apiece.

Most popular items: pre-1945 jointed bears made of mohair, old
and new Steiff bears, and the original Teddy from 1907.

Good sources: thrift and goodwill stores, flea markets and garage sales.

IT IS A DEPRIVED ADULT who cannot fondly recall those
scary nights when the thunder was cracking, the lightning flashing, and noble "Teddy" lay atop the pillow to guard against all
manner of dangers. Because of the mythic quality attributed to
these cuddly, warm creations, they have recently become extremely popular, and it seems only a matter of time before the
genuinely rare ones will begin showing up at the major auctions.

HISTORY. The actual origin of the Teddy bear is hotly de-
bated among "bearthusiasts." The most agreed-upon story, however, begins with President Theodore Roosevelt on a hunting trip
in Mississippi sometime in 1902. As the story goes, the president's
hunting party was in pursuit of some quarry. The advance team,
alerted by howling hounds, came upon a cornered old bear that
was almost dead from exhaustion. The hopeless creature was tied
to a tree, and the party awaited the president's arrival. When he
got there, Teddy (as he was known to his friends) was so taken
by the pitiful bear that he refused to shoot it or to have it shot;
and after a moment's contemplation he decided to have it set free.
The president's act of kindness was flashed across the nation during the following days in the form of a cartoon entitled "Drawing
the Line in Mississippi," which showed the president with his back
to a bear cub and his arm outstretched in refusal to do the bear in.
During the weeks that followed the press continued to publicize
the incident, and it was at this time that a struggling shopkeeper

in Brooklyn named Morris Michtom was thinking of how he could sell his wife's most recent sewing efforts. She had made some toy bears out of old pieces of fabric, excelsior, and shoe buttons. Morris brought the bears to his store to capitalize on the fuss being made over the president's incident. Thinking about the whole thing he had a brainstorm—why not call the toys Teddy's Bears. He sought the permission of the president and was granted it.

In no time the bears were selling faster than his wife could produce them. They hired workers and in the first two years of production sold over 8,000 pieces. By 1907 Morris and his wife were manufacturing over one million bears a year and had moved into a large factory. They became the Ideal Novelty Company (later to become the Ideal Toy Company).

Prior to 1907 the main competitor (and actually the largest seller of bears) for Morris and his wife was the German company Steiff. Their founder, Margarete Steiff, had fashioned a beautiful jointed bear in 1902, and it had become very popular all over the world. After 1907 many other American companies joined in producing bears. Since this time millions upon millions have been produced in every conceivable shape, size, expression, and quality.

COLLECTING. The most important thing to know is that collectors generally regard only those bears made before 1945 as antiques. More recent bears are also collected but are not regarded with the same reverence given to their ancestors. One must learn to tell which bears are old and which are not, so one won't end up paying the antique price for a recent item.

The best way to start is by going into a large toystore and examining the bears for sale there. The better stores will stock a large selection and will also carry the more expensive Steiffs (some of which cost over $100 new). The best pieces being produced today are made of mohair. Common, but still lovable, bears are made of a variety of compositions, including cotton, wool, synthetics, and even plastic. By handling the new product, you can become knowledgeable enough not to mistake brand-new bears for old ones. My recommendation for beginning collectors, however, is to buy only new bears or old ones that sell for prices in the low end of the low value range. A beautiful collection can be assembled this way and you avoid the possibility of making a mistake and getting stuck with an expensive fake or an inaccurately dated bear. If you have to buy the really expensive old pieces, work with a knowledgeable dealer.

The most popular ways of collecting are by *size* (bears from 4″ to 6′ have been made); *manufacturer* (Steiff still being the most popular); *color* (with brown by far the most popular); and *breed* (koala, panda, grizzly, black, etc.).

Serious collectors pay particular attention to whether a piece is in original condition or has been mended along the way. Repaired bears are worth less than their untouched counterparts. If you are handy with a needle and thread, and a new leg or eye does not offend your aesthetic sense, you can benefit by buying damaged bears and restoring them. Look for likely acquisitions at thrift stores and goodwill shops. Often, broken Teddys are overlooked at these places.

Collectors also collect according to whether a Teddy is "jointed" or "fixed." A jointed bear has his arms and legs attached so that they can be rotated 360 degrees. A fixed bear's limbs are sewn into position and cannot be arranged without crippling the animal. Some bears have "squeeze boxes" contained in their chest cavities, which produce various sounds when squeezed.

Although many collectors choose a particular category to pursue, the nice thing about bear collecting is that it doesn't have to be approached in a systematic way. Some collectors simply choose to buy bears that "speak" to them in some special way. What person could resist, for instance, purchasing the guardian Teddy of their childhood should he be encountered at a show or sale?

BOOKS

Bialosky, Peggy and Alan. *The Teddy Bear Catalog.*
New York: Workman, 1980.

Cantine, Marguerite. *Beggar T. Bear.* Published in 1981
by Elizabeth Kilpatrick, Box 798, Huntington, NY 11743. The book traces the history and significance of the American Teddy between 1903 and 1945.

Schoonmaker, Patricia N. *The Collector's History of the Teddy Bear*. Order from: Doll Research Projects, 6117 Denny Avenue, No. Hollywood, CA 91606.

PERIODICALS

The Teddy Bear
900 Frederick Street
Cumberland, MD 21502

   1 yr./4 issues/$9.95; for Teddy bear lovers.

The Teddy Bear News
Box 8361
Prairie Village, KS 66208

   1 yr./10 issues/$15; sample, $2; for true bear lovers.

CLUB

Good Bears of the World International
Box 8236
Honolulu, HI 96815

   1 yr. membership/$8, includes subscription to the quarterly *Bear Tracks*, which features articles and buy/sell ads on Teddy bears.

TOBACCO AND SMOKING COLLECTIBLES

Value range: low–medium. Most late 19th and 20th century smoking collectibles are available for prices within the low value range.

Most popular items: anything that is visually appealing and identifiable, e.g., an early pack of cigarettes marked with the company name and address.

Good sources: flea markets and collectible shows, old candy shops, tobacco stores, and other places where tobacco was sold 20 years ago.

HISTORY. The first Europeans to smoke tobacco were the Portuguese and Spanish explorers and seamen who reached the New World during the 15th century. Friendly natives were more than happy to share their primitive pipes with the "white gods." By 1550, tobacco was being grown in Europe for use as a medicinal plant. A Frenchman named Jean Nicot had isolated an element in tobacco he believed could cure a number of diseases. For his discovery, this element, nicotine, was named after him. Within 50 years the notion of tobacco as a curative had largely been abandoned, and tens of thousands of Europeans began smoking pipes simply for the pleasure of it. By 1604 the number of people smoking pipes in England had become so great that King James I, a noted hater of tobacco, published an anonymous pamphlet called *Counterblaste to Tobacco* in which he excoriated what he considered a disgusting, filthy habit. During the following 100 years tobacco went in and out of favor in different parts of Europe. As an alternative to smoking, the French perfected the art of sniffing it in a finely powdered form.

In 1815 cigar smoking became popular in France and Britain. Before this time cigar smoking had been limited to Spain, Portugal, some of the colonies, and to the Indians, who taught them all. The novelty of smoking tobacco in rolled form soon became the rage, and in 1844 the first cigarettes appeared in France. The French, happy to be the leaders of a new style, embraced the cigarettes with a passion, and soon all of Europe was ingesting smoke through hand-rolled cigarettes. By 1869 machinery had been developed to mass produce cigarettes, and they began their rise to an extraordinary popularity that did not wane anywhere until the first major discoveries, in the early 60's, that cigarette smoking was tied to lung cancer.

COLLECTING. Collecting tobacco and smoking items can be enriching from an historical standpoint. Collectors have a wide range of items to choose from, and most are not very expensive. Below is a list of the smoking items that are collected:

advertising pieces	cigar cutters
cigars	cigar labels
cigar boxes	cigarettes

cigarette dispensers
cigarette holders
cigarette packs
cigarette papers
lighters
match containers
match safes
matches
measuring blocks
measuring jars
pipe racks

pipe stems
pipes
smoking garments
snuff
snuff boxes
snuff pouches
snuff spoons
tobacco
tobacco cutters
tobacco pouches
tobacco stoppers

Following is a look at three of the most popular tobacco and smoking collectibles.

Cigarettes and tobacco: American companies began producing packs of cigarettes in the 1870's. These were marketed under brand names like Sweet Capporal, Piedmont, Polar Bear, Hindu, Sovereign, Old Mill. During this same period tobacco was also sold loose in paper pouches. Today collectors of cigarette packs and tobacco pouches consider pre-1900 examples of tobacco products (still unused and unopened) very rare and desirable.

Most collectors begin by trying to buy an example of every domestic brand of cigarettes or tobacco available. This base collection can be enlarged by (1) pursuing foreign brands, a pursuit especially popular with collectors who travel a lot, and (2) searching for older examples of cigarettes and tobacco at flea markets, collectible shows, old drugstores, candy shops, stationery stores, and tobacco shops. Prices at the shows range between $2 and $15 a pack. Occasionally one runs across a dealer who has found several cartons of an old brand and is selling them cheap.

Regarding the old stores as a source, a collector must be willing to develop his sleuthing abilities and "gabbing" skills if he hopes to find and buy old products. Often, owners of stores that are likely to have an antique carton of cigarettes nestled somewhere gathering dust need to be prodded gently before they will go into their storerooms to look for old products. The way you speak to them will often determine whether they brush you off by mumbling a negative or look up with interest and invite you back for a look. Collectors have told me of pretending to be professors doing research on the history of tobacco, writers doing an article on smoking in the U.S.A., and lawyers looking for a particular brand needed to win a lawsuit. Clearly, one must use imagination. Many eastern collectors have assembled wonderful collections of products dating back to the early 20th century by methodically combing likely stores and leads in the small towns that dot the eastern seaboard.

Lighters: The first cigarette lighters were made in France in the mid-19th century. Many of these were ingeniously devised but required too much fiddling with to make them practical. The first useful lighters, and the ones collectors more regularly encounter, appeared in the United States in the early 1900's. These lighters were primitive-looking metal contrivances consisting of a wick that had been dipped in some flammable liquid and a flint that would spark when a grooved little circle of steel was flicked. Today, collectors save lighters by *type, age,* and *size.* This first category consists of rechargeable butane, disposable butane, fluid, electric, flint, and non-flint lighters. There are combinations of the above types as well. There are no limitations on the way one can go about collecting lighters. I remember being at a party when a non-collector friend, finally motivated by all the collectors she knew, decided to collect, of all things, disposable butane lighters. None of us took her very seriously until a year later when she displayed her collection of over 200 different kinds of "disposable butes" from all over the world.

In terms of age, the most interesting lighters available are those that were handmade by soldiers in the trenches during World War I. These cleverly crafted lighters were made from buttons, coins, and a variety of other scrap metal objects that the soldiers had at their disposal. Tens of thousands of these lighters were made and then brought home after the war. Over the years they have made their way into the inventory of dealers and private collections. I have bought several, paying as little as $2 for one that was in a junk box. They are truly a bargain considering the history behind them.

Collectors who save lighters by size pursue examples sometimes as small as a nickel all the way up to large tabletop units imbedded in marble. It is best to decide on a general size range before you begin collecting. The best place to look for lighters is at flea markets, thrift shops, and garage sales. They have not yet become desirable collectibles, and you should never have to spend more than $20 unless, of course, the piece has some further value, as in the case of sterling silver lighters or one placed in an art deco holder.

For additional information on smoking collectibles, see under Ephemera (Paper) for matches and cigar labels and under Advertising.

PERIODICAL

The Pipe Smoker's Ephemeris
Tom Dunn
20-37 120th Street
College Point, NY 11356

> An irregular quarterly for pipe smokers and anyone else. Free copies may be obtained by writing to Mr. Dunn.

TOYS

> Value range: low–very high. For an explanation of pricing, see the particular categories of toys below.
>
> Most popular items: tin robots made in Japan in the mid to late 50's and early 60's. American tin toys featuring comic strip characters like Mortimer Snerd, Charlie McCarthy, Blondie and Dagwood, Superman, etc.
>
> Good sources: toy shows, general antique and collectible shows, and old stationery, candy, and five and dime shops that might have old stock in the storeroom or on the shelves.

TOY COLLECTING HAS always been popular, and for decades prior to the collectibles boom sophisticated hobbyists enjoyed the pleasures of collecting early tin, wood, and cast iron toys. Today, however, after 12 years of mounting collector interest, toys have become one of the most popular collectible groups. At toy auctions wealthy collectors regularly bid prices into the stratosphere. No price is too much it seems when a toy possessing special significance is being offered. There are over 70 different categories of toys that can be collected. Following is a list of these categories. Some of the headings refer to a genre, as, say, boats, which describe many varieties of floating toys. Other of the headings describe specific toy groups such as battery-operated or tin.

aircraft	friction
animal	frog
automobile	golf
banks	guns
battery-operated	horses
blocks	jack-in-the-box
board games	jacks
boats	jigsaw puzzles
busses	kitchen
candy	leaden
cap guns	Lincoln Logs
cast-iron	marbles
cats	marionettes
clockwork	motorcycles
comic-character	movie toys
Cracker Jack	owls
cyclist	paper
dogs	plastic
dolls	pop-up
elephants	premiums
erector sets	pull-toys
ferris wheels	puppets
figure	radio
fire	robot
flying saucer	rocket
folk art	rocking horse

Santa	trains
ship	trolleys
soldiers	vehicles
space	wagon
sports	Walt Disney
tanks	water pistols
Teddy bears	western
television toys	windup
tin	wooden
Tinker Toys	zeppelins

In addition to deciding which category (or categories) one would like to pursue, a collector must also determine which composition, country, and era he wants to collect. (In some cases the nature of the item will obviate the need for choice, as say with Lincoln Logs, which were made of wood, in this country, during a specific period.) The five main categories are *tin, cast iron, wood, glass,* and *plastic.* The four main toy-producing countries are England, the United States, Germany, and Japan. And the eras, though they vary among categories, are early 19th century, late 19th century, 1900–1925, 1926–1948, 1949–1969, and current.

Recently, Japanese tin, friction, and battery toys made during the 50's and 60's have joined older toys in capturing the interest of collectors. Prices have risen exponentially on some items. Certain robots that sold new for only a few dollars during the early and mid-60's are now worth over $1,000. They are popular because they mark the beginning of a new direction in toy production.

Toys appeal to collectors on several levels: (1) they are attractive; (2) they provide a link with one's childhood; (3) they are miniature examples of the technological level of a nation; and (4) they reflect the drives and mood of a society for a particular era.

An example of this last point is the plethora of space toys made during the 60's. They were a manifestation of this country's preoccupation with getting to the moon. Similarly, the video games of the late 70's and early 80's reveal our fixation with computer technology. Sociologists have said that if one wants to understand a society, one should start by examining its playthings.

Because the number of toy categories is far too numerous to

cover each separately, I have chosen to look at four major groups which encompass most of the toys produced in the last 300 years. These groups are *primitive, tin, cast-iron,* and *plastic* toys. Before going on to them, however, I have included some information that, although covered in Part One, is particularly important concerning toys.

The hobby is complex and full of the kind of pitfalls to which beginners are susceptible. When I first began collecting toys, I spent $1,400 on a collection of tin cars I was certain were from the 30's and 40's. They were not. In fact, they were from the late 50's and worth only $700. Let my blunder serve as a lesson teaching that *the way a toy looks does not always reveal its true age.* I have seen authentic 19th century tin toys that look like they were made yesterday. Which nicely leads to the point that some ostensibly antique toys *were made only yesterday.* Many companies have produced reproduction cast-iron fire engines, carriages, and automobiles. These are usually marked "reproduction" in the castings and are painted in modern colors; however, there are unscrupulous people who file them, pour acid over them, burn and bake them, and even bury them in coffee grinds in an effort to efface their reproduction stamp and modern color. Repainted in antique style, these toys then appear at antique and collectible shows and are sold for hundreds of dollars. One *must* put in the necessary time studying and learning about toys. You will make enough mistakes once you think you know what you are doing, so avoid buying until you have read books, attended auctions and toy shows, and picked dealers' brains.

PRIMITIVE TOYS. Before the earliest known tin and cast-iron toys, children had a variety of handmade wooden, paper, ceramic, and cloth toys. Such toys, made before the 1840's, are extremely rare today. The ones that have survived mostly reside in museums as examples of early American folk art. The advent of manufactured tin and cast-iron toys during the 1840's and later did not stop creative parents from making wonderfully imaginative and beautiful toys for their children.

Today, there are many collectors who pursue handmade toys of the mid to late 19th and early 20th century. For those who wish to pursue this field, the best place to begin is at a museum of American folk art, where one can view examples of what has been made and develop a feel for the look of desirable pieces. Some of the popular primitive toy categories are dolls, blocks, arks with animals, and models of ships, trains, and carriages. One should supplement the museum trip with readings on the subject of folk art and American primitive art. There is much to learn before one can tell the difference between a piece that has been poorly made and one that reflects the charming naiveté so desirable in primitive toys.

TIN TOYS. The earliest American toys manufactured to be sold were made of tin. Beginning in the 1830's craftsmen used hand presses to cut out patterns from sheets of tin, soldered these die-cut pieces together, and then hand painted and finished the toy. As the century advanced, industrial techniques improved toy manufacture. One of these improvements was a steam-generated machine that could mass produce die-cut parts. Another was the development of offset lithography, which eventually made possible the transfer of color images to tin.

During the 1850's tin toys began arriving from England and Germany. Later, French toys with complex clockwork mechanisms began appearing for sale to wealthy industrial families. The 1860's and 70's, however, were the years of great growth in American tin toy manufacture. Utilizing new techniques, companies produced thousands of tin horse-drawn carriages, milk carts, and moving vans.

Beginning around 1900, lithographed tin toys were produced in abundance. They began to outsell their hand-painted counterparts. At the same time, many windup toys began to appear, which were an inexpensive alternative to the elaborate clockwork mechanisms. From the turn of the century on, the toy business, spurred by industrial advances and a rapidly growing reservoir of new designs from the fledgling aviation and growing automobile industries, grew considerably. Every decade produced new wonders and themes, which would immediately be reproduced in miniature as toys. The popularity of 30's and 40's radio personalities and comic strip characters, for instance, led to the manufacture of Amos 'n' Andy, Popeye, Mortimer Snerd, Buck Rogers, and Blondie and Dagwood toys. Many of these toys marked the first use of new synthetics in toy manufacture. Prior to this time, only rubber, cloth, string, and glass has been used to adorn tin toys.

The 1950's is largely the story of the Japanese toy. Japan, just beginning her industrial revolution, began turning out inexpensive tin toys with friction, windup, and battery-operated motors. While many of these toys did not equal earlier American toys in quality, the Japanese models ushered in the new technology of gadgetry. The Japanese made robots that could walk, talk, bump into walls, and automatically reverse; vehicles with flashing lights and whirring sirens; and comic character toys that were imitative of U.S. versions. The Japanese domination in tin toys lasted until the late 60's, at which point it stopped, primarily because Japanese companies saw that they could be more profitable producing color TVs and stereos rather then 89¢ toys. Also, a series of safety laws were enacted in the late 60's requiring that tin toys meet certain regulations. Many children had been severely cut by sharp tin edges and exposed metal tips. By 1975 one could no longer buy an all-tin toy in the United States. The companies in Taiwan and Hong Kong that had bought die patterns from defunct Japanese toy companies began producing toys with plastic bodies and, occasionally, a little tin.

Recently, China, just beginning her industrial revolution, has started exporting beautiful tin toys that are reminiscent of the best ones produced during the 50's and early 60's (of which many of them are in fact copies). They are brought into the United States classified as adult consumer goods, thus evading the stringent toy safety laws. One high-class New York department store chain launched a major advertising campaign pushing some of the more elaborate Chinese "battery ops" as the perfect Christmas gifts of nostalgia.

For collecting purposes, tin toy production can be divided into eras. There are four major divisions: the early period, 1830–1899; the second wave, 1900–1919; the new style, 1920–1941; and the modern period, 1945–1969. Generally, the first two eras are the most expensive to collect from. Early tin toys in desirable condition usually cost a minimum of $300. Most sell for over $500, and it is not exceptional to see examples bring thousands. The best, and sometimes the only, places to buy them are at antique toy shows and auctions. Dealers there usually know about what they are selling, and you will have the opportunity to browse.

Third-era toys are more affordable to collect than those produced earlier. Many small windup vehicles and animals can be obtained in fine condition for as little as $20 from dealers at flea markets and general collectible shows. More popular items like the comic strip character toy are going to cost much more. A pair of Amos 'n' Andy walking toys, mint in their original boxes, brought over $1,800 at one toy auction. Record prices have also been set by high-grade Walt Disney character toys.

Toys from the fourth era are the best ones to begin collecting today. They are plentiful (many still in their original boxes) and usually cost less than $50. If one is thinking of investing in toys, this is the area that will likely see the most appreciation in coming years. Except for certain robots, space, and comic character toys, which already have become extremely expensive, Japanese friction, windup, and battery-operated toys from the 50's to mid-60's are underpriced.

When buying toys from this era, look for the ones that have a special "look." Having a look usually describes a toy *made in a style that is no longer popular*. One can develop an appreciation for the desirable look by first becoming familiar with the look of toys presently being made. You will probably feel an immediate affinity for the Japanese toys of the 50's and 60's if you grew up in those decades.

When buying toys from the modern era, try to obtain them in top condition. The original box is desirable and can increase the value up to 30 percent. Be particularly careful to look for rust or corrosion in the battery box caused by leakage from past batteries. Also be careful to check for a MADE IN JAPAN mark on toys that are supposed to be of Japanese origin. There has been a fair amount of cheating done by disreputable individuals who sell recent Chinese and Taiwanese imports as 50's vintage Japanese toys. The former are not nearly as well made as the toys they imitate and often will have a number of plastic parts. Plastic is presently undesirable in collecting circles and is often the tipoff that a toy is not old. Desirable vintage Japanese tin toys seldom have more than a small piece or two of plastic ornamentation. (Plastic toys are discussed later in this chapter.)

Following is a list of the larger manufacturers producing tin toys during the last 100 years:

American	German	Japanese
Automatic Toy	Bing	Alps
Carter	Fisher	Bandai
Chein	Lehmann	Cragstan
Girard	Marklin	HoriKawa
Gilbert	Nifty	Modern
Marx	Schucco	TM
Selrite	Stock	TN
Straus		ST
Unique Art		SSS International
Wolverine		Yone

CAST-IRON TOYS. The first cast-iron toys appeared after the Civil War and were made by American companies. Very few cast-iron toys ever came from abroad. These were produced through a variety of processes, the most common of which was sand casting. The most popular of the ones made before 1900 were the mechanical banks (see pages 211–217). Cast-iron vehicles of all sorts did not become very popular until the 1920's. The war years hurt the cast-iron toy business because industry and raw materials were needed to produce armaments. After the war a few companies tried to resurrect the cast-iron toy but could not compete with the growing popularity of inexpensive tin windup toys. Today, the only cast-iron toys being sold are reproductions of earlier models.

The most important first step in collecting authentic cast-iron toys is learning how to detect fakes. As mentioned earlier, there are a number of ways in which reproductions are transformed into ersatz originals. Acquiring the ability to spot these clinkers can only be accomplished through handling a number of originals and reproductions and seeing the differences between them. The repros are usually not as well cast and will feel grainy to the touch. The way the piece has been fit together may also be a clue; reproductions are notoriously uneven.

Another problem frequently encountered is the original piece that has been repainted. Many collectors will not buy these, feeling that they have been altered. A repainted piece should sell for 20 to 40 percent less than a similar untouched example.

One also finds toys that have had their original parts replaced with reproduction pieces. These "mutts" are even less desirable than repainted toys. Don't buy on your own until you are certain you can tell the difference between good and bad toys. Test yourself when in the company of someone who knows more than you. There are a large number of fakes on the market.

The best place to buy is at toy and antique shows. The most popular cast-iron toys are colorful horse-drawn sulkies and fire engines and early gasoline-powered vehicles. Early examples (pre-1910) bring $300 to $5,000, depending on size and condition. Later toys can be obtained for less. The Stanley Company produced several lightweight cast toys during the late 40's and 50's that sell for only $40 to $100.

PLASTIC TOYS. Many toy collectors are repulsed by plastic. They identify it with all that has gone wrong with toy production. To them, it is the epitome of uncreative manufacturing processes. Except for a few robots, which are plastic but still desirable because they are robots, plastic toys have few supporters. Most collectors of Japanese and American toys will only tolerate owning pieces that sport at most a plastic figure or a bit of plastic ornamentation. Some of the finest collections of toys conspicuously stop at the beginning of the all-plastic (or mostly plastic) era in the mid-60's.

It is for these reasons that I think plastic toys will one day be quite valuable. In my travels to various shows and sales of all kinds, I seldom see American or Japanese plastic toys from the mid- to late 60's. Few collectors realize that although dyed plastic is not as attractive as tin lithography, the former is more fragile and fewer pieces will survive. The irony of the situation is that many toy collectors used to regard the early Japanese tin toys (now worth hundreds of dollars in some cases) the same way they now regard plastic toys. Because the Japanese tin toys were ignored until their production ceased, many are now scarce and have become valuable. I suspect the same thing will happen with plastic toys.

For toy collectors who are either cash poor or do not mind plastic, now is the time to begin purchasing American and Japanese plastic toys made between 1964 and 1975. Trends reveal that toys that portray space, television, and movie themes and characters will be particularly popular during the next 15 years. Examples of such toys would be rocket ships with the NASA insigne, vehicles and guns from *The Man from U.N.C.L.E.* and *Star Trek* television series, and toys based on models from James Bond films and other movies. As always, try to obtain examples that are in the best possible condition. Toys that are still in their original boxes are especially desirable. Avoid pieces with broken plastic parts, as these are impossible to repair without leaving traces of the mend.

BOOKS

Ayers, William S. *The Warner Collector's Guide to American Toys.*
New York: Warner Books, 1981.

Harmon, Kenny. *Comic Strip Toys.*
Des Moines: Wallace Homestead Books, 1975.

O'Brien, Richard. *Collecting Toys.*
Florence, AL: Books Americana, 1982.

Schoss, Martyn L. *A Guide to Mechanical Toy Collecting.*
Order from: Performance Media, 167 Terrace Street, Haworth, NJ 07641

PERIODICALS

Antique Toy World Magazine
3941 Belle Plaine
Chicago, IL 60618

1 yr./12 issues/$15. This is *the* magazine for toy collectors, featuring articles, buy/sell ads and convention information for the whole country.

Playthings
Box 1129
Dover, NJ 07801

1 yr./12 issues/$15; sample, $3. A magazine geared to merchandisers

of toys and crafts. Good for those collectors who wish to see what kinds of toys are currently available.

RELATED COLLECTIBLES

MARBLES

Marble Collector's Society of America
Box 22
Trumbull, CT 06611

1 yr. dues/$10. Entitles members to all the club's publications during the year.

PLASTIC MODELS

Kit Collectors International
Box 38
Stanton, CA 90680

1 yr./$12, includes a subscription to the bimonthly *Vintage Plastic*, as well as other club publications and discounted offerings. For all collectors of model kits.

TOY SOLDIERS

Johnson, Peter. *Toy Armies*.
    New York: Doubleday, 1981.

Old Toy Soldier Newsletter
209 N. Lombard
Oak Park, IL 60302

1 yr./6 issues/$12. Contains articles on toy soldier companies like Britains, Barclay, Manoil, Mignot, Lineol, Elastolin, Johillco, and others. Also has ads for buying and selling.

TRADE CARDS

Value range: Except for some extremely rare "clipper ships" cards, which can go into the high value range, most trade cards are available for between 50¢ and $12.

Most popular items: cards with brilliant color lithography depicting recognizable brand names, such as Hershey's Cocoa, A&P, etc., and cards depicting children, horse sports, agriculture, and cosmetics.

Good sources: from dealers who will sell an entire album that can be processed to produce a number of collectible cards; through the mail.

THE TRADE CARD WAS most popular in America during the years 1870–1900. During this time millions of these often beautiful cards advertising goods and services were produced and circulated through the mail, by salesmen, and at stores. Today, they are collected for a variety of reasons, the most popular of which are historical and aesthetic.

HISTORY. Trade cards have been produced for hundreds of years, but the ones collectors are concerned with became popular during the 1870's. At this time the art of printing had reached the stage where inexpensive production of color lithographed cards became possible. This occurred at the same time as a major spurt in the growth of American consumer business. Unlike their modern counterpart, the business card, trade cards usually featured color artwork depicting a scene indicative of the type of business being advertised. A chemist, for instance, might have a picture of medicine bottles drawn up; a dairyman might use a drawing of cows.

Cards came in many different sizes, ranging from very small to almost ten inches in length. Most were around three by five, however. Cards were used to promote events, advertise the services of a tradesman, and to push a particular product. The cards flourished between the years 1880 and 1900. All businesses used them, and millions of cards were produced. After 1905, for no special reason, the country seemed to lose interest in them and within ten years hardly any companies still used them. It was as if their novelty had worn off all at once.

COLLECTING. In the last several years the trade card has begun to follow most other collectibles in an inflationary spiral. Cards that were once around a half a dollar are now selling for three dollars and up. The hobby is still young, however, and this information is not meant to discourage budding collectors, who can still assemble a nice collection rather inexpensively.

To actually hold and examine a wide variety of cards, the best place to begin is an antique paper show. Another avenue, though, is flea markets and collectible shows. Many dealers know about the popularity of the trade card and bring shoeboxes full of them to their shows.

Condition is very important with cards, and the most desirable ones are crisp, clean, and free from any errant marks, tears, or creases. The perfect card looks just as it did when it was made. Collectors usually find that in order to assemble a collection, however, they must be willing to compromise in terms of condition. Trade cards were very popular among collectors even in the late 19th and early 20th centuries, and many were pasted into albums and scrapbooks. These books often surface and can serve as an inexpensive source for obtaining a wide variety of cards. Most dealers are willing to sell them for much less than the total of the value of the cards in them because of the amount of work that must be invested to remove the cards from the album.

To remove cards from an album, take the album apart and soak its pages in tepid water until the old paste begins to loosen. Once this happens, the tricky part begins—pulling each card off without destroying its back or ripping it. If you work carefully, you should get the card off intact. Residual glue must be rubbed off with the fingertips so that the card will not stick to the newspaper on which it will be placed to dry. Drying usually takes a day. When almost all of the moisture has evaporated out of the cards, the last step is to place the cards on a dry newspaper, cover them with more newspaper, and then press them with books. If done correctly, the collector will end up with beautiful examples for his collection. The process is actually very similar to the one stamp collectors use to remove stamps from envelopes. With practice, one can become quite adept.

Cards are collected by category. The most popular categories are *music, sports, sewing, agriculture, cosmetics, horses,* and *children.* There is no limit to the way one can collect. There are some who pursue cards originating from a particular town or city. Others collect cards of only one size. Try to find a category that appeals to you.

Another source for obtaining cards is to establish contact with one of the reputable dealers who sell through the mail on approval. Receiving cards through the mail can be nicer than having to contend with the various pressures of a convention atmosphere. Most mistakes are made when you are too tired to remember to look for signs of a card having been cut down or repaired. Many times dealers inadvertently attempt to sell pieces that resemble trade cards but which are not, having been cut out of larger paper items. Remember that the generally accepted rule with paper is that one can do anything to an item that does not add or subtract a natural ingredient. Therefore, soaking away glue or removing a stain or pencil mark is permissible, while trimming an edge or coloring in a section is not. Do not buy cards that have been altered.

BOOK

Barry, Kit. *The Advertising Trade Card.* Published by the
   author and available from him at 86 High Street, Brattleboro, VT
   05301.

TRAINS

Value range: low–very high.

Most popular items: Lionel trains are the most widely collected toy trains. Of the Lionel line, "post-war O gauge" is the most popular.

Good sources: train meets and private connections.

HISTORY. The first toy trains made in this country were produced by the Ives Company during the 1880's. These early trains were powered by a clockwork mechanism that propelled the engine when wound. Children and adults alike were fascinated by trains, and during the late 19th century German and French manufacturers exported toy trains to the United States. In 1900 the Lionel Train Company was founded by Joshua Lionel Cowen. By 1915 Cowen's large "standard gauge" electric trains were becoming well known among wealthy families who could afford to provide extensive layouts for their children. In this year Cowen produced an "O gauge" line, which was smaller and more affordable than the standard gauge.

Ives and the European companies could not compete with the quality and appeal of the Lionel product. By 1928 Lionel had bought Ives out and was number one in the country with an extensive line of trains and accessories. In the 30's this line was expanded to include magnificently detailed steam engines and such famous sets as the Blue Comet and the 408-E Apple Green. The Depression, however, hurt Lionel, and many of their most beautiful, but expensive, trains remained in inventory until the economy began to improve. In 1934 Lionel came out with the now-famous Mickey Mouse Hand Car, which sold for a dollar (collectors now pay over $500 for high-grade examples) and helped revive the company.

Lionel's main domestic competitor was the Louis Marx Company, which began producing an inexpensive line of light tinplate trains. These were popular only with those who could not afford Lionel. In terms of their design, quality, and appeal, Marx trains were no match for Lionel.

During the war, toy train production decreased markedly as companies concentrated on war contracts. Lionel did not resume full production until 1946, the year the company began an incredible publicity campaign to promote its expanding O-gauge line. During the next ten years, Lionel became the largest toy company in the world. Their new O-gauge engines and cars were extremely popular. Their only real competition came from American Flyer Trains (a line begun by the Gilbert Company of Erector Set fame).

In the late 50's, toy-train sales had begun to decline as national tastes changed. This decline worsened in the early 60's as American children became hypnotized by the allure of the wondrous battery toys constantly being advertised on the television. American Flyer was the first to go, selling out to Lionel in 1966. By the late 60's, the Lionel empire, which had been so mighty 15 years earlier, had greatly eroded, and the company suspended production. In 1969 it was sold to General Mills, which began, in the early 70's,manufacturing reproductions of some of the more popular 1950's O-gauge trains.

COLLECTING.   While there are Ives, Marx, and American Flyer train collectors, Lionel, always considered best by children, is number one among train collectors today. In fact, 95 percent of all train collectors save Lionel. With this in mind, the following section has been devoted exclusively to Lionel train collecting.

The passion of train collectors for Lionel trains and accessories is founded on the amazing quality of the items Lionel produced. The detail, materials, execution, depth, and design of the Lionel product manufactured up until the late 1950's is of a quality unmatched by any other company.

The best way to begin collecting Lionel is to attend a train meet. Meets are held all over the country and are forums where collectors rent tables and then buy, sell, and trade trains and accessories. Several good books have been written on collecting Lionel. There is much to learn, and beginners are advised to read before buying. Lionel produced hundreds of different trains and accessories. These range in value today from 50¢ for a "lockon" clip to over $8,000 for a high-grade State set. Of the books that have been written, the value guides to the various Lionel eras will give you an *idea* of prices. This idea will become more definitive when you start dealing (with other collectors and at meets) in the marketplace.

Lionel trains and accessories are all identified by a *number* and the name *Lionel* stamped somewhere on the toy (true of all Lionel products except for the earliest trains, which sometimes had *J.L.C.*, Cowen's initials, marked on their bases). In the case of engines and cars, the number is usually incorporated into the design. This numbering system, which all collectors use, makes it possible to immediately identify the train or accessory you are looking at.

There are three major divisions into which Lionel trains can be divided. These are *standard gauge*, *pre-war O gauge*, and *post-war O gauge*. Gauge indicates the distance between the inside of the rails the trains run on. Standard-gauge trains were the largest made and run on track that has a space of $2^{1}/_{4}''$ between the outer rails. O-gauge trains are smaller (the size most people are familiar with from their childhoods) and run on track that has a distance of $1^{3}/_{8}''$ between the outer rails. Of the three divisions, post-war O gauge is the most popular because it is the most plentiful, diversified, and easy to operate of the three categories.

It is also affordable. While some of the rarer or more desirable post-war engines like the 2341 Jersey Central Diesel, the 2373 Canadian Pacific Diesel, and the 2363 Illinois Central sell for over $300 in top condition, there are many attractive engines and cars that sell for prices within the low value range. Unlike some of the standard gauge accessories that sell for over $400, post-war accessories are also affordable, and a collector can enhance his collection with railway station houses, billboards, and water towers.

There are three kinds of collectors. Those who operate, those who display, and those lucky few who operate and display. An operator is a collector who acquires all the necessary components and then builds a layout to run rolling stock over. I have seen layouts that are simply extraordinary. One collector from Pennsylvania has one that measures 20' x 30', is able to handle 10 trains at once, and is replete with vintage Lionel accessories like depots, crossing signals, metal figures of conductors and travelers, buildings, tunnels, and bridges. He has spent thousands of dollars equipping it.

A displayer is someone who does not operate but rather ex-

hibits his trains and accessories. Displayers often build shelf systems just the right size to accommodate their collections. Some
even paint backdrops so that the display becomes a diorama of a
train in a railroad setting. Whether one becomes an operator or
a displayer usually depends on space limitations. Many displayers
would like to be operators but haven't the room.

The beginning Lionel collector should be aware of reproductions, repairs, and replaced parts. Lionel engines, cars, and accessories that have an 8000 or 9000 number are reproductions of
earlier Lionel items. Repros have been produced since the early
70's and are currently available. Serious collectors will have nothing to do with them.

Many of the items one encounters at train meets and collectible
shows have been repaired. A repair can vary from a replaced
wheel to an entire paint job. Repairs involving the replacement
of wheel and rod assemblies or trim are acceptable to most collectors. Trim describes any of the small metal and plastic bells,
flags, handles, horns, etc., that adorn a train. At the train meets
there are dealers who specialize in selling replacement trim and
other parts that have a tendency to break. A collector can obtain
anything from a headlamp to a whole new motor.

A "repaint" describes a train that has either been partially or
fully repainted. Such trains are the bane of all serious collectors.
Repainted trains should be avoided. To learn to spot them, first
become familiar with the way the finish looks on an original train.
Lionel trains are known for coming with "beautiful paint." A train
that has been sloppily painted would tip you off. Better quality
repaints are harder to spot, and unless you are sure of yourself,
it is better to consult with someone who knows before buying a
questionable piece.

Many collectors like to buy trains that still have their original
boxes. Before the war most of the Lionel products were sold in
sturdy corrugated boxes that were meant to double as shipping
containers should the toy have to be mailed back for repair. These
pre-war boxes are more common than some of the boxes made
with flimsy cardboard after the war.

BOOKS

Greenberg, Bruce C. *Greenberg's Price Guide to Lionel*
Trains: Postwar O and O-27 Trains.
Available with several other books on Lionel from the author at 729
Oklahoma Road, Sykesville, MD 21784.

Hollander, Ron. *All Aboard!* New York: Workman, 1981.
This is the story of Joshua Lionel Cowen and his Lionel train
company.

O'Brien, Richard. *The American Premium Guide to American*
Trains.
Florence, AL: Books Americana, 1983.

CLUBS

Toy Train Operating Society
25 West Walnut Street
Suite 305
Pasadena, CA 91103

1 yr./$15, with a $15 one-time initiation fee. Members receive a monthly
bulletin and other club publications.

DEALER

Greenberg Publishing Company
729 Oklahoma Road
Sykesville, MD 21784

Send for a catalog listing numerous books on the subject of toy trains.
Mr. Greenberg is also an authority on Lionel and could be of help
to those who have questions.

WORLD'S FAIR AND EXPOSITION COLLECTIBLES

Value range: low.

Most popular items: souvenirs from the 1876, 1894, and 1904 events.

Good sources: at general antique and collectible shows and through the mail from other collectors and dealers.

COLLECTING THE MEMORABILIA of World's Fairs and Expositions has become quite popular in the last 10 years. These monumental events have always generated a prodigious quantity of souvenirs. Does anyone remember going to a World's Fair and not returning home with a bagfull of free samples from the various pavilions?

HISTORY. The first World's Fair was held in London in 1851. It was launched by the British as an experiment to see if an international exposition to promote new inventions, world commerce, and industrial manufacturing processes could be viable. The event was a resounding success, and two years later a second fair was held in New York. Since then there have been 44 World's Fairs held in different major cities throughout the world. All of the fairs have had themes, the most common of which has been the promotion of trade between nations and the exhibition of technological advances. Some fairs have been held to commemorate a famous historical figure or event. Following is a listing of all the World's Fairs and Expositions from the beginning:

1851	London, Crystal Palace	1867	Paris Universal
1853	New York, Crystal Palace	1873	Vienna International
1855	Paris International	1876	Philadelphia Centennial
1862	London Universal	1878	Paris Universal

1889	Paris Universal	1931	Paris, French Colonial
1893	Chicago, World's Co-lumbian	1933	Chicago, Century of Progress
1894	San Francisco, Califor-nia Midwinter	1935	Brussels Universal
		1935	San Diego, California-Pacific
1895	Atlanta, Cotton States		
1898	Omaha, Trans-Missis-sippi	1936	Cleveland, Great Lakes
		1937	Paris, Arts and Tech-niques
1900	Paris Universal		
1901	Buffalo, Pan-American	1938	Glasgow, British Empire
1904	St. Louis, Louisiana Pur-chase	1939	San Francisco, Golden Gate International
1905	Portland, Lewis and Clark	1939	New York, World of To-morrow
1907	Norfolk, Jamestown Tercentenary	1951	London, Festival of Brit-ain
1909	Seattle, Alaska-Yukon	1958	Brussels Universal
1910	Brussels Universal	1962	Seattle, Century 21
1915	San Francisco, Panama-Pacific	1964	New York, World's Fair
		1967	Montreal, Man and His World
1915	San Diego, Panama-California		
		1968	San Antonio, HemisFair
1924	Wembly, British Empire	1970	Osaka Universal
1925	Paris, Modern Decora-tive & Industrial Arts	1974	Spokane, The Environ-ment
1926	Philadelphia Sesquicen-tennial	1975	Okinawa, International Ocean
1929	Barcelona and Seville	1982	Knoxville, Energy Expo
1930	Stockholm		

COLLECTING. The best place to begin is the library. A pleth-ora of general and specific books and articles have been written about the World's Fairs. Learning about them provides you with (1) a way of determining which fair or fairs you would like to center your collecting interest on and (2) the necessary back-ground information for intelligent collecting.

The most popularly collected items are books, buttons, clocks, jewelry, literature, matchbook covers, medals, postcards, posters, pictures, souvenirs, stamps, tickets, and toys that have the logo or name of their fair or exposition printed on them. For instance, the logo of the 1893 Columbian Exposition was Columbus's head in profile; the logo of the 1939 fair was the Trylon and Perisphere, and the logo of the 1964 fair was the Hemisphere. Collectors look for items that are *colorful, interesting,* and *capture the mood of the world at the time of the fair*. Items from the fairs of 1876, 1893, and 1904 are the most desirable to American collectors. Material from these fairs has survived in abundance, and one can buy many beautiful souvenirs for under $15. Exceptional pieces that were not sold in quantity during a fair can bring over $200, but in general the value of fair collectibles stays in the low range.

Potential collectors should choose to collect items from only one or two fairs. So many items were produced for each event that even one fair can overwhelm the average collector. Locating desirable pieces can be accomplished best by placing classified want ads in the *Antique Trader* and other collectibles publications. Many general antique and collectible dealers also bring fair material to the shows. As always, try to obtain pieces in the best possible condition.

CLUBS

Expo Collectors and Historians Organization
Edward J. Orth
1436 Killarney Avenue
Los Angeles, CA 90065

> 1 yr./membership $5, includes *Expo Info*, a quarterly guide, and free advertising in same. For collectors of World's Fair memorabilia and history.

World's Fair Collectors Society
148 Poplar Street
Garden City, NY 11530

> 1 yr. dues/$7, includes *Fair News*, the *WFCS Bulletin*, and the right to free advertising.

Appendix I

Publications Relating to Collectibles and Antiques

Following is a list of publications relating to collectibles and antiques. Most charge nominally to send samples. I strongly advise beginners to write to several of them requesting copies.

By subscribing to one or more of these publications, you avail yourself of (1) information about the dates and locations of collectible shows, conventions, and museum exhibits; (2) the advertisements of dealers selling the gamut of collectible items; (3) information about current price trends; and (4) other collectors looking to buy, trade, and sell.

LEGEND

N = National coverage

R = Regional (area)

A = Publication concentrates on antiques but includes articles and advertisements for collectibles

C = Publication concentrates on collectibles but includes articles and advertisements for antiques

E = Publication pays equal attention to antiques and collectibles

Americana
Subscription Office
381 West Center Street
Marion, OH 43302
  1 yr./6 issues/$11.90 Articles
  about life and times in the
  United States
  N, E

American Collector
Drawer C
Kermit, TX 79745
  1 yr./12 issues/$20
  N, E

American Collector's Journal
Box 407
Kewanee, IL 61443
  1 yr./6 issues/$4.25
  N, E

Antique and Auction News
Box B
Marietta, PA 17547
  1 yr./26 issues/$12
  R (East Coast), E

Antiques and Collectibles
230 Arlington Circle
East Hills, NY 11548
  1 yr./12 issues/$10
  R (New York area), E

Antique Gazette
929 Davidson Drive
Nashville, TN 37205
  1 yr./12 issues/$9
  R (Tennessee area), A

Antique Monthly
2320 7th Avenue Box 2274
Birmingham, AL 35201
  1 yr./12 issues/$14
  N, A

Antiques and the Arts Weekly
The Newtown Bee
Newtown, Ct. 06470
  1yr./52 issues/$23
  R (East Coast), A

Arts and Antiques
One Worth Avenue
Marion, OH 43302
  1 yr./6 issues/$21
  N, A

Arts and Antiques Antiquarian
Box 798
Huntington, NY 11743
  1 yr./12 issues/$20
  N, A

Barter News
P.O. Box 407B
Kewanee, IL 61443
  1 yr./4 issues/$14 Thousands
  of listings of people who want
  to trade one thing for another.
  N

Bazaar Gift Handicrafts
Tower Press Inc.
Box 428
Seabrook, NH 03874

   1 yr./4 issues/$4 Lists instruc-
   tions with photos on how to
   make things that can be sold
   at flea markets.
   N

Collect America International
Box 777
Waynesboro, TN 38485

   1 yr./12 issues/$10
   N, C

Collectibles Illustrated
Depot Square
Peterborough, NH 03458

   1 yr./6 issues/$11.50
   N, C

Collector Editions
Acquire Publishing
170 Fifth Avenue
New York, NY 10010

   1 yr./4 issues/$8.50
   N, C

Collector's Journal
Box 601 421 First Avenue
Vinton, IA 52349

   1 yr./ 50 issues/$17
   R (Iowa, Minnesota), A

Collector's Showcase
Box 27948
San Diego, CA 92128

   1 yr./6 issues/$20
   N, C

Flea Market Forum
355 Great Neck Road
Great Neck, NY 11021

   1 yr./12 issues/$10 Magazine
   filled with advertisements of
   wholesalers desiring to sell to
   flea market vendors.
   N

Hobbies: The Magazine for Collectors
Circulation Dept., Hobbies
1006 S. Michigan Avenue
Chicago, IL 60605

   1 yr./12 issues/$14
   N, E

Jersey Devil
P.O. Box 202
Lambertville, NJ 08530

   1 yr./11 issues/$6 Publication
   concentrates on listings of flea
   markets and advice on how to
   be a vendor
   R (East Coast)

Maine Antique Digest
Box 358
Waldoboro, ME 04572

   1 yr./12 issues/$23
   R (eastern seaboard), A

National Journal of Antiques and Collectibles
Box 3121
Wescosville, PA 18106

   1 yr./12 issues/$12
   N, E

New England Country Antiques
4 Church Street
Ware, MA 01082

  1 yr./12 issues/$8.95
  R (eastern seaboard), A

Ohio Antique Review
Box 538
Worthington, OH 43085

  1 yr./11 issues/$18
  N, A

Rarities: The Magazine of Collectibles
17337 Ventura Boulevard
Encino, CA 91316

  1 yr./6 issues/$10
  N, C

Spinning Wheel: Antiques & Early Crafts
Pegasus Ltd.
1981 Moreland Parkway Bldg. 4A
Annapolis, MD 21401

  1 yr./6 issues/$15
  N, E

The Antique Trader
Box 1050
Dubuque, IA 52001

  1 yr./52 issues/$19
  N, E

The New York Antique Almanac
Box 335
Lawrence, NY 11554

  1 yr./10 issues/$10
  R (New York City area), E

Tri-State Trader
27 N. Jefferson Box 90
Knightstown, IN 46148

  1 yr./52 issues/$13.50
  R (Ohio, Kentucky, Indiana, Michigan, Illinois, Western Pennsylvania, West Virginia, Tennessee, Wisconsin, Missouri, New York), E

West Coast Peddler
P.O. Box 988
Lakewood, CA 90715

  1 yr./12 issues/$10
  R (California), E

Wooden Nutmeg
87 Nutmeg Lane
Box 504
Glastonburg, CT 06033

  1 yr./26 issues/$9
  N, E

Appendix II

Where to Obtain Books on Collectibles

Following is a list of dealers who specialize in the sale of books on collectibles. This list has been included because there are so many new books coming out each month that the chapter bibliographies will be incomplete by the time of publication. As well, the reader may find, in trying to obtain copies of books listed in the bibliographies, that certain titles are out of print or unavailable. The reason for this stems from the fact that many of the specialized books on collectibles being produced today are privately published in small editions. When they sell out, they often are not reprinted and therefore become unavailable.

Should you wish to find out what *is available* on a particular collectible group, contact the dealers listed below and request information. They are professionals in the field and will be happy to help you.

Mrs. John Houghmaster
539 Second Avenue
Troy, NY 12182
(518) 235-7690

Does not publish a catalog but, rather, works from collectors' want lists.

Lamplighter Books
Leon, IA 50144

Write to them for current lists or with particular requests.

The Reference Rack
Box 445C
Orefield, PA 18069
(215) 395-0004

The Reference Rack is expertly managed, and its owners, Betty and Jim Johnston, are especially good at working with collectors needing out-of-print or hard-to-find books.

Appendix III

General Books

Appraisers Directory. Order from: Appraisers Association
of America, 60 East 42nd Street, New York 10165. Lists appraisers
by geographic area and by specialty.

Ketchum, William C. Jr. *The Catalog of American Collectibles*.
New York: Mayflower Books, 1979.

Kovel, Ralph and Terry. *Know Your Antiques*.
New York: Crown, 1981.

———. *Know Your Collectibles*.
New York: Crown, 1981.

———. *The Antiques Price List*.
New York: Crown, 1981.

Michael, George. *The Basic Book of Antiques*.
New York: Arco, 1982.

Miller, Martin and Judith, eds. *Miller's Antiques Price Guide*.
Rutland, VT: Charles E. Tuttle, 1982.

Rinker, Harry L. *Warman's Antiques and Their Prices*.
Elkins Park, PA: Warman Publishing, 1982.

Appendix IV

Books, Periodicals, and Clubs for All Types of Collectibles

Following is a list of books, clubs, and periodicals pertaining to collectible groups not covered in this book. Some of these groups are collected by only a handful of serious individuals, while others are very popular and have many supporters. This list is included to provide a starting point for collectors interested in any of the categories; give specific examples of some of the more esoteric items being collected; and be an inspiration for collectors contemplating forming a club or writing a book.

AUTOMATIC MUSICAL INSTRUMENTS

Bowers, David Q. *Encyclopedia of Automatic Musical Instruments.*
Order from: Vestal Press, Vestal, NY 13850.

AMICA International
Box 172
Columbia, SC 29202.

1 yr./$25, including initiation fee. Members receive news bulletins that include articles and buy/sell ads.

BRICKS

International Brick Collectors Association
Dr. Ronald P. Anjard, Sr.
10942 Montego Drive
San Diego, CA 92124

Write for information.

318

BUTTONS

National Button Collecting Society
Miss Lois Pool, Secretary
2733 Juno Place
Akron, OH 44313

1 yr./$10, includes various club benefits, plus 5 issues of the *National Button Bulletin*.

CLOCKS

Clockwise
Miller and Miller
1236 East Main Street
Ventura, CA 93001

Published quarterly for clock and watch enthusiasts. It centers on the how-to aspects of the hobby; subscription, $24.

COOKIE COLLECTIBLES

Weitherill, Phyllis S. *An Encyclopedia of Cookie Shaping*.
Order from: Cookies, 5426 27th Street N.W., Washington, DC 20015.

Cookie Cutter Collectors Club
Ruth Capper
1167 Teal Road S.W.
Delroy, OH 44620

1 yr./$5; members can also subscribe to *Cookies*, a newsletter devoted to cookies and cookie shaping; 1-yr. subscription, $15.

COUNTRY COLLECTIBLES

Emmerling, Mary Ellisor. *American Country, A Style and Source Book*.
New York: Crown, 1980.

Smith, Carter, ed. *Country Antiques and Collectibles*.
1981. Order from: Southern Progress Corp., Box 2463, Birmingham, AL 35201.

CUP PLATES

Pairpoint Cup Plate Collectors of America
9308 Brandywine Road
Clinton, MD 20735

1 yr./$6, includes quarterly newsletter, *The Thistle*.

DOORKNOBS

Antique Doorknob Collectors of America
Arnie Fredrick
221 Second Street S.E.
Waverly, IA 50677

Write for information.

ELECTRICAL COLLECTIBLES

Fredgant, Don. *Electrical Collectibles: Relics of the
Electrical Age*. Order from: Padre Productions, Box 1275, San Luis
Obispo, CA 93406.

HATPINS AND HATPIN HOLDERS

Baker, Lillian. *Handbook to Hatpins and Hatpin Holders*.
Order from author: 15237 Chanera Avenue, Gardena, CA 90249.

International Club for Collectors of Hatpins and Hatpin Holders

1 yr./$15, entitles members to a year's worth of the club's publications.
Write to Ms. Baker at address above.

ICE CREAM COLLECTIBLES

The Ice Screamer
Ed Marks
1042 Olde Hickory Road
Lancaster, PA 17601

Newsletter about the history of ice cream collectibles; includes buy/
sell ads.

ILLUSTRATIONS

Illustration Collectors Newsletter
53 Water Street
South Norwalk, CT 06854

   1 issue/$3; a catalog of illustrations offered for sale, useful for gaining
   a sense of the market.

JEWELRY

Ornament
Box 35029
Los Angeles, CA 90035

   1 yr./4 issues/$16. A magazine covering all types of jewelry and other
   forms of personal adornment. Mostly scholarly articles on the history
   of jewelry in certain regions, etc.

KEYS

Stewart, Don. *Standard Guide to Key Collecting.*

   Order from: Box 9397, Phoenix, AZ 85068. Mr. Stewart also publishes books on specialized areas of key and lock collecting. Write for
   a catalog.

Key Collectors International
Don Stewart (same address as above)

   1 yr./membership/$18, includes 5 issues of their journal and a
   certificate.

KITS

Kit Collectors International
Box 38
Stanton, CA 90680

   Publishes a newsletter, *Vintage Plastic.* Write for information.

LOCKS

American Lock Collectors Association
36076 Grennada
Livonia, MI 48154

   Publishes a newsletter 6 times a year. Membership $4.50.

LURES

Luckey, Carl F. *Old Fishing Lures*.
     Florence, AL: Books Americana, 1980.

MEDICAL AND SCIENTIFIC INSTRUMENTS

Fredgant, Don. *Medical, Dental, and Pharmaceutical Collectibles*.
     Florence, AL: Books Americana, 1981.

Turner, Gerard, L'E., *Collecting Microscopes*.
     New York: Mayflower Books, 1981.

MINIATURES

Miniature Collector
Acquire Publishing Company
170 Fifth Avenue
New York, NY 10010

   1 yr./6 issues/$12.

OWL COLLECTIBLES

The Owl's Nest
Howard's Alphanumeric
Box 5491
Fresno, CA 93755

   1 yr./6 issues/$10. Newsletter for owl collectors. Contains articles and
   classifieds; subscribers allowed a free ad.

PAPERWEIGHTS

Selman, Lawrence H. *Collector's Paperweights*
     Available from author: 761 Chestnut Street, Santa Cruz, CA 95060.

PENS

Pen Fancier's Club
1169 Overcash Drive
Dunedin, FL 33528

> 1 yr./$25; sample, $2. Publishes a monthly magazine, *The Pen Fancier's Magazine*, which includes articles on the history of fountain pens, and buy and sell ads.

The Fountain Pen Exchange
Box 64
Teaneck, NJ 07666

> 1 yr./12 issues/$15; sample, $2. Includes letters, ads, repair tips, and general information on fountain pens. They also have published a book, *Collecting and Valuing Early Fountain Pens*, available for $10.75, including postage.

PRINTS

Luckey, Carl F. *Collector Prints Old and New.*
    Florence, AL: Books Americana, 1982.

American Print Review
Box 6909
Chicago, IL 60680

> 1 yr./6 issues/$18. Subscribers can place two free classifieds per issue. Essentially a review of current prices realized at auction for American prints. Also contains buy/sell ads.

REED ORGANS

The Reed Organ Society
The Musical Museum
Deansboro, NY 13328

> Issues a newsletter about reed organs. Write for information.

RUBBER STAMPS

Miller, Joni K. *The Rubber Stamp Album*
New York: Workman, 1978.

SEWING COLLECTIBLES

Whiting, Gertrude. *Old-Time Tools and Toys of Needlework.*
New York: Dover Books, 1971.

SILVER COLLECTIBLES

Silver Magazine
Box 22217
Milwaukie, OR 97222

> 1 yr./6 issues, $12; sample, $2. Publication specializing in the entire field of silver items. Buy/sell ads, articles, club advertisements, convention news, etc.

SILVER FLATWARE

Turner, Noel D. *American Silver Flatware 1837–1910.*
La Jolla: A.S. Barnes & Company, 1972.

SNUFF BOTTLES

The International Snuff Bottle Society
2601 North Charles Street
Baltimore, MD 21218

> 1 yr. $50, includes a quarterly journal featuring scholarly articles and information about collectors and collections of snuff bottles throughout the world.

SPOONS

American Spoon Collectors
Bill Boyd
Box 260
Warrensburg, MO 64093

> To join there is a one-time fee of $15, which includes a spoon pin

and certificate. Members can subscribe to *Spooner's Forum*, a monthly newsletter including articles and buy/sell ads; 1-yr. subscription, $10.

THIMBLES

Thimbletter
Mrs. Lorraine M. Crosby
93 Walnut Hill Road
Newton Highlands, MA 02161

1 yr./6 issues/$10; sample, $1. A newsletter for thimble collectors.

Thimble Collectors International
Box 143
Intervale, NH 03845

Write for information.

TIN CONTAINERS

Tin Containers Collectors Association
Peter Sidlow
11650 Riverside Drive
North Hollywood, CA 91602

1 yr./$20, includes the monthly newsletter, *Tintypes*, and other mailings. The ideal club for collectors of tin advertising pieces.

TOOTHPICK HOLDERS

National Toothpick Holders Collectors Society
Joyce Ender
Red Arrow Highway
Sawyer, MI 49125

1 yr./$8, entitles members to the monthly bulletin, which keeps collectors informed about price trends, reference material, meetings, and reproductions.

TYPEWRITERS

Post, Dan R. *Collectors Guide to Antique Typewriters.*
Order from: Post-Era Books, Box 150, Arcadia, CA 91006.

WALT DISNEY COLLECTIBLES

Terison and Morrison. *Walt Disney Price Guide*.
Order from authors: Box 1177, North Windham, ME 04062.

The Mouse Club
13826 Ventura Boulevard
Sherman Oaks, CA 91423

1 yr./$17.50, includes 6 newsletters. For serious collectors of Disneyana.

WATCHES AND CLOCKS

Ehrhardt, Roy. *American Pocket Watch Identification and Price Guide*
Order from: Heart of America Press, Box 9808, Kansas City, MO 64134. The Press also publishes other books on watches; write for information.

National Association of Watch and Clock Collectibles
Box 33
Columbia, PA 17512

Dues/$20, includes the various Association publications, 6 issues of *The Mart*, a forum for sellers and buyers.

Index